THE CINEMA
OF
TONY RICHARDSON

THE SUNY SERIES

CULTURAL STUDIES IN CINEMA/VIDEO

Wheeler Winston Dixon, editor

THE CINEMA
OF
TONY RICHARDSON

*Essays and
Interviews*

Edited by

JAMES M. WELSH
and
JOHN C. TIBBETTS

Foreword by
JOCELYN HERBERT

STATE UNIVERSITY OF NEW YORK PRESS

Published by
State University of New York Press, Albany

For information, address State University of New York Press,
State University Plaza, Albany, N.Y., 12246

Production by Marilyn P. Semerad
Marketing by Patrick Durocher

Library of Congress Cataloging-in-Publication Data

The cinema of Tony Richardson : essays and interviews / edited by
  James M. Welsh and John C. Tibbetts : foreword by Jocelyn Herbert.
      p.   cm. — (The SUNY series, cultural studies in cinema/video)
    Filmography: p.
    Includes bibliographical references and index.
    ISBN 0-7914-4249-7 (alk. paper). — ISBN 0-7914-4250-0 (pbk. :
  alk. paper)
    1. Richardson, Tony, 1928–1991—Criticism and interpretation.
  I. Welsh, James Michael. II. Tibbetts, John C. III. Series.
  PN1998.3.R53C56 1999
  791.43′0233′092—dc21   98-55482
                                                               CIP

10 9 8 7 6 5 4 3 2 1

This book is dedicated to two distinguished professors at the University of Kansas, Hal Orel, of the Department of English, and Marilyn Stokstad, of the Art History Department, both of whom have been mentors and friends to both of us and taught us how to be productive.

CONTENTS

LIST OF
ILLUSTRATIONS

FOREWORD

Remembering Tony

JOCELYN HERBERT

What was it that made Tony such a unique and unforgettable character? His boundless energy, both physical and mental, a very quick mind, and an amazing memory. He was a great manipulator. He once told me that, as an only child, he lived with his parents, two grandmothers, and an aunt. He found that if he could not get what he wanted from one, he would get it from one of the others. So at an early age, he learned the art of "divide and rule." This skill he chiefly used to persuade one or another relative to house the wounded animals and birds that he brought in from his walks in the country, which his mother did not approve of. A lonely child, hating and hopeless at games, he spent hours wandering the fields, learning about flowers, birds, and trees, which remained an obsession all his life.

The two places Tony loved most were Nid le Duc, an old farm house in France, and his house and garden in Hollywood. On arriving at his house in Hollywood, the first thing you saw was an enormous toucan with a gigantic beak guarding the front door. When you went inside, you were greeted by a large, very colorful parrot on his perch, who went upside-down onto the ceiling. There was a wonderful garden filled with exotic flowers and an open aviary, where beautiful birds flew in and out and made their home. And then there were orchids, which Tony nurtured with loving care.

Nid le Duc was an old farm house with many outbuildings, in the mountains in the south of France. Tony turned the outbuildings into bedrooms and built a magical swimming pool cantilevered out over the valley. You swam in warm water, the sky above you and a view down the valley to the mountains beyond. Here his family and his friends came and stayed, eating at a long wooden table on the terrace outside the house, a large mulberry tree providing shade in the summer. In the spring, mimosa trees descending the mountain to the stream below filled the air with their glorious scent. There were dogs and cats, chickens and ducks and, above all, peacocks, sitting on the walls with their beautiful tails draped below them. You were often woken by their piercing shrieks. Many film and theatre projects were planned and discussed in these wonderful surroundings. Tony certainly knew something about the art of living.

I first met Tony, I think, in 1954. He was then a young, aspiring director trying to put on plays or get work in television. He had recently met George Devine, and they became friends. George told Tony of his ideas for creating a writers' theatre and how he was trying to get financial backing and find a theatre. Tony was enthusiastic and offered to help raise money. They had no luck, but eventually the English Stage Company was formed, and, having heard of George's ideas, they asked him to become their artistic director. When George took over the Royal Court Theatre, he asked Tony to be his associate. Tony was invaluable in helping to find new young directors and suggesting new writers. In his youth in Salford and later at Oxford, Tony had staged many plays, and he drew on people who had worked with him then to invite them to work at the Court.

The first break came when John Osborne sent George his script of *Look Back in Anger*. George loved the play and gave it to Tony to read. Tony subsequently directed it with great success, and this was the beginning of his long and often stormy friendship and collaboration with John Osborne. Tony directed many plays in the early days at the Court, but with his increasing success, he was away more and more frequently in the States, which he loved, taking productions of plays from London to New York and doing films in Hollywood. Tony and John Osborne formed a company called "Woodfall," with the aim of trying to do for films what George was trying to do for the theatre. They produced many memorable films based on books and plays by contemporary writers, filming as much as possible on location rather than in big studios.

In 1957 Tony asked me to design *The Chairs* by Ionesco, and while working with him, I really began to know him. He would announce that he knew exactly how it should be designed and what it should look like and talk about the play in a very interesting and inspiring way, but I found that when I tried to produce exactly what he had suggested, it never seemed to look right to me—or to him. I did a lot of drawings and gave them to Tony to look at. He looked carefully through them all and then picked out the one I liked best. It was wonderful, and somehow our working relationship developed from that moment on, as well as a feeling of trust and collaboration that would permeate all our future work together in the theatre, and, later, in films. This was also the beginning of our long and lasting friendship.

We did many plays together at the Court, and in the West End, culminating with *Hamlet* at the Round House. During the run with Nicol Williamson playing Hamlet, Tony decided to make a film of the play. So in the daytime we removed all the seats and made the film, using all the Round House, including the tunnels in the basement for the different scenes. It was utterly exhausting for all concerned, but the challenge to get through the shooting schedule for the day, in time to get the seats back for the evening performance, galvanized everyone into action. I think Tony was at his best and most creative in those kinds of circumstances.

In 1961 Tony decided to make a film of Henry Fielding's *Tom Jones*. It was to be his first film in period and in color. I was astonished when he asked me to work on it. He already had a brilliant production designer, and he asked me to be color consultant and to design the costumes. I knew nothing about making films and disliked most of the color films I had seen, but Tony said that was exactly why he wanted me to do it, to see if color could be more controlled and meaningful. It was a challenge I could not refuse. Tony assembled a wonderful cast, nearly all actors from the theatre, and every part was brilliantly played. Tony brought out the humor and also Fielding's wry comments on the manners and modes of the times in the imaginative and beautiful way he shot the film.

Why did Tony have such a bad time with the critics, even with *Tom Jones*, which, in spite of very bad reviews, was an enormous financial success and eventually won three Oscars in Hollywood? Perhaps Tony's films were difficult to fit into the normal categories. He did not really make "Art" films (though some, such as *Mademoiselle*, fit that category), and his feature films always had a serious side—a point of view—that Tony wanted to get across, so he kind of fell between two stools from the critics' point of view. More fools them!

An example is *The Charge of the Light Brigade*, which was a brilliant film, imaginative, inventive, satirical, and very moving. The critics disliked it. Was it because Tony was interested in showing up the hypocrisy and incompetence of the class-dominated generals? For he showed the "charge" to be the unforgivable, tragic mistake that it was, stemming from the rivalry and pigheadedness of two generals and ending in the massacre and butchery of the Light Brigade, shot by Tony in all its horror, with no holds barred. By some quirk, Lord Cardigan survived the slaughter, and, in an unforgettable shot, he emerges out of the smoke and devastation, a single figure riding back, oblivious that his horse is trampling on his soldiers, who lay dead and dying on the field.

Tony Richardson was unique. There will never be anyone quite like him again. I think it would be true to say that although he worked a lot in the theatre, especially in the early days, his real love was films, and he was never happier than when he was standing beside the camera, waiting to call "*Action!*"

ACKNOWLEDGMENTS

As with any book, the authors are indebted to many people who helped this project along and made it happen. Wheeler Dixon was encouraging from the beginning, and we are grateful to him and to Clay Morgan, who has since left the press, to James Peltz, our final editor, for extending our deadline, and to Marilyn Semerad, who supervised production. Next are our splendid contributors, who stole time from projects of their own to help us make this one better. Becky Pauly, for example, stalled her continuing work on *A Month in France*, a CD-ROM project, in order to help us cover Tony Richardson's French films. Bill Horne faxed thirty pages of his first draft to us from Britain, where he was visiting his family, so we would know how his work was progressing. On very short notice, Linda Cahir stole time from research on her forthcoming book *Solitude and Society in the Works of Herman Melville and Edith Wharton*. Ken Nolley postponed work on his summer home on the Oregon coast to share his thoughts on issues of class in Richardson's Fielding adaptations. And so it goes.

We are especially pleased about the interviews we were able to get from people in England who had worked directly with Tony Richardson. Kevin Brownlow, whose enthusiasm for early cinema we share, opened many doors for us, not only his own, but also those of his London neighbor Karel Reisz and of David Watkin, in Brighton, who not only spent half a day with us, but also fed us breakfast, and then lunch. After the long interview with David Watkin, we concluded that would-be critics should be more attentive to the art of cinematography. Without these interviews, the book might still have merit, but it certainly would be more "academic" and far less lively. Thanks to Kevin, it contains several industry voices to whom we believe it is well worth listening.

We are also indebted to Kevin for putting us in contact with theatre-designer Jocelyn Herbert, who knew Tony Richardson from his earliest associations with George Devine, when the English Stage Company was formed. She and George Devine were witnesses as maid of honor and best man when Tony Richardson and Vanessa Redgrave were married on April 28, 1962. She worked as color consultant on *Tom Jones* in 1963 and as production designer on other film projects, such as *Hamlet* (1969), *Ned Kelly* (1970), and *The Hotel New Hampshire* (1984). We were therefore delighted when she agreed to write the Foreword for this book.

Assembling the book was a continuing nightmare of electronic technology, made possible only through the kindness of Shawn Punga and Shannon Benner at Salisbury State University, who helped us to convert disks and merge computer files. One should not need a degree in computer science to write or edit a book, but the world is changing around those of us who still prefer the fountain pen. Shannon, an excellent copy editor, also input and edited one of the essays so that we would not miss our final deadline. Shawn works wonders on sophisticated computers by which people twice his age are mystified. These are good, deserving, knowledgeable, skilled people who pitched in at the final hour and to whom we are grateful. Gabriela Alexandra Vlahovici, a talented graduate student from Romania and the research assistant for *Literature/Film Quarterly* at Salisbury State, also helped with copyediting and last minute emendations as the manuscript was prepared for the press. With friends like these, scholarship could be a pleasure.

CHAPTER ONE

Introduction:
Running the Distance

JAMES M. WELSH

Although in his later years he favored filmmaking, and although he was one of the founders and innovators of the British New Wave, Tony Richardson (1928–1991) was originally a man of the theatre. His London debut as stage director was an unsuccessful production at Wyndham's Theatre of Thomas Middleton's *Changeling*, which opened (and closed) on May 16, 1954. His last stage production came thirty-four years later, when he directed Shakespeare's *Antony and Cleopatra* at the Los Angeles Theatre Center in July 1987, casting John Goodman as Enobarbus and helping thereby to advance that actor's film and television career, as was his habit.

As co-founder of the English Stage Company, Richardson helped to usher in a revolutionary style of theatrical production when he directed John Osborne's play *Look Back in Anger* at London's Royal Court Theatre on May 8, 1956. After 151 performances at the Royal Court and an additional three-week run at the Lyric Theatre in Hammersmith, Richardson took the production to Moscow for the International Youth Festival and, in October 1957, to Broadway, where it was a tremendous success and was voted the season's Best Foreign Play by the New York Drama Critics' Circle. The play was later adapted to cinema in 1959 as the first feature

1

FIGURE 1.1. The Royal Court Theatre. Photo by John C. Tibbetts.

film Richardson would direct. His first short film, *Momma Don't Allow*, co-directed with Karel Reisz in 1955, predates the Royal Court production of *Look Back in Anger*, prefiguring the fact that he would ultimately be, first and foremost, a filmmaker.

Cecil Antonio Richardson was born in Saltaire, Shipley, Yorkshire, on June 5, 1928, the only son of a pharmacist. After grammar school he was educated first at Ashville College, a private boarding school in Harrogate, twenty miles from Shipley, described by Richardson as "a black gloomy stone mansion" that he considered "a halfway station to Siberia" (Richardson 1993, 24). After graduating Ashville College in 1946, he prepared for entrance exams for Oxford and Cambridge, founded the Shipley Young Theatre group, and mounted local amateur productions. Even at such an early age, Richardson influenced other talents. William Gaskill, who went on to become a distinguished theatre director with the English Stage Company (1957–59, then 1965–72), the Royal Shakespeare Company (1961–62), and the National Theatre (1963–65), before becoming director of the Joint Stock Company in 1973, for example, was first introduced to the theatre through Richardson's amateur group in Shipley, and he would later follow Richardson from Bradford to Oxford. Gaskill described Richardson to Kathleen Tynan as "creative and destructive, encouraging and disheartening, serious and flippant. Without him I would never have become a director" (Tynan 1992, 116).

In 1948 Richardson was accepted by Wadham College, Oxford. At Oxford, Richardson did not excel in scholarship, but he was certainly creative in other ways. "Find Yourself" was his mantra, as he explains in his memoirs (1993, 44), and he achieved this goal by involving himself in Oxford's dramatic societies, first the Oxford University Experimental Theatre Club (the ETC), then the more prestigious Oxford University Dramatic Society (the OUDS), both of which he joined. He soon became theatre critic for the Oxford journal *Isis* and went on to impress his colleagues with an innovative production of *Peer Gynt*. Following Kenneth Tynan, Richardson was elected president of the ETC, and by the end of his second year he was elected president of the OUDS as well. His second Oxford Playhouse production was Webster's *Duchess of Malfi*.

He graduated Oxford with a B.A. in English literature, and in 1952 he was offered a contract as a trainee director by the British Broadcasting Corporation (BBC). He continued to write criticism for the film journal *Sequence*, founded by Gavin Lambert and Lindsay Anderson (1923–1994) in 1947 and edited by Anderson until 1952. By 1954 he was an independent director for BBC and writing film criticism for *Sight and Sound*, published by the British Film Institute and edited by Gavin Lambert, which kept him in touch with Lambert, Anderson, and Karel Reisz and would later link Richardson to the "Free Cinema" movement in Britain.

Richardson was not favorably impressed by the six-month BBC training course. He would later describe the BBC as an "out-front-and-proud-of-it bastion of mediocrity and its pensioners: an aggressively complacent and Philistine bureaucracy; the lowest common multiple of talent and intelligence; a world of the self-congratulating, the would-bes—whether they're journalists or politicians or interviewers or directors who think they're the ace" (Richardson 1993, 56). The only BBC production from that period he mentions in his memoir is the Giraudoux play fantasy *The Apollo of Bellac* (1955, with Denholm Elliott and Natasha Perry, he notes), but he worked on the six-part series *Happy and Glorious* (1952) and with the writer J. B. Priestly on the series *You Know What People Are* (1955, six episodes), among other projects. Priestly then contracted Richardson to direct his satirical play *Mr. Kettle and Mrs. Moon* at the Duchess Theatre in September 1955.

The first BBC program Richardson directed after completing the training program was *Sound of Stillness* (1952). Through the BBC Richardson first met George Devine (1910–1966), an older, established theatrical figure who also had graduated from Wadham College and had also served as president of OUDS. Through his persistence, Richardson managed to persuade Devine to play the lead in the television production of Anton Chekhov's *Curtain Down* he directed in 1953. In 1960 Richardson would direct *A Subject of Scandal and Concern* for BBC, the first play John Osborne wrote for television. In 1956 the excerpt of *Look Back in Anger* Richardson directed for BBC helped to generate national attention for his stage production at the Royal Court.

Though Richardson may have been disillusioned by the mentality of the BBC, working freelance for the BBC helped him to launch his career as director and enabled him to make useful contacts, most obviously with George Devine, which led to his involvement with the English Stage Company as assistant artistic director, which ultimately factored out as an "equal partnership between the older, more experienced and responsible" Devine and the "young, inexperienced, capricious Richardson" (Radovich 1995, 6).

George Devine was therefore one of Tony Richardson's first theatrical friends and the collaborator who brought him into the English Stage Company and the Royal Court Theatre. He had served as director and manager of Saint-Denis's London Theatre Studio (1936–39) and had taught at the Old Vic School before he founded the English Stage Company in 1956. From the turn of the century, the Royal Court Theatre had earned an avant-garde reputation. As Artistic Director of the English Stage Company Devine was determined to promote new and experimental drama. In Richardson he found an eager and willing collaborator in achieving this goal.

Years later Richardson would pay a special tribute to Devine by casting him as Squire Allworthy (the name is emblemmatic of the character, in the eighteenth-century way) in *Tom Jones*, a character described by Henry Fielding as "an agreeable person" possessed of "a sound constitution, a solid understanding, and a benevolent heart" (Fielding 1962, I:3). In his introduction to the Everyman Library edition of *Tom Jones*, A. R. Humphreys describes Allworthy as an agent of God, "somewhere between a realistic and a morality figure, the generalization of Fielding's friend and benefactor Ralph Allen into the Christian ideal (Latitudinarian style)" (ix). Allworthy represents goodness and wisdom, as George Devine also must have done for Richardson.

Important as his work in theatre was, Richardson has claimed that he saw the theatre as a means to an end: "I wasn't going to be a diplomat, or a lawyer, or a politician, as my parents hoped," Richardson wrote. "I was going to be a film director, and the way to start was in the theatre" (qtd. in Tynan 1992, 116). By 1958 Richardson had formed Woodfall Films with his playwright collaborator John Osborne and producer Harry Saltzman in order to break into feature filmmaking with *Look Back in Anger*, featuring Richard Burton as Jimmy Porter, and *The Entertainer*, starring Laurence Olivier as Archie Rice. Both films were extensions of his work in the theatre and therefore theatrical by definition and style, but at the end of his life, in *A Tribute to Tony Richardson*, published by the Bradford Playhouse and Film Theatre in June 1996, Grizelda Grimond (the daughter of Liberal party leader Joe Grimmond, who disapproved of his daughter having had an affair with Richardson) wrote: "I think *The Entertainer* is his masterpiece and a perfect epitaph for one whose raison d'être was entertainment."

THE FREE CINEMA MOVEMENT

Lindsay Anderson and Gavin Lambert founded the film journal *Sequence*, which operated on auteurist principles in England before the *Cahiers du cinéma* theorists and filmmakers began writing in France. François Truf-faut, for example, did not publish his first *Cahiers* essay until 1953. Anderson, born in 1923 and, like Tony Richardson, a graduate of Wad-ham College, Oxford, described the origins of the Free Cinema move-ment as follows:

> In 1956 Karel Reisz, Tony Richardson and I (all struggling inde-pendents) launched a series of shows at the National Film Theatre under the title of Free Cinema. Partly as a result of the quality of our work and partly through our canny manipulation of publicity, these attracted a good deal of critical attention. But they also aroused a good deal of resentment—both from the old Establishment and from the new Establishment which was growing up in and around television—and when the Ford Motor Company withdrew its spon-sorship, we found it impossible to get further funding to make the kind of films (individually expressive, free from propagandist obli-gations) that interested us. (qtd. in Wakeman 1988, 46)

In the later 1950s, Anderson goes on to explain that "the frozen surface of British society began to break up" after the Suez Crisis of 1956, which, according to historian C. J. Bartlett, strengthened the "angry young man" movement in British theatre that dates to Richardson's Royal Court pro-duction of *Look Back in Anger* by "confirming for some the fallibility of the British leadership, suggesting moral bankruptcy to others, or, by revealing the limitations of British power in the world, fuelling their sense of impotence and frustration" (1977, 153). Anderson considered himself lucky "to be involved in that pioneering movement, inspirited by a Left which had been both stimulated and liberalised by the events of 1956—Suez and Hungary." Richardson invited him to direct plays at the Royal Court, such as John Arden's *Serjeant Musgrave's Dance* and *Billy Liar* (by Willis Hall and Keith Waterhouse).

One goal of the Free Cinema was to capture "the poetry of everyday life," resisting traditional British documentary approaches and the con-ventions and techniques of the commercial cinema. "These films are free," the organizers explained, "in the sense that their statements are entirely personal." The film journal *Sequence* produced the intellectuals who cre-ated the Free Cinema movement parallel to but also embracing similar principles as the Angry Young Men of the Royal Court, for obvious rea-sons. The movement was the first manifestation of the British New Wave.

Richardson's *Momma Don't Allow* was a classic example of a first film effort, an unpretentious twenty-five-minute documentary about kids dancing at a jazz club in the London working-class district Wood Green. Richardson's collaborator, Karel Reisz, knew about the club and, having taught school, was aware of how young people were thinking about the changes that were taking place in England under the Labor government. After the war, a social revolution had taken place in England, bringing about the welfare state, the National Health Service, and the Education Act, all of which changed the country substantially.

One might speculate that a realistic treatment of the concerns of working-class people, through either stage or screen, might have been influenced by the Italian neorealists, but, when asked about this, Karel Reisz noted one significant difference, that the films of the British New Wave were very much writer-led. In his early years, François Truffaut claimed that the French cinema was in such a dreadful state that it could be rescued only by the amateurs. A similar point could be made about the state of the commercial cinema in England. One of his friends noted that though Richardson had no coherent political views, he certainly knew where the action was.

In his *Companion to British and Irish Cinema*, John Caughie contends that the British New Wave "can be read as the backwash of a wave which had happened elsewhere" (1996, 38), but that is patent nonsense. Anderson, Richardson, and Reisz had completed their short films *before* the premiere of *Look Back in Anger* at the Royal Court and had shaped their critical stance in *Sequence* and *Sight and Sound.* They were writing in *Sequence* before François Truffaut published his first criticism in *Cahiers du cinéma* in 1953. Moreover, Richardson and Reisz completed *Momma Don't Allow* a year *before* Truffaut made *Les Mistons* in 1957. Rather than a backwash, the Wave was already breaking in England before it crossed the Channel.

RICHARDSON'S TRANSITION: THE FIELDING ANALOGY

One could argue that Tony Richardson was essentially a man of the theatre and that film was his secondary occupation, were it not for the fact that after he had "gone Hollywood" he spent more time making films than directing theatrical productions. Once he had bolted for Hollywood, leaving the West End behind, Richardson was firmly committed to filmmaking. In a famous little polemic, Ingmar Bergman once asserted that theatre has nothing to do with film, but one can easily argue a contrary position, by analogy to the career of Henry Fielding (1707–1754), the author of two novels Richardson would adapt to the screen, *The History of the Adventures of Joseph Andrews* (1742) and *The History of Tom Jones, A Foundling* (1749), if filmmaking is examined in its narrative function. Both Fielding and Richardson would be remembered mainly for the achievements of *Tom Jones* rather than, respectively, for the success of *The Tragedy of Tragedies, or Tom Thumb* (1730) and *Look Back in Anger* (1956), even though the latter production became a benchmark for a theatrical revolution in Britain and lent its name to the revolutionaries, the so-called Angry Young Men, with Richardson in the forefront.

W. Somerset Maugham clearly explained how theatrical experience could be useful to a playwright who turned to storytelling through the craft of fiction, and the lessons to be learned on stage Maugham saw of value also would apply to a director making the transition from stage to screen who would also need to master the components of narrative storytelling. Although many "eminent novelists have tried their hands at playwriting," Maugham remarked, he could not "think of any that have succeeded," because the experience of writing a novel "is of no help when it comes to writing a play." The novelist had time to develop themes, characters, and motivation: "[I]f he is skilful he can give verisimilitude to improbabilities; if he has a gift for narrative he can gradually work up to a climax which a long preparation makes more striking; he does not have to show action but only write about it; he can make the persons explain themselves in dialogue for as many pages as he likes" (1962, 62).

However, plays depend on action: "[T]he power of attention that an audience has is very limited, and must be held by a constant succession of incidents; something fresh must be doing all the time; the theme must be presented at once and its development must follow a definite line, without digression into irrelevant by-paths; the dialogue must be crisp and pointed, and it must be so put that the listener can catch its meaning without having to stop and think; the characters must be all of a piece, easily grasped by the eye and the understanding and however complex, their complexity must be plausible" (1962, 62).

If the successful playwright then turns to writing novels, he will have an advantage: "He has learned to be brief, he has learned the value of rapid incident, he has learned not to linger on the way, but to stick to his point and get on with his story; he has learned to make his characters display themselves by their words and actions without the help of description" (1962, 62–63). It is debatable that Fielding was able to apply all of these "lessons," when he wrote his first novel, *Joseph Andrews*, notorious for its so-called digressions; but it is not debatable that John Osborne applied all of these lessons when he wrote the screeenplay for *Tom Jones* and certainly that Richardson had "learned the value of rapid incident" when he transformed that screenplay brilliantly into his Academy Award-winning motion picture. Both the director and the playwright who had collaborated on theatre and film productions instinctively knew how the action could be dramatized so as to display Fielding's characters through their words and actions.

This Fielding analogy has a further application to both Richardson's career and the goals of the Free Cinema. Dr. Samuel Johnson took the high moral ground in responding to the "corrupt" novels of Henry Fielding, whom he dismissed as a "blockhead" and "a barren rascal." Boswell defended Fielding, however: "Will you not allow, Sir, that he draws very natural pictures of human life?"—to which Dr. Johnson responded, dismissively, "Why, Sir, it is of very low life" (qtd. by Maugham 1962, 66–67). In his early features, Tony Richardson also drew "very natural pictures of human life." Somerset Maugham contended that in *Tom Jones* Fielding "described for the first time in English fiction a real man" and quoted Austin Dobson, who wrote that Fielding "made no pretense to produce models of perfection, but pictures of ordinary humanity, rather perhaps in the rough than in the polished, the natural than the artificial, his desire is to do this with absolute truthfulness, neither extenuating nor disguising defects and shortcomings" (qtd. by Maugham, 1962, 66). One senses echoes here of the "first principles" of Italian Neorealism as expressed by Cesare Zavattini and his cohorts who made "pictures of ordinary humanity" in post-war Italy, just as Richardson would later make his own "pictures of ordinary humanity" in postwar Britain.

Which brings us to the question of What was neorealism? and the larger issue of the realistic and the artificial in cinema, questions that have teased British critics out of thought. Simply put, cinema is a realistic medium—that is a commonplace—but the issue of screen realism has been thoroughly debated by critics in Britain, and this is not the place to rehearse that larger argument. (Those particularly interested in so-called kitchen-sink realism and nice distinctions between "surface realism" and "moral realism" may find such matters discussed at length in Andrew Higson's anthology *Dissolving Views*, published by Cassell in 1996.) Suffice it to say that Richardson welcomed the opportunity to escape the artificial limitations of the stage. He much preferred location shooting to studio sets. *Look Back in Anger* takes the viewer to Jimmy Porter's street stall, to the cemetery, to the jazz club, and, at the end, to the train station, but opening up the play in this way does not necessarily make it "realistic" or free it of artifice. Watching the film, as good as it is, the viewer does not and cannot entirely forget that it has been adapted from a stage play. The exterior settings work better as cinema in *A Taste of Honey* to make viewers forget that film's theatrical antecedents, and, to a degreee this is also true of Richardson's second feature film, *The Entertainer*, also adapted from a John Osborne play. But in *The Entertainer* Archie Rice is, after all, a stage performer, a fact one is not likely to forget if that character is played by Laurence Olivier.

The Italian neorealists believed that filmmakers should work with nonprofessionals, that trained actors could not give entirely "natural" performances because of their stage training. Professional actors could not be spontaneous and honest when "performing" before the camera. Of all the British New Wave filmmakers, only Peter Watkins and Kevin Brownlow would attempt to observe this principle, but after *Culloden* (1964) and *The War Game* (1965), even Watkins was forced to compromise when he made *Privilege* for Universal Studios, London, in 1967. Although his protagonist pop singer Paul Jones and Jean Shrimpton (a model) were not trained actors and Watkins was able to tease "natural" performances from them, the supporting cast consisted of professionals. Only in his later films, most notably *Edvard Munch* (1974), would Watkins return to the neorealist ideal in terms of casting.

Richardson, by contrast, always drew his talent from the theatre and favored professional actors, an absolute necessity if he were to become a mainline Hollywood film director. Artifice was the stuff of his cinema, though he did take chances, as when, for example, he cast the unknown but distinctive Rita Tushingham in the lead role of *A Taste of Honey*, adapted by Richardson and Shelagh Delaney from her play in 1961. Moreover, could anyone criticize Richardson for casting Olivier, Richard Burton, Tom Courtenay, Albert Finney, Anthony Hopkins, or any other actors who had mastered their craft on stage? Peter Watkins started his career by making documentaries and knew he could work without seeking star talent; Tony Richardson started his career in theatre and knew actors willing to work under his direction. Watkins would specialize in documentary and do his best work adapting history and biography to the screen. Richardson would specialize in adapting drama and literature to the screen and would pursue an entirely different and more conventional track of filmmaking. Indeed, as will be discussed in some detail later, Richardson had a special talent for adaptation.

Take, for example, *The Loneliness of the Long Distance Runner*, adapted from Alan Sillitoe's story that demonstrated the integrity of a criminal psychopath, seduced into performing for the benefit of others but ultimately deciding to resist authority in order to become his own man. The character's "anger," his developing sense of *ressentiment*, a kind of supercharged resentment that comes of an awareness that one is being manipulated by others, and his entrapment as a consequence of class are themes that recur in the cinema of Tony Richardson.

In general, as was noticed at the time of its release, Richardson's film resembled Truffaut's *Les quatre cents coups* (1959), a benchmark of the French New Wave, especially in the way Richardson redefines his protagonist, Colin Smith, who is seen in the film as the product of a squalid, working-class environment, a boy who, under better circumstances, might have turned out differently. But there is far more anger in Sillitoe's protagonist, whose first-person narration shows him to be a social outcast—and proud of it. Like Antoine Doinel in Truffaut's film, Richardson's Colin Smith is given to mischief, stealing an automobile on a lark and robbing a bakery, which gets him thrown into the Borstal, a juvenile detention center. The main difference between these two films is that *Les quatre cents coups* is partly autobiographical and far more personal. Truffaut sees his character from the inside out. As Roy Armes has written, Truffaut "makes similar material into an extremely vital filmic experience because the work is deeply felt by the director and its style is shaped so as to convey from within the social vision of the protagonist" (1978, 269).

Because Antoine Doinel is so much younger than Smith, the audience is more sympathetic about his attempts to deal with the adult world, his uncaring parents, and his foolish, dictatorial teachers. Both Antoine and Colin are seen being interviewed by a psychiatrist after their incarceration. Antoine cooperates as best he can, and the psychiatrist seems to sense the troubles he has had at home. However, Colin turns the interview into a cynical game and does his best to make the interviewer look like a fool when giving his perfectly absurd word-association responses. Richardson, by contrast, seems to be an outsider looking in, detached from the boy's feelings, distanced from the boy's experience by education and class. "Perhaps because of his own distance from such sentiments," Armes speculates, Richardson is unable to find "a stylistic equivalent to this first-person narration," and his "failure of empathy and often clumsily derivative visual style are compounded by the way in which he stridently dominates his films at the expense of his writers" (1978, 269).

A SPECIAL TALENT FOR ADAPTATION,
OR A "MODEST" ONE?

From almost the beginning, Richardson had his detractors. "If directors may be compared to horses," Dwight Macdonald wrote, for example, "I see Antonioni as a thoroughbred flat-racer, Truffaut as a steeplechase jumper soaring lightly over obstacles." Extending this metaphor, he described Tony Richardson "as a hackney, by which I don't mean 'hack,' for he is ambitious and serious, but merely the dictionary definition: 'a horse for ordinary driving and riding'" (1969, 426). His films offer "simple transportation," Macdonald continued, "a virtue—most movies don't get you anywhere—but a modest one." Richardson's defect, indeed "his directorial trademark," was his inability to achieve unity. Macdonald reached this conclusion after comparing *The Loneliness of the Long Distance Runner* to Truffaut's *Les quatre cents coups*, which might in fact be the better film, but it does not necessarily follow that Richardson's film lacks unity, even though the film's chronology may be fragmented, shifting frequently between past and present to tell the runner's story. In fact, one could just as easily argue that the film is extraordinarily well structured and unified. It begins and ends with Colin Smith running, whereas Truffaut's film ends with Doinel in flight. Richardson's whole film could be regarded as a record of Smith's thoughts and memories as he runs and attempts to make sense of his disadvantaged young life.

Of course, Smith is not so endearing as Truffaut's Antoine Doinel, who is six years younger than Smith, but Smith at the age of eighteen is better able to make sense of his experience, to realize that he is being exploited and manipulated. An epiphany occurs to him as he approaches the finish line of the big race—that he is his own person, that he is free to choose his fate and whether or not he will win the race that the warden of the Borstal so wants him to win for the warden's own glory. Smith chooses to lose and to resist authority, and Richardson's film clearly explains his reasons for doing so. Even Macdonald concedes that Richardson's film has "realism, pathos, an interesting performance by a new young actor," Tom Courtenay, and "a cinematic liveliness rare in British films about working-class life." Are these not significant accomplishments? After all, Richardson cannot be blamed for not being Truffaut.

Maybe in comparison to Truffaut and Antonioni, Richardson is not a "thoroughbred," but his films establish a track record that certainly has held up over time to the output of his Free Cinema colleagues Lindsay Anderson and Karel Reisz. One could argue (as has been done) that Richardson lacks the "signature" style that Truffaut was able to sustain through his early career and the Doinel features. Richardson's forte was adapting literary and dramatic works to the screen. His early experience was in theatre, and his play adaptations are better than most that had been done by the time Richardson started making films. Moreover, there is a kind of thematic signature that holds his early films together, emanating from his concerns with the working class and the "anger" of the so-called Angry Generation transformed from theatre into film. And there is a sly, winking, distinctive signature that defines the comic style Richardson developed to translate the fiction of Henry Fielding to the screen.

THE ADAPTOR AS CREATOR

What is it that they say about a prophet in his own country? During the course of his career Tony Richardson had more than his share of detractors, both in Britain and in the United States. Was he stylish enough to be truly distinctive? He had a wicked sense of humor, according to those who worked with him—people who genuinely seemed to enjoy working with him (with some exceptions, of course, such as Marianne Faithfull, and, possibly, Anthony Hopkins)—and boundless enthusiasm for new projects, an enthusiasm that could be infectious. That sense of humor served him well when he came to deal with satirical projects, though he might have better resisted the temptation to translate satire into farce. He had a knack for social realism, as is demonstrated by his first feature films in Britain. The same signature is clearly present in *The Loneliness of the Long Distance Runner* and *A Taste of Honey*, for example.

Richardson was multitalented: He had a talent for working with actors and a talent for furthering (or reviving) their careers. He knew how to get the best out of his actors and crew, as the interviews that follow confirm. He was an outstanding entrepreneur. In fact, as Angela Allen told us in her interview, "What I think was his forte, his strongest talent, was that he was a brilliant entrepreneur," also noting that "that side of him hasn't been fully appreciated." She went on to praise his generosity: "He gave so many chances and breaks to people."

Because he made many films that were adapted from novels, short stories, and plays, he was attacked for lacking originality, but he had a special talent for adaptation, and he made more than his share of excellent movies. Critics sniped at him because they claimed, as already noted, *Long Distance Runner* was merely imitative of Truffaut. Indeed, there may be parallels, but Richardson was, in his defense, merely following the general design of Alan Sillitoe's story, though one might rightly criticize him for sentimentalizing Colin Smith and giving him motives that his criminal psychopath counterpart in the story lacked. As William L. Horne points out in his essay on *A Taste of Honey* and *The Loneliness of the Long Distance Runner*, Richardson had a special empathy for characters who were outsiders, on the fringe of society.

Richardson's first success as film adaptor followed upon the theatrical success of *Look Back in Anger*, the play that elevated both to celebrity status. Neither Richardson nor John Osborne was entirely comfortable with the "angry young man" label that critics had affixed to them, to the play, and to the character of Jimmy Porter. "The original character of JP was widely misunderstood," Osborne wrote in the London *Observer* in January 1992, "largely because of the emphasis [placed] on the element of 'anger'" (1992, 45). "Wearisome theories about JP's sadism, anti-feminism, even closet homosexuality are still peddled to gullible students by dubious and partisan 'academics,'" Osborne continued, "who should know better." According to the playwright, Jimmy Porter is a "comic character," a man "of gentle susceptibilities, constantly goaded by a brutal and coercive world." Osborne believed it was neither necessary nor advisable "to express bitterness bitterly or anger angrily."

By 1992 Osborne had written a new play, *Déjà vu*, which brought back Jimmy Porter and other characters from *Look Back in Anger*. Richardson, by contrast, was not given to looking back in anger or resentment: "I never look at my old movies," he wrote, "—once done, they're over; the faults can't be changed, the achievements are what they are, so there has never seemed any point to me" (1993, 98). But, he added, "I'm sure *Look Back in Anger* remains in the category of that hybrid, the filmed play," admitting that one of his "greatest weaknesses as a director" was that he "loved writing too much and respected it too much." Unlike Osborne, Richardson was never a man to dwell on the past. In adapting *Look Back in Anger*, he certainly "opened up" the play by moving the action to exterior London locations, but the viewer is still reminded that this is a film adapted from a play. This was also his approach in adapting Shakespeare to the screen.

"A KING OF INFINITE SPACE"?

Reviewing Franco Zeffirelli's *Hamlet* for *The Christian Science Monitor*, John Tibbetts borrowed this phrase from Shakespeare's play ("Oh God, I could be bounded in a nutshell and count myself a king of infinite space, were it not that I have bad dreams" [II.ii.251–53]) to title his review, then Paul Meier reborrowed it as the title for his essay that follows here. It is a good phrase to use in the theatrical context for Tony Richardson, who could be "bounded in a nutshell" while working within the confines of the stage, though he preferred to liberate himself when filming, "opening up" stage plays by extending the action to exterior locations. The whole wide world was waiting outside the theatre, and "outside," as John Tibbetts writes in his chapter following our interviews with Richardson's co-workers, "in every sense of the word, metaphoric, realistic, artistic, was where he always wanted to go."

One obvious exception to this preference is the "bold" and experimental *Hamlet* Richardson filmed at the Roundhouse Theatre in 1969. The film has particular interest because it provides a visual and aural record of Nicol Williamson's definitive performance as the prince in the justly famous London production Richardson mounted, with Anthony Hopkins as an oily and devious Claudius. Though not especially "cinematic," the production is interesting in many ways. Richardson chose not to emphasize Hamlet's denial of life, for example. Instead, Richardson makes him the victim of a very corrupt world. All the characters are portrayed as the hostile and melancholy Prince would be likely to perceive them. Claudius is stripped of the rhetorical elegance Shakespespeare has given him and reduced to the besotted satyr of Hamlet's imaginings. Judy Parfitt's Gertrude is voluptuous and given entirely to carnal luxury. Ophelia as played by Marianne Faithfull is merely a tart, incestuously intimate with her brother, Laertes. Richardson interprets the Court through the disturbed and cynical prism of Hamlet's imagination.

In filming the play, however, Richardson made no attempt to open up the play or disguise the fact that it was a classic play, unlike Franco Zeffirelli, whose later *Hamlet*, released in 1991 and starring Mel Gibson as the prince, was filmed by David Watkin at Dunnottar, a fourteenth-century castle some fifty miles south of Aberdeen on the North Sea, at Blackness on the Firth of Forth, outside Edinburgh, and at Dover Castle in Kent, where the shooting began on April 23, 1990, Shakespeare's presumed birthdate (Stivers 1991, 50). But what Richardson understood, that Zeffirelli apparently did not, was that the real challenge of filming this play is to place the viewer inside the prince's *mind*, not his castle.

The play *Hamlet* is a masterpiece of construction. What Zeffirelli also did not apparently understand, unlike Richardson, was that the blocks of text which constitute the mystery of *Hamlet* cannot be capriciously restructured without rearranging the puzzle, and once that puzzle has been mutilated, the enigma will be magnified and damaged. A good film adaptation of any play or novel will both simplify and clarify the text, but Zeffirelli simply muddles the meaning of *Hamlet* by tampering with the text.

Reviewing the Mel Gibson *Hamlet* in 1991, Stanley Kauffmann noted that "little of the play is used," and that Zeffirelli "cut a good deal more than 50 percent of the original" (1991, 24). In his chapter on *Hamlet* that follows in this collection, Paul Meier notes that Richardson reduces the text of the play by about 50 percent, too, as Michael Mullen definitively demonstrated by actually counting the lines excised from the text—and listing them—in an essay published in *Literature/Film Quarterly* in 1976. But, as should be obvious to anyone who really knows the play, the problem is not so much in simply cutting lines from the text (though, as Kevin Kline remarked to an interviewer when he was making the version that aired on PBS in 1990, "In *Hamlet*, every cut bleeds!"); the problem with Zeffirelli's *Hamlet* is the way the screenplay rearranges, restructures, and purposefully misplaces lines in unexpected contexts where they cannot make sense ("Get thee to a nunnery," for example, absurdly inserted to the Mousetrap scene), making a jumble of the text and of Shakespeare's design. By contrast, Richardson's cuts are nearly seamless, creating the illusion that the whole play is intact (excepting the Fortinbras business at the end), when in fact, it is not. Much more is required than the $15 million budget Zeffirelli had to do that kind of *Hamlet* properly, but Richardson accomplished a lot more than Zeffirelli with far less money.

The film is a tribute to Richardson's theatrical sense. It gives Horatio his due, as played by Gordon Jackson, and Anthony Hopkins is a far better Claudius than Alan Bates in the Zeffirelli version, who is stripped of too many lines and simply not convincing in his villainy. In the Zef-firelli film, Mel Gibson is an agitated and animated Hamlet, but his is no more inventive an interpretation of the prince than Nicol Williamson's, which Gibson seems to have imitated, a smartalec prince with attitude problems. Otherwise, Richardson's casting is splendid, even the tempera-mental Marianne Faithfull, whose Ophelia is worldly wise rather than innocent and fragile.

The casting is also amusingly flamboyant. Richardson's Claudius, for example, is given to hedonistic excess and because of the cuts made in Act I, Scene ii, not sufficiently attentive to foreign policy. A paragon of lust, avarice, and luxury, Hopkins's Claudius has more bite and back-bite than the ineffectual buffoon played by Alan Bates. Richardson under-stood, as Zeffirelli apparently did not, that Claudius has to be convinc-ingly dangerous and a worthy opponent of Hamlet. When Polonius enters the royal bed chamber with news of Hamlet and addresses the king and queen, who are lolling with dogs and fruit and indulging in "reechy kisses" shamelessly, Richardson provides a unique context for Polonius's opening line, "to expostulate what majesty should be" (II.ii.86–87). Whatever "majesty should be," it is not the gross and vulgar spectacle that Polonius is witnessing. Mark Dignam's Polonius is more comic-likable than Ian Holm's more "businesslike" Polonius in the Zeffirelli, who is less foolish and less rambling and less the "tedious old fool" that Hamlet rec-ognizes him to be.

The point that really needs to be made about Richardson's bare-bones low-budget *Hamlet* is that the director manages to turn liabilities into assets. It is filmed in a made-for-television style that depends mainly upon close-ups and two-shots. As a consequence, Richardson places the emphasis squarely upon the text, the language, and the actors, which is a perfectly agreeable way of capturing Shakespeare on film, even if it does not attempt to utilize the advantages of the medium fully. It is a carefully executed, well-performed rendering of the definitive production of the 1960s, and it has special relevance because it records for posterity the remarkable performance of Nicol Williamson.

OR, "A FELLOW OF INFINITE JEST"?

Hamlet is packed with usable, quotable phrases for critics to pillage, and perhaps this one, wrenched from the gravedigger's scene, best describes

Tony Richardson himself, the man, not the artist: "Alas, poor Yorick! I knew him, Horatio, a fellow of infinite jest, of excellent fancy" (V.i.172–75). By all accounts from those who knew and loved him, Richardson was also "a fellow of infinite jest" as well as one of "excellent fancy," whose imaginative powers were extended to the cinema, a merry prankster given to mischief and practical jokes, as the examples cited by David Watkin and Kevin Brownlow in the interviews that follow give ample evidence.

Other stories abound. When he made *The Charge of the Light Brigade*, for example, Richardson wanted to use a particular breed of Arab horses in the interest of historical accuracy. Richardson went to a breeder of these horses to ask if he could use them, but he was promptly turned down. Undaunted, he persevered, and eventually a contract was signed. At the signing of this contract, Richardson was reputed to have joked: "Well, I do want you to know that we are going to be doing this film in a realistic way, so you won't mind if we mutilate some of them, will you?" "Anyone will tell you twenty stories like that," one source said of Richardson's sense of humor.

All of our sources pointed out that Richardson was very responsive to actors, but he was not above trickery. David Warner had a story about *Tom Jones*. "I would like to play this role," he told the director, "but you know I can't ride a horse." Richardson assured him that would be no problem, but on the first day of shooting he found himself on horseback, next to Albert Finney. "You know I can't ride, don't you," the actor reminded him, and Richardson answered, "Yes, I know. We'll just rehearse the dialogue." Then he said, "All right, then. Now we're going to shoot. I want you to speak your lines and then I want you to give the horse a little bid of a nudge with your heels, and I want you to ride into the distance, and then you can do whatever you want." Richardson was more considerate of Sir John Gielgud, who was also afraid of horses, since he had been thrown during his first riding lesson in Turkey, where *Charge of the Light Brigade* was filmed. According to Michael Munn's *Trevor Howard: The Man and His Films* (Scarborough House, 1990), Richardson saw to it that Gielgud's horse's reigns were secured by extras standing on either side of him to keep the horse from bolting.

Richardson was a sociable person, famous for his parties in South Kensington, Paris, Hollywood, and at his home in the south of France, Le Nid du Duc, north of Saint-Tropez, near La Garde Freinet, frequented by friends such as David Hockney, Christopher Isherwood, John Mortimer,

John Osborne, Sam Spiegel, Joan Didion, John Gregory Dunne, Jack Nicholson, John Gielgud, Jessica Mitford, Rudolf Nureyev, his former wife Vanessa Redgrave, and their daughters Joely and Natasha. "We spent holidays together," Joan Didion wrote in her introduction to the American edition of Richardson's memoirs. "His daughter Natasha was married in our house. I loved him" (1993, 17). Cinematographer David Watkins told us, "I *adored* him." John Osborne, who had a falling out with Richardson over *The Charge of the Light Brigade*, was to write in the second volume of his memoirs, "No one has inflamed my creative passions more tantalizingly than Tony, nor savaged my moral sensibilities so cruelly. Whatever wayward impulse of torment he inflicted, his gangling, whiplash courage, struggling within that contorted figure, was awesomely moving and, at the last, unimpeachable" (1991, 116).

Richardson peaked early in Hollywood and suffered a decline after the tremendous popular success of *Tom Jones*. One might have assumed that he later turned to *Joseph Andrews,* one of his favorite projects, because he genuinely liked the writing of Henry Fielding, but critics assumed that he was merely exploiting Fielding further, and imitating himself in hopes of repeating his earlier success. They tended to overlook the film's many witty and inventive performances and the skill with which an oversized novel was compressed and simplified; they failed to realize that Richardson was temperamentally drawn to Fielding's satire and humor.

Pauline Kael once remarked that Richardson was "one of the most gifted directors, and one who hasn't had the breaks he deserves." Richardson was not one to be upset by the critics, whom he ridiculed as "a group of acidulated intellectual eunuchs hugging their prejudices like feather boas" (qtd. in Tynan 1992, 85, 118). After adapting John Irving's *Hotel New Hampshire* in 1983, he had to settle for television assignments for seven years before getting the opportunity to make *Blue Sky* in 1990. For reasons quite beyond his control, *Blue Sky* was then shelved for four years and not released until nearly two years after his death in November 1991. When it was finally released in 1994, it earned an Academy Award for Jessica Lange and critical acclaim as well. Richardson was then praised for his "old-fashioned" storytelling abilities. This praise was no doubt well intended and well deserved, but it came too late. However, it reminded the world that Richardson was one of the premiere filmmakers of his generation, and thus justice was done, belatedly.

In his introduction to the British edition of Richardson's memoir *Long Distance Runner*, Lindsay Anderson underscores the significance of

Richardson's work, of Woodfall Films (the production company Richardson founded), "the ground-breaking production of *Saturday Night and Sunday Morning*, which Karel [Reisz] directed," as well as of Richardson's own *Look Back in Anger, The Entertainer,* and *A Taste of Honey.* "Together with *The Loneliness of the Long Distance Runner* and the hugely successful *Tom Jones*," Anderson wrote, "those were films which changed the face of British cinema" (1993, xvi). Anderson went on to say that Tony Richardson "still remained true to himself and his beliefs: films like *The Loved One, The Border, The Hotel New Hampshire* (especially) and *Blue Sky*, his last work, were uneven, but they bore the unmistakable imprint of his personality and his convictions." In other words, such personally directed films were marked with Richardson's signature and were uniquely his own. Richardson therefore should be considered one of the very first *auteur* directors of the *British* New Wave, by the logic of the critic-filmmaker who introduced the *auteur* concept into England before it had been fully formed by the French. To conclude otherwise would do the man a disservice by dismissing the importance of his life's work in cinema.

Tony Richardson, then, was not only obviously and indisputably one of the defining talents of British theatre at mid-century but also a very important filmmaker. He started his career with Karel Reisz and Lindsay Anderson, both of whom have been accorded more critical attention. Allison Graham's *Lindsay Anderson* was published in 1981, for example, and Georg Gaston's *Karel Reisz* was published in 1980, both in the Twayne Theatrical Arts Series then edited by Warren French. And yet Tony Richardson directed more feature films than Karel Reisz and Lindsay Anderson combined, films that were critical successes and Hollywood films that earned Academy Awards, yet no book on Richardson was to appear in the Twayne series.

Good as the best films of Anderson and Reisz were, Richardson had the more impressive career *as filmmaker*. And yet the first critical treatment of Richardson's career—Don Radovich's *Tony Richardson: A Bio-Bibliography*—was not published by Greenwood Press until 1995, four years after the director's death. The time has come for a critical reassessment of Richardson's work in cinema. It is hoped that the essays and interviews that follow will revive a reputation that has been sadly neglected. Tony Richardson was far more important than the usual surveys of British cinema would seem to suggest. Radovich explained that his book was "not designed to be a defense of Tony Richardson's work. That will surely come later" (1995, xi). This book was not designed with that goal exactly in mind, but, as it turned out, it may well serve the purpose. If so, the authors have no regrets.

WORKS CITED

Armes, Roy. *A Critical History of the British Cinema.* New York: Oxford, 1978.

Bartlett, C. J. *History of Postwar Britain, 1945–1974.* London: Longman, 1977.

Caughie, John, with Kevin Rockett. *The Companion to British and Irish Cinema.* London: BFI/Cassell, 1996.

Fielding, Henry. *The History of Tom Jones.* 2 vols. Ed. A. R. Humphries. London: J. M. Dent Everyman's Library, 1962.

Gaston, Georg. *Karel Reisz.* Boston: Twayne Publishers, 1980.

Graham, Allison. *Lindsay Anderson.* Boston: Twayne Publishers, 1981.

Kauffmann, Stanley. "On Film." *The New Republic* 28 (January 1991): 24–25.

Macdonald, Dwight. *On Movies.* New York: Berkley Medallion Books, 1969.

Maugham, W. Somerset. *The Worlds Greatest Novels: Great Novelists and Their Novels.* Greenwich, CT: Fawcett Publications/Premiere Books, 1962.

Mullin, Michael. "Tony Richardson's *Hamlet:* Script to Screen." *Literature/Film Quarterly* 4.2 (Spring 1976): 123–33.

Munn, Michael. *Trevor Howard: The Man and His Films.* Chelsea, MI: Scarborough House, 1990.

Osborne, John. *Almost a Gentleman: An Autobiography, 1955–1966.* Vol. 2. London: Faber and Faber, 1991.

———. "Jimmy Porter, 35 Years On." *The* [London] *Observer* (26 January 1992): 45–46.

Pickering, David. *Dictionary of the Theatre.* London: Penguin/Sphere Books, Ltd., 1988.

Radovich, Don. *Tony Richardson: A Bio-Bibliography.* Westport, CT: Greenwood Press, 1995.

Richardson, Tony. *The Long Distance Runner: A Memoir.* London: Faber and Faber, 1993.

Shakespeare, William. *The Tragedy of Hamlet, Prince of Denmark.* Ed. Willard Farnham. Baltimore, MD: Penguin Books, 1957.

Stivers, Cyndi. "'Hamlet' Revisited." *Premiere* 4:6 (February 1991): 50–56.

Tynan, Kathleen. "Exit Prospero." *Vanity Fair* 55.2 (February 1992): 82–85, 116–19.

Wakeman, John, ed. *World Film Directors, 1945–1985.* Vol. II. New York: H. W. Wilson, 1988.

CHAPTER TWO

"Let's Talk about Tony":
Interviews with Colleagues
(Karel Reisz, Kevin Brownlow,
David Watkin, and Angela Allen)

JOHN C. TIBBETTS AND JAMES M. WELSH

KAREL REISZ INTERVIEW

Karel Reisz was born in 1926, the son of a Jewish lawyer, in Ostrava, Czechslovakia, and was sent to England in 1939, shortly after the Nazi invasion of his native country. He was educated at Emmanuel College, Cambridge, then taught in London for two years at the St. Marlebone Grammar School. In 1949, he turned to journalism and soon was writing film criticism for *Sequence* and *Sight and Sound,* which put him in company with Tony Richardson, Lindsay Anderson, and Gavin Lambert. He was director of the National Film Theatre (1952–53) and wrote *The Technique of Film Editing* (1952), commissioned by the British Film Academy. His first film, *Momma Don't Allow,* was a twenty-two-minute documentary about a jazz club in London, directed in collaboration with Tony Richardson and photographed by Walter Lassally in 1956. This documentary, which launched the filmmaking careers of both Reisz and Richardson, was showcased in the first Free Cinema program at the

National Film Theatre in February 1956. By 1960 Reisz had directed his first feature film, *Saturday Night and Sunday Morning*. Later films included *Morgan!* (1966), *Who'll Stop the Rain* (1978), *The French Lieutenant's Woman* (1981), and *Sweet Dreams* (1985). He was interviewed on January 18, 1997, at his home in North London, where he lives with his wife, the actress Betsy Blair.

JIM WELSH: As the editor of *Literature/Film Quarterly*, I thought you might be surprised by the number of essays we've published on *The French Lieutenant's Woman* and the continuing academic interest in the achievement of that adaptation.

KAREL REISZ: Yes . . . well . . . good. But let's talk about Tony.

JOHN TIBBETTS: First, however, would you set the scene for us, where we are exactly, maybe how long you've been here?

KAREL REISZ: I've lived in North London for, oh, forty-five years, and this is my home . . . where I've been for twenty-five years. This room is my nest.

JOHN TIBBETTS: And surrounded by books, more art books than any other individual subject.

KAREL REISZ: Well, it's not the only room where there are books. The film books are downstairs.

JOHN TIBBETTS: When did your association with Tony begin?

KAREL REISZ: I'm hopeless about dates. It was when I was running the programs at the National Film Theatre . . . the early fifties . . . at a time when I hadn't made any movies yet. I'd worked on a magazine, a film magazine. Tony rang me out of the blue. Did you know Tony?

JIM WELSH: No, unfortunately, we didn't.

JOHN TIBBETTS: But we had a nice personality sketch from Kevin Brownlow, very amusing.

KAREL REISZ: Yes. He was very good company—eccentric, opinionated, charming. Absolutely fearless. And he had this weird voice. You'll find, as you talk to people about him, they'll all be doing his voice for you.

JOHN TIBBETTS: We knew that would come up. Kevin said everyone does the voice. Why?

KAREL REISZ: Because it was so bizarre. And he was unaware of it. Gavin Lambert once picked up the phone and there was Tony— "Hello Gavin." "Hi Tony." Tony was absolutely astounded: "How on *earth*," he enquired in his baroque, breathless drawl, "did you guess it was me?"

JOHN TIBBETTS: How did you meet?

KAREL REISZ: He rang me at the BFI and said . . . "You sound like an interesting person. Let's have lunch." Which was absolutely the way he worked. If something interested him, he picked up the phone and did something about it. Anyway—we became friends and quite soon started talking about doing a 16mm. film together.

JOHN TIBBETTS: *Momma Don't Allow?*

KAREL REISZ: Yes, with money from the BFI experimental film fund.

JOHN TIBBETTS: Did he know about or had he read your book on editing?

KAREL REISZ: No, I don't think so. It's the kind of book he would run a mile to avoid.

JOHN TIBBETTS: And you were working on *Sequence* at that time already?

KAREL REISZ: Well, *Sequence* had been before that. *Sequence* collapsed in the early 1950s when Gavin Lambert (who had run the magazine with Lindsay Anderson) became the editor of *Sight and Sound.* There were another two or three issues, and I joined Lindsay as editor. Tony would have seen *Sequence*, yes. He had already had a rather striking career as a theatre director at Oxford—some spectacular undergraduate productions that had made a stir. And he did odd productions, at Stratford East, the Joan Littlewood Theatre . . . one of *The Changeling*, I remember. Then he and George Devine started the English Stage Company at the Royal Court. But you don't need me to talk about all that—the Court's work has been fully documented by people much better qualified than me. And of course it was very important—the new writing, *Look Back in Anger*, all that. Tony was at the very center of it. Yet strangely, for all his importance and success in the theatre of the time, it was the cinema which was his main center of interest and ambition.

JIM WELSH: Was that ever expressed to you directly? Did you talk about films as opposed to theatre?

KAREL REISZ: Not *opposed* . . . For Tony, one led naturally to the other.

JOHN TIBBETTS: How did his production company—Woodfall Films—come about?

KAREL REISZ: Well . . . John Osborne's play *Look Back in Anger*, was an enormous critical and commercial success—both in London and in New York. David Merrick put it on in New York. Tony saw immediately that this success could open doors into the cinema. He and John Osborne formed a production company—Woodfall Films. Its capital was the film rights of *Look Back in Anger*. That's what they had to sell—and they could do it on their own terms. And so—Woodfall was born. Oh yes . . . they brought in a third person—a rather strange, unexpected partner, Harry Saltzman.

JOHN TIBBETTS: Why do you say "strange"?

KAREL REISZ: Well, Harry was a very charming, exuberant sort of rascal, really. He had never made a feature film before in his life, but he had any amount of energy and cheek. He persuaded Tony that they'd need a star—so they got Richard Burton, and Harry took the project to Warners.

JIM WELSH: You mean for *Look Back in Anger?*

KAREL REISZ: Yes. After that, they hung out their shingle and invited projects from kindred spirits. Tony said to me, "If you've got anything you want to make, bring it, and we'll get you the money." And then there was suddenly this golden period of Woodfall, where we were all making films.

JOHN TIBBETTS: Well, *Saturday Night and Sunday Morning* as much as *Look Back in Anger*, certainly in America gave us our first view of what was going on. The two are often almost inseparably linked together.

KAREL REISZ: Yes . . . for a period of four or five years there, Woodfall films became a very important part of the British scene, mainly because the films opened up new territory, I mean new in subject matter. And the pictures were popular.

JOHN TIBBETTS: How did Tony function as a producer?

KAREL REISZ: Well, he and Harry were the nominal producers of *Saturday Night and Sunday Morning*, as you know. But Tony wasn't around when we were shooting. He was doing *Sanctuary*, in Hollywood, by then. He arrived, I think, during the last week. Nor would he have had any desire to interfere in the sense of wanting to control me. His attitude was, "You have a go." And, actually, it wouldn't have interested him to do more.

JOHN TIBBETTS: That was what so impressed Kevin Brownlow, that Richardson was willing to let people "have a go," as you say, and, moreover, people who weren't really tested yet.

KAREL REISZ: Absolutely. I mean, a film like *A Taste of Honey* or a film like *Saturday Night and Sunday Morning* or *The Loneliness of the Long Distance Runner*, they were all made by writers who had never written, directors who had never directed, and actors who had never acted, and so on, all the way down the line. It was Tony's confidence and impresario genius which made it all possible.

JIM WELSH: Could you tell us a little about *Momma Don't Allow*?

KAREL REISZ: It's a little 16mm. film that we shot . . . I think in six Saturday evenings. We went to this jazz club in Wood Green for several months with still cameras so people got used to our presence. And then we attempted a kind of "fly on the wall" treatment: then cobbled together some sort of continuity.

JOHN TIBBETTS: So your intent in making this film was . . .

KAREL REISZ: Just to make a movie about something we thought would be interesting.

JOHN TIBBETTS: Almost as a lark?

KAREL REISZ: No, I think that's to undersell it. I mean, we wanted to make films, and you have to start somewhere. And this seemed like a good subject on which to start. Don't forget that these were pretelevision times, and the opportunities for young filmmakers were very, very scarce. It was very difficult to break in. I think the film cost £350.

JOHN TIBBETTS: Were you working with hand-held equipment, single-track sound?

KAREL REISZ: 16mm. Walter Lassally shot it, and John Fletcher did the sound—under the sort of uncontrolled, spontaneous conditions that were quite new to British filmmaking. These two men were absolutely central to the whole movement of films which developed in the years to follow. The idea was to confront the new realities which the years of labour government had brought about, to catch the extraordinary social changes which were in the air. You have to remember that the British Cinema was very tight-assed and class-bound then: the films were mainly theatre-centered. There were interesting people working in the commercial cinema, I'm not saying there weren't. But, in general, the response of the British cinema to what had actually happened in England in those quickly changing times was minimal. A very substantial change took place in England, and the commercial cinema really ignored it. The most important thing our films did was to take notice. Even when they weren't good, they were about subjects that the cinema had ignored.

JOHN TIBBETTS: And what did you learn about Tony as a man and as a filmmaker by means of this project? I suppose you were first getting to know each other with this film?

KAREL REISZ: We had quite a bumpy ride. It's a ridiculous notion, really, to try and co-direct anything. There were six couples in the film, roughly. I did three, and he did three, and since what you get is what you want in this kind of cinema, the thing was really created in the cutting room. And there was one thing about the film that was interesting. Four or five of the characters were shown in a sort of cross-cutting pattern between work and play. I mean, there was one girl, the carriage cleaner at the railways, and a boy singing in the choir, and so on—that confidence of the postwar generation, when people in their teens had money for the first time. Making the connections between work and play—that's something that was central to the film—and most of the so-called Free Cinema films that followed.

JOHN TIBBETTS: How close an association did you maintain with Tony during the later years?

KAREL REISZ: When he was in London, we met socially. We didn't see each other all the time, no. But we remained friends. We had a bit of a tiff at the end of *Saturday Night*, but it didn't last. And then, in later years, he spent a lot of time in Europe and in America. He really didn't like England in the later years. He certainly didn't like *living* in England. He thought it was very stultifying and anti-enterprise. And he'd lost interest in the Court; his whole life was devoted to movies, and he made a lot of them. Maybe too many. But he loved shooting. Preparation was a necessary evil, and editing was something that he mainly subcontracted to editors. He loved shooting; he loved *activity*.

JOHN TIBBETTS: You worked in America later on. It must have been interesting when you got together to compare notes about working in America.

KAREL REISZ: I don't think we did talk much about it. He was a person of a very untheoretical turn of mind. What interested him was the next project or a new group of actors and a new set of friends, a new environment, and gossip. That doesn't mean he wasn't serious. I think *The Charge of the Light Brigade* is a very serious film. He was given to much horsing around and bitching, but he was very serious, too. With him it was all of a piece.

JIM WELSH: Do you have any recollection of the last time you saw him?

KAREL REISZ: I don't remember the specific occasion. We were probably playing cards. He had this house in King's Road—in Hollywood. I remember I arrived one day, and there was this house, and he said, "I seem to have bought Linda Lovelace's house."

JOHN TIBBETTS: Was he amused by that?

KAREL REISZ: I don't think it particularly interested him, except it was a very, very nice house. Tony had a great gift for houses and gardens, and he was crazy about birds. There were always cages full of toucans and parrots, and newts in aquariums. . . . He had difficulty in later years getting money for his films; but he always seemed to have three projects on the simmer, right to the end.

KEVIN BROWNLOW INTERVIEW

Kevin Brownlow, director, editor, film historian, collector, preservationist, filmmaker, and television producer was born in Crowborough, Sussex, June 2, 1938. He was educated at University College School. While still a boy at school, he developed a passion for collecting films after being hooked on the old movies that his headmaster would project in 9.5 mm. By 1954 he was writing essays on film collecting for *Amateur Cine-World* and at work on his first amateur film, *The Capture*, adapted from "Les Prisonniers," a short story by Guy de Maupassant. He learned to edit film in 1955, when he found a job with World Wide Pictures, a London firm that specialized in industrial documentaries. His first feature film, *It Happened Here*, was made in collaboration with Andrew Mollo. It was started in 1956 but not completed until 1964 and was helped along in its final stages by Tony Richardson. Brownlow worked with both Lindsay Anderson and Tony Richardson at Woodfall Films from 1965 to 1968 and edited, among other films, *The Charge of the Light Brigade* for Tony Richardson. In 1968 Brownlow published *The Parade's Gone By . . .*, a groundbreaking collection of interviews with pioneering filmmakers, and completed his documentary *Abel Gance: The Charm of Dynamite*, made for the BBC "Omnibus" television series. In 1975, working again with Andrew Mollo, Brownlow directed *Winstanley*, named for the seventeenth-century visionary Gerrard Winstanley and adapted from David Caute's historical novel *Comrade Jacob*. All the while, Brownlow had been working on a tremendously important project, restoring Abel Gance's epic *Napoléon* to the five-hour length of its premiere in 1927, including the tryptich "Polyvision" finale, which set the world standard for widescreen projection. For his outstanding contribution to French culture—his restored *Napoléon* was presented in London, Paris, New York, Washington, and Telluride, where it premiered in September 1979—Brownlow was named *Chevalier des Arts et des Lettres*. With David Gill, Brownlow produced and directed the thirteen-part *Hollywood* series for Thames Television in 1980, followed by *Unknown Chaplin*, a three-part series that used never-before-seen footage from Chaplin's archives to demonstrate how the comedian made his pictures. His work on Chaplin was then followed by *Buster Keaton: A Hard Act to Follow* and *Harold Lloyd: The Third Genius*. Brownlow's most recent book is the massive biography *David Lean* (1996). He was interviewed at his home north of London on January 17, 1997.

FIGURE 2.1. Kevin Brownlow, Filmmaker. Photo by John C. Tibbetts.

KEVIN BROWNLOW: How did I first come in contact with Tony Richardson? I'll tell you how it happened. Andrew Mollo and I were making *It Happened Here*, and we were running out of everything and desperately needed a sponsor to get us to the end. Andrew took a job as personal assistant to [Woodfall producer] Harry Saltzman, who produced *Saturday Night, Sunday Morning* with Tony Richardson, and Andrew became assistant director on that. He went on to others like *Loneliness of the Long Distance Runner* and spoke to Richardson, who said to him: "How much would you want to finish the film?" And, plucking a figure out of his head, Andrew said £3,000. Richardson said, "If you can make it for £3,000, I'll get you the money." Of course, we knew we couldn't, but said we could in the hope of hooking him, and so he produced the money. We became a subsidiary of Woodfall. We had the same note paper, but the name of the company we were given was Rath Films, God knows why; it sounds like something out of Lewis Carroll. And then it was changed to Long Distance Films, when the other film entered production. And that helped, on telephone calls, I can tell you: "Who's speaking?" "Long Distance!" "Oh, just a minute, I'll get him for you!" So I met Richardson, who was a sort of character that you might joke about. He was very languid and talked [imitating Richardson] "just like this, and had a very distinctive voice." He came from Bradford, and he would have talked like [the artist] David Hockney once. But he came into the theatre at a time when it was necessary to speak with an Oxford accent, so he did his best, and it ended up [again imitating Richardson] "talking like that, and it sounded most peculiar." Everybody had Tony Richardson jokes, but he was an encourager. He was one of the very few people in the British cinema who wasn't festering with jealousy about everyone else they knew. And he would give people a start. He made Desmond Davis, his camera operator, into a director. He was the one who took up the cause of *Kes* for Ken Loach, and got it released! He did all sorts of wonderful work that was never acknowledged. He was also a very mischievous character.

Richardson was very interested in the cinema, but he veered too much towards [Jean-Luc] Godard, for my liking. He was a man essentially of the theatre, who didn't think very strongly in filmic terms. And yet he became a very fine film director—and certainly *Charge of the Light Brigade* proves it—a pure film director. But it took a bit of time. I think the first ones are pretty heavygoing. He's simply putting a theatrical event on film. But as far as we were concerned, he left us alone, and we were able to continue with the film [*It Happened Here*]. Richardson had linked up with [John] Osborne to create Woodfall Films. Then Richardson went away to France for *Mademoiselle* and *Sailor from Gibraltar*, and he was completely out of the running. Osborne took over just as we came to the end of production, and we had gone over our budget, and we desperately needed more in order to finish the film. Osborne came to see the film, and at the end of it, he turned around and said, "Congratulations" [and] shook our hands, then went out to where the [Woodfall] producer Oscar Lewenstein was standing and said, "God, I hated it!" and froze any further progress. We then waited until Richardson came back, and he saw it and said, "Of course, it's marvelous," and started the whole thing up again and enabled us to get a United Artists release, which, for what was essentially an amateur film, was unique. That was due to him. . . .

I was still an editor, and Lindsay Anderson hired me to edit *The White Bus*. At that time Lindsay Anderson, Peter Brook, and Tony Richardson were supposed to be the three top art-house directors, and United Artists had the idea of making a film combining their talents, called "*Red, White, and Zero*," the last one being Zero Mostel. The first one was called "*Red and Blue*" [1967], one I also cut, which was heavily influenced by *Umbrellas of Cherbourg* [1964, directed by Jacques Demy]. It was a musical in that style, but it did not work, although it was beautifully photographed by Billy Williams and had Vanessa Redgrave and Douglas Fairbanks. *The White Bus* was very experimental, very avant-garde, and wasn't going to work with any mainstream audience. But it got me hired to do *Red and Blue*. Tony Richardson left me completely alone to do the editing, which surprised me, and simply commented on it in the projection room, rather like a Hollywood director. I watched some of the filming of that, I think [even] filmed some of the shooting. Eventually, United Artists got fed up with the Peter Brook one never being finished, and they put out *Red and Blue* as a short subject with *The Graduate*. Now *The Graduate* was the latest thing in risqué cinema at that period. And *Red and Blue* was so out of date from that point of view, it was laughed off the screen. They took it off after two or three days, and it was never shown again. But because

Richardson had made that mega-hit *Tom Jones*, he was able to sail on for ages making films which didn't make money. *Hamlet* was an example of that, with Nicol Williamson, which was just a version of a play he put on at the Roundhouse [theatre]. I remember being there for the opening night, and Nicol Williamson said, "To be, or not to be . . . *Oh, fuck!*" and walked off the stage. Then you heard Richardson in the audience say, "Come back, Nicol!" And at that point in the play, you didn't even have Marianne Faithfull to look at while he was off-stage. It was a sort of happening, which was very popular in the sixties, so it didn't matter.

In 1967 I felt if I wasn't directing professionally by the end of the year, I never would make it. (I proved to be right.) And so, when Richardson offered me *The Charge of the Light Brigade* as editor, I turned it down. He then got another editor he didn't get on with. When I started seeing the rushes, I thought they were absolutely stunning and wished to God I hadn't turned it down because I still hadn't found work as a director. So I came on it halfway through, when they came back from Turkey. He had a second-unit director, and it was fascinating to compare the second-unit work on the events which he also filmed. The second-unit work was like film school, but Tony's was exceptional. He was a really first-rate director. His stuff was very high standard, and he once said—because he had Gielgud and Harry Andrews and Trevor Howard, he said that he felt that half of the job of directing was solved if you did the casting correctly. So that by having Trevor Howard as Cardigan, you were halfway there. It is true, but you still have to present visually. That's the difficult part. He was lucky enough to have David Watkin.

One of the things David Watkin did on *Charge* with that was to use old lenses to get an old look, which worked wonderfully most of the time, but I remember seeing one set of rushes that involved the Household Cavalry in the uniforms of the time. (Incidentally, the family of my partner, Andrew Mollo, were now deeply involved in this picture, and John Mollo's career started [there], and it climaxed with him getting an Academy Award for *Star Wars*. I think he got another one for *Gandhi*. And this was all due to the fact that Andrew was too busy with me to work on those pictures for which, of course, he would have got the Academy Award. However, that's show business.)

We saw these Household Cavalry rushes, and there was quite serious bleeding of light into the horsemen. The sky was too hot, and Tony says, "What's the matter? Why's it doing *that*?" The cameraman wasn't there, so I said, "Well, my guess is that these lenses are designed to be used at 5.6 [f-stop] ideally, and here were wide open at 2.5 because it was a dull day, and they're not designed for English weather." Well, of course, being a man who loved mischief, he went straight to David Watkin, and in front of the whole cast says, "Kevin Brownlow says that you're not using those lenses properly!" Can you imagine? So then he said to me, "Oh, do come down to the set Kevin, David Watkin wants to have a word with you!" So I went down to the set, in all innocence, and you can imagine what David Watkin said. . . .

JIM WELSH: A colleague of mine interviewed Richardson twenty years ago. I had read Cecil Woodham-Smith's *The Reason Why* (McGraw-Hill, 1953) within a year or two of when I saw the film, and it seemed to me Richardson's film followed the book's interpretation of events very closely indeed. But when asked, Richardson denied any link between the book and his film . . .

KEVIN BROWNLOW: Well, that [book] was what would have been made, but Laurence Harvey bought the rights to it, so that he could make it. John Osborne then wrote a script for *Charge of the Light Brigade* and was sued for plagiarism on behalf of Cecil Woodham-Smith and lost. The situation was settled with a great deal of money; the script was rewritten by Charles Wood. Laurence Harvey, as part of the settlement, said, "I want a part in the film." Since he obviously wasn't going to be Nolan or Cardigan, Richardson gave him the part of Prince Radziwill, who was in charge of the Heavy Brigade. But when we were cutting the picture and we had to shorten it, Tony Richardson said, "I'd love to cut Laurence Harvey out of this picture. Shall we just take him out? Let's cut the charge of the Heavy Brigade completely! Then we won't have Laurence Harvey." So we did; we took that out. Not just because we were tight for time. It was four hours, like Branagh's *Hamlet*. I thought it actually played better at four hours than it did in its final length. You can just glimpse [Laurence Harvey] in the theatre scene, but, otherwise, he was eliminated.

JOHN TIBBETTS: Any feedback from him about that?

KEVIN BROWNLOW: I never heard any, but there must have been. Yes, there must have been. We were all desperately disappointed in the failure of that film. We all thought we were off to the races and this was going to be a huge hit. I thought it was terrific.

JOHN TIBBETTS: Well it certainly was making the right kind of message at the right time, and it did have David Hemmings . . .

KEVIN BROWNLOW: What it didn't have was Errol Flynn. That's really what people wanted to see. They wanted a thrilling charge. They didn't want to see horses falling over and blown up and people being killed and injured; [they didn't want to see] what war was really like. They really didn't. It sounded as though it was going to be a fantastic romantic adventure.

JOHN TIBBETTS: Was it difficult for Richardson, then, the fate of the film? Did he take it hard?

KEVIN BROWNLOW: Well, he left the country then. I think he did *Laughter in the Dark*, which I didn't cut. I went to the American Film Institute then, and Richardson gave it to my assistant, Charles Rees, again taking a chance on a complete beginner, which is typical of him. But Charles showed me some rushes, which would give you some idea of how Richardson went on. Nicol Williamson was in it, and there was a scene looking up at a Spanish mansion, and behind the slate board you could hear Tony's instructions: "Acting away, Nicol, acting away!"

JOHN TIBBETTS: How many other associations were there, then, after that?

KEVIN BROWNLOW: After *Charge*, did I have with Richardson? Well, I'm sure that was the finish of it because he went off, and I don't think I ever saw him again. Isn't that extraordinary? I don't think I ever saw him again. Occasionally I ran into Neil Hartley [a production manager for David Merrick Richardson befriended, who, Richardson wrote in his memoir, "knew nothing about making movies" before their association and before becoming producer for *Charge of the Light Brigade*]. He would be a very, very valuable man to interview, because he was Richardson's producer, an American, World War II-vintage American, who was a very nice bloke. He wasn't at all a producer, not the type you normally get. All the

FIGURE 2.2. *Laughter in the Dark* (Nicol Williamson and Anna Karina)

people around him were extremely pleasant, extremely relaxed, very funny. It was a totally different atmosphere from the usual British film company. I felt an aversion to most people in the British film industry, which was why I never really wanted to go into it. And the beautiful thing about Richardson was that he thought, "It's all a lot of nonsense. Why do we have to sit in studios all the time? Let's go out into the street and take a house and use that as a studio, but have some *fun!*" And in the cutting room (not mine, because I don't go for such things), he had bottles of champagne lined up on the rack. That really summed him up. There was a bitter and twisted side to him. He loved to get relationships breaking up on pictures, and he would quite happily set married couples at each other's throats. And at the end of *Charge of the Light Brigade* I remember being present at a showing of a rough cut and the crew had given him a present. What would you give your director after a picture like that? They gave him a boa constrictor. And he was saying to his Polish chauffeur, Jan, "You'll have to give it the mice! I'm not going to feed it!" So there was something very strange about him.

JOHN TIBBETTS: I imagine the news of his death was a shock to you if you hadn't seen him in all that time?

KEVIN BROWNLOW: Absolutely! I was amazed. He was very gregarious, but he wasn't social, I suspect. He didn't keep in touch with people. He used to hold the most extraordinary parties. He was going to do *Ned Kelly* with Ian McKellen, and Ian McKellen told me recently that he was studying the part and doing an enormous amount of research. He had just come out of the shower, and he got a note or a telephone call that said, "We're using Mick Jagger," just like that, and he was absolutely devastated. So I think Tony had great problems with relationships. Like so many artists.

DAVID WATKIN INTERVIEW

David Watkin, a world class artistic cinematographer, was born in Margate, England, in 1925. His first film assignment was *The Knack—and How to Get It* in 1965, the first of several films lensed for Richard Lester, including *Help!* (1965), *How I Won the War* (1967), *The Bed-Sitting Room*

FIGURE 2.3. David Watkin, Cinematographer. Photo by John C. Tibbetts.

(1969), *The Three Musketeers* (1974), *The Four Musketeers* (1975), and *Robin and Marian* (1976). His genius for color and composition is evident in the films he shot for many gifted directors—Ken Russell (*The Devils* and *The Boy Friend*, both in 1971), Franco Zeffirelli (*Endless Love* [1981] and *Hamlet* [1990]), Hugh Hudson (*Chariots of Fire*, 1981) and Sydney Pollack (*Out of Africa*, 1985, for which he won an Academy Award and the British Academy Award as well). He worked with Tony Richardson on several pictures: *Mademoiselle* (1966), *The Charge of the Light Brigade* (1968), *A Delicate Balance* (1973), *Joseph Andrews* (1977), and *The Hotel New Hampshire* (1984). He also started *Mahogany* (1975) with Richardson, though Richardson left the project, which was taken over by Barry Gordy, who took directing credit. Mr. Watkin was interviewed at his home in Brighton on January 20, 1997. The interview was more like a monologue.

> DAVID WATKIN: Certain people are like a lighthouse, an influence you never lose. Tony was one of those people to me. One of the things that Tony had was that he was very, very particular about human behavior. He didn't like any form of dishonesty, but he was extremely mischievous. If I were to say, for instance, to Tony, that Jim was a bit of an idiot, the very next time we would all be together, Tony would say to Jim, "David says you are a bit of an idiot!" That was Tony. If someone has a sense of humor, I can work with him. If they don't, then it's hard.
>
> We first met when I was doing documentary films. I started in 1948, and my first film as a cameraman was in 1955. I had wanted to be a musician. But my father wasn't having that. I came out of the Army at twenty-four, and I was determined not to go into a suit-and-tie job. So, I thought films might be fun. In those days, the unions were very powerful, and I was told there was no room for me. My father was a solicitor for one of the railway companies. I found out it had a tiny documentary unit, and I went to work there. We had a socialist government after the war, which was a very good thing, and it nationalized all forms of transport, like the railways, the roads, the canals, etc. A large documentary film unit was needed to put this across. As a result, I got my union membership right away.
>
> I freelanced with commercials with Richard Lester. I had evolved a kind of lighting, using reflectors, that was quite success-

ful. As a result of this, Lester asked me to film *The Knack* in 1964, a Woodfall film (which had nothing to do with Tony). Tony must have seem some of it, and he asked me about working on *Mademoiselle*. Tony and Richard were very different. Richard didn't really enjoy shooting. What he loved was being in the cutting room. Tony was bored out of his mind in the cutting room. He wanted to be out on the shoot.

Tony was a very strange man. He certainly quite liked to take over people's lives, if he had the chance. If you didn't let him, you kept his respect. And I was having none of that. Anyway, we did *Mademoiselle*, and about halfway through he told me he wanted me to do all his films. *Sailor from Gibraltar* and *Charge* were coming up. By that time, I'd seen a bit of him. And I told him if I agreed, we might get sick of each other. I suggested I not do *Sailor from Gibraltar* but resume working with him after that on *The Charge of the Light Brigade*. Now Tony couldn't believe this; he tried all sorts of tricks. I never did do *Sailor*, but I did do *The Charge*.

I found that Tony and some of the others at Woodfall, like another cameraman, Walter Lassally, had a kind of group dislike of studio filmmaking. They had this idea that if you wanted the truth, you had to go on location. I never had this. Not for a minute. I knew what they meant, and I sympathized; but that doesn't mean to say that I can't come in to a studio and do things that still look entirely natural. Tony would say, "Oh, the actors can't perform in a studio." Rubbish! The other thing with Tony was that you knew you would never win. Even if you could influence him, he'd never let you know it. But I did tell him many times, "You give me a location, and I will make it look like a bad set. Give me a decent set on a stage, and I'll make it look absolutely real." He never took me up on it. As far as I knew, while I was working with him, Tony never set foot in a set. Never. For him the fun was shooting the damned thing out on location with his "family" about him, to play with them and wind them up and get them at each other.

Like me, Tony was never bothered by bad language. Unless you're angry and cross, these words are no different from other words. If you were in trouble, there was no one better than Tony. He was so resourceful, so positive a person.

When you meet a director, you very quickly know what he would and wouldn't like. I make my movies for an audience of one, the director. I've never had an agent; I've never been "sold" to anybody. This gets you off on the right foot with people. Tony helped to crystallize my ideas, but the ideas were there to begin with. The best things on the screen, very often, are accidents. You just have to arrange things so accidents can happen. For example, on *The Charge*, we had a big establishing shot of the battle, one of those things with explosions and effects that takes a day to set up. The camera was on a high rostrum looking down a valley and beyond. Finally, we were ready to go and the light was right. An ideal day. What we then had was a combination of smoke and wind that was unpredictable. All of a sudden, it looked like a Delacroix painting. I didn't know it at the time, but during the rushes it looked breathtaking. There was a foreground explosion marked by a black flag. There it was, the black flag visible in the corner of the frame. Everybody reacted, "Dear, dear, we can't have that there!" I answered, "Who cares? What the hell does it matter? It's something we could never get again. It's silly to worry about it." Then Tony's voice pipes up: "Well, Mr. Watkin is obviously the only person with any sense!" That gives you an idea of the sort of way he saw things.

Another example is in *Mahogany*, with Diana Ross. Tony was to direct, originally. There was a scene where the camera follows two actors as they enter a Chicago ghetto apartment. The camera was on a dolly following all this. They enter the room, and the camera keeps following them as they go into a bedroom. It was a complicated shot, with a light change and lots of movement. After a couple of false starts, we got the shot right, except that there, visible on the pillow, was my light meter. The light meter I used in those days had a distinctive appearance with a very clear dial. And Tony immediately said, "Don't make a fuss, David, we'll say it's just a little transistor radio!" (Tony didn't like the way the project was going, and he eventually talked Berry Gordy into firing him.)

I had the sense not to take silly chances, of course, but that apart, Tony would far rather I came unstuck trying to do something interesting rather than being perfectly secure doing something boring. And that is a tremendous quality to have in a director. That kind of support meant you could relax and have a great time.

He rarely looked through the viewfinder; only if he wanted to annoy me. On one scene in *Mademoiselle*, he announced to me that he was going to light it. I told him to go ahead; and I watched him get into more and more of a mess. What Tony would have loved, would have been for me to refuse him. *Mademoiselle* was the first time I had done anything in wide-screen format. I said to Tony, "Why not just keep the camera absolutely still and use the space; let all the movement take place within the shot?" We did it.

Tony's overriding interest, his big passion was people, human behavior. He was very interested in that sort of thing. He really understood actors. He used to say that actors carried everything. The only reason we were here was because of the actors. It changed my own attitudes about actors. Of course, *Mademoiselle* was basically a French production with a French crew. Tony loved to wind people up. There was a scene with some French widows, dressed in black. They were trying to make an impression on Tony, so they were overdoing things. Tony just sat back, laughing, egging them on.

Ken Russell was enormous fun. A big, nice kid. Quite, quite different from Tony. I don't think they ever met. I was never as close to Ken as I was with Tony.

I did *A Delicate Balance* with Tony. I couldn't come to his rehearsals because I was shooting *The Homecoming* with Peter Hall. Tony laughed and said, "He won't even read the script; come to my rehearsals!" He was right. One only reads the script to find out what's happening and how many nights there are and what clothes to bring. The idea was to put on significant contemporary plays with the original casts. Albee was there all the time. The text was to be kept sacrosanct. Tony thought that was pretty silly. He'd been a theater director, but he didn't really like it. He loved making films. We shot it on location in a house in Crystal Palace. It wasn't any different from shooting on any other location. Tony and Albee got along all right. I don't think I ever saw him in a real dispute with anyone on the set.

JIM WELSH: What about *Joseph Andrews?*

DAVID WATKIN: At the time of *Tom Jones* everybody at Woodfall despised traditional cinematography. It was a different approach, all right. I think it's a better film than *Tom Jones*. I thought *Tom Jones* was one of the worst photographed films I'd ever seen. Walter Lassally shot it in the full flood of saying, "We're going to do this differently!" The antistudio, antiprofessional attitude was there. What

I have always done is combine the two; you don't have to be either a hide-bound pedant or a wild anarchist. Of course, *Tom Jones* was a huge hit.

For a start, what wonderful actors in *Joseph Andrews!* Beryl Reid, for example. I believe in casting a crew for a picture. I get the best possible camera operator, for example. You can list them on the fingers of one hand. He works with the director. I don't want to get involved in the details; I want my time to think about how I want the picture to look on the screen. The secret is getting someone who can be my contact with the director. If he's any good, he'll know instantly if something the director might want will compromise me; he'll contact me about that. He must understand both sides of things. In this case, it was Freddy Cooper and Paul Wilson. You see, I think we had both of them. For *Charge*, it was Alan McCabe. Years ago the National Film Theater asked me to select three outstanding examples of my work. I chose *Marat/Sade, Charge, Catch-22.* They are superbly operated films. They give you a superb idea what they do, yet they're largely unknown. Nowadays, many younger cinematographers expect to do their own operating. It's awful. Many producers don't realize the importance of an operator. I've had producers tell me not to have one, since he might interfere with my relationship with the director. That is nonsense! They find that out soon enough! The only person who has an easy time of it is me.

I wish there had been more work with Tony. I adored him. *Hotel New Hampshire*, for example. By that time, Tony was no longer at the peak of what Hollywood regarded as success. I've always had the good fortune to work on pictures with directors where you didn't really feel you'd wasted three months of your life. There have been things that I think will last and that I've been thrilled to have done. *Hotel New Hampshire* was the last time we worked together. I don't think Tony made anything at all on that one. They shot in Montreal, and I went out there a week before. The first evening there, I was with Tony and Jocelyn [Herbert, the production designer], and we were the only people who knew at the time that the money was not guaranteed. It was possible at the end of the week we would have to have come home. That was the sort of atmosphere we worked with. It was the one time I saw him in such an uncertain situation. Not that it bothered him, really; Tony was always Tony. Even so, we all had a good time. You always had a good time with Tony. But it was a sad contrast to the first time I worked with him, when they would give him anything. The cast was wonderful on that. Jodie Foster was terrific. Jocelyn was there. The only picture I did with her.

I used to wonder how Tony could stand to live in Hollywood. I lived in his house on North King's Road while I worked on *Journey to the Center of the Earth* with Emo Phillips. I don't think it ever got finished. Hollywood really resented my being there on *Catch-22*. A real horror story. Anyway, Tony'd say, "It's the only place where you can live in the open air." True, if you're there, it's easy to get projects off the ground. Everybody deplored Hollywood, except Tony. His friends there were Christopher Isherwood and David Hockney. Three exiles who actually loved the place.

The last time I saw Tony? He kept very quiet about his illness. I spoke to him on the phone. I never saw him when he was really ill. I was doing *Used People* with Shirley MacLaine. She told me he was ill and what it was. I didn't know whether to phone him up or not. But I know my Tony. If I phoned him or he phoned me, he'd wonder, "What is he phoning for?" Somehow, I thought it was better not to. I miss him.

ANGELA ALLEN INTERVIEW

Angela Allen was in charge of continuity on *The Charge of the Light Brigade*. Like David Watkin, she speaks extensively about her craft, but she offers some vivid memories about Tony Richardson, in comparison to other directors with whom she has worked. She was interviewed in central London on January 20, 1997.

ANGELA ALLEN: I'm what they used to call a "continuity girl." It's the attention to detail; you have to be there for every shot, watching every movie, every gesture, making sure you can cut it together smoothly when it goes into the cutting room. You have to be with the director all day long.

I was lucky. I started at the Korda studios; I worked for John Huston on *The African Queen,* then I stayed with him for fourteen films. I got along with him very well. He was very easy to get along with. He never ever lost his temper with people. He was always calm. But for writers it was a different story. For Ray Bradbury, for Arthur Miller. I used to say to John, "For God's sake, I've had enough; pick up the bloody pencil and do it yourself!" But he didn't with Arthur.

And now I've been working with Franco Zeffirelli. I did *Jane Eyre* with him, and *Hamlet*. I hope that I'm good at my job. I'm very observant. I'm not frightened to point out defects—to say that the scene is terrible, or to tell the actor to pick up the pace. I can remember one film when the director forgot he'd killed off a character in an earlier scene. I told him he'd have to shoot a resurrection scene! If I let somebody come on in the wrong costume, on the other hand, I can cause a lot of unneeded expense later when you have to re-shoot.

I only worked with Tony on one film, *The Charge of the Light Brigade*. With Tony, he'd had other continuity people before. He was a quite extraordinary person, a bit like Franco. I'd heard he was sort of mercurial and mischievous and could be devious. I went along for an interview and told him what I'd done. What I think was his forte, his strongest talent, was that he was a brilliant entrepreneur. He found so much talent in this country, from designers to actors. And he was brilliant at it. That side of him hasn't been fully appreciated. He gave so many chances and breaks to people. But you never knew him. He could be quite impossible.

On *The Charge*, he was quite impossible on one scene: It's in the end when a man gets killed and falls on his right side. Later, when we shot the wide shot, Tony wanted him to lie on his left side. I told him, "They don't turn over, you know." He argued about it: "I don't care; I don't care." He prevailed: "Nobody will notice," he said. But they did!

Tony didn't really care about continuity. He could be willful. That's the word. Hilarious things happened on that picture. But I must say, it was great fun to work on. We were in Turkey. We had the Turkish cavalry. They'd got the horses from America (they were still marked). They were old. Trevor Howard was on a horse when it fell asleep and fell down. We used to have the Turks as extras, some as Highlanders and some as Russians. They didn't want to be Russians. We explained that some of them would have to be Russians! They'd slash their clothes in protest. They were like children. Tony was very good with people. The crews also enjoyed him. We all knew how mad he was. And in those days, we used to have champagne in plastic cups around eleven o'clock.

One day we had a lot of rain, and our tents were blowing down. I can remember striding down the hill, trying to follow him through the mud. He was so tall and thin. All the horses and actors were down in the mud. We had so many laughs. There was a breezy spirit about everything. He could be quite devious. He was wicked. He talked about everybody. He would pull everybody apart at night. Of course, he could snap his fingers and stamp his feet. Not like Huston. At bad weather and things, John would just sit down and read a book and wait for everything to sort itself out. Tony got on well with all the actors. At times he might have felt David Hemmings was a bit of a pill. Most of us felt he was badly cast. Osborne wasn't allowed on the set because of the plagiarism issue. Larry Harvey was there, but he got cut out. Tony didn't want him there, but they were polite. He even got Gielgud on a horse. Gielgud hates horses.

I didn't keep contact with him afterward. I would have liked to. I never really knew whether he liked me or if he didn't. He could be charming to you to your face, but you never knew what he might be saying behind your back.

What about new projects? You just wait for the phone to ring.

CHAPTER THREE

Breaking the Proscenium: Tony Richardson, the Free Cinema, the Royal Court, and Woodfall Films (Look Back in Anger *[1959]* and The Entertainer *[1960]*)

JOHN C. TIBBETTS

FREE CINEMA

When Tony Richardson joined forces with Lindsay Anderson and Karel Reisz in the so-called Free Cinema movement of the mid-1950s, he had virtually no experience in the film medium. Most of his work had been confined to the stage and television. Yet, if he had any reluctance tackling this new challenge, it was not apparent to any of his associates; nor does he admit any self-doubts in his writings. Filmmaking for Tony just seems to have happened, as naturally and inevitably as most of the opportunities and endeavors that came his way. "In the movies, as far as we were concerned," he recalled in his memoirs, "you worked as you liked" (1973, 94).

That was all. But that was everything. And that—as so many of his friends and associates would say time and time again over the next four decades—was Tony.

Tall and lean, with puckish features and an irresistibly gregarious nature, the twenty-eight-year old Richardson was the most amiable of the Free Cinema revolutionaries. However, as he recounts it, he had been a very different sort of character in his early years. He was born in the shadow of the woolen mills of the West Riding region of Yorkshire, to a lower-middle-class family (his father was a pharmacist). Sheltered and withdrawn, he spent many of his hours alone watching movies in the local cinema. After dreary years spent in Harrogate boarding schools— "It is impossible to exaggerate the misery, the sordidness, the continual and recurring nastinesses of a sentence to a gulag from which there was no escape" (1973, 45)—he went to Ashville College and later Oxford University's Wadham College. It was here, in a less repressive and creatively stimulating atmosphere, that he blossomed and indulged his new-found passion for the theater. He directed a variety of productions, ranging from Shakespeare to Marlowe to Ibsen. He graduated in 1951 and promptly enrolled in a directors' training program at the British Broadcasting Corporation (the BBC). Meanwhile, he was reading a film journal, *Sequence*, edited by a very noisy and persuasive young man named Lindsay Anderson.

At thirty-three, Lindsay Anderson was the patriarch of the Free Cinema movement. He was a force of nature, rather stern and magisterial, face and form hewn from flint and stone, aflame with a passionate devotion to social concerns that was genuine and unflagging. He was born in Bangalore, South India, the son of a Scottish major general, and educated at Cheltenham College. After the war, where he served in the Army Intelligence Corps, he co-founded the Oxford film journal *Sequence* in 1947. He began making short documentary films of his own. His admiration for the work of documentarian Humphrey Jennings— especially in his "sensitivity to human regard," as Anderson put it (qtd. in Walker 1974, 26)—bore fruit in his own attempts to render truthfully on film the life of the working classes: *Meet the Pioneers* (1948) depicted the workers in a northern England factory; the Oscar-winning *Thursday's Children* (1953), the doctors and patients in the Royal School for the Deaf; and *Every Day Except Christmas* (1953), the fruit and vegetable and flower sellers at Covent Garden. By the time Free Cinema launched itself upon the world, Anderson was by far the most experienced filmmaker in the movement.

Joining Anderson and co-editor Penelope Houston at *Sequence* during its last months was Karel Reisz, Anderson's junior by three years.

Like Anderson, he was a transplant. He was born in Czechoslovakia and, with the rise of Nazism, was sent out of the country by his parents to be educated at Cambridge University. His tenure as a teacher of working-class youngsters at a secondary-modern school gave him insights into the social realities concerning which he had been hitherto unaware in the encapsulated environment of academia. Convinced that the film medium could be an outlet for his newfound social consciousness, he began writing for *Sequence* in 1952, became program officer at the National Film Theatre that same year, and wrote The *Techniques of Film Editing* in 1953.

When *Sequence* disbanded in 1952, Richardson, Anderson, and Reisz, a mixed triumvirate of hotheads if there ever was one, planted their flag in the journal *Sight and Sound* (established during the 1930s and overdue for a makeover), where they found a common forum for their attacks on the establishment cinema of the day, the Ealing Studios, the Rank Organization, and the Associated British Picture Corporation (ABPC). "This is a permanent revolution that we all have to fight," stormed Richardson in *Sight and Sound.* "What is so disheartening about the British cinema is that few of the producers have any convictions at all, not even determinedly commercial ones. Behind all their actions and decisions is a timidity which leads to a falling between every stool, so that their products are totally without vitality" (1959, 64). Such declamations, Richardson ruefully recalled later, made them appear "ridiculous to everyone within the [film] industry" (1973, 94).

Nonetheless, with partial financial support from the British Film Institute's Experimental Film Fund, they collectively arranged to present a program of films at the National Film Theatre in February 1956. The films were loosely classified as documentaries, although, as Richardson noted at the time, "they differ completely from the conventional documentary in that their interest is entirely in the people and they are concerned with both environment and activity only in its human effects" (1956, 17). Apart from the Grierson-inspired English documentary movement, then in its last gasp—which they criticized as overly leftist propaganda—the Free Cinema approach was avowedly neither didactic nor political, but, as Alexander Walker has noted, politically conscious only in a "romantic, simplistic way" (1974, 31). Their motto was Free Cinema, a term which Anderson had coined as a publicity gimmick. Appended to it was the following declaration of principles:

As film-makers we believe that
No film can be too personal.
The image speaks. Sound amplifies and comments. Size is irrelevant.
Perfection is not an aim.
An attitude means a style. A style means an attitude.

It was, Anderson admitted later, a masterstroke of publicity: "I honestly believe the Press would have paid us no attention at all. . . . It was a successful piece of cultural packaging." Richardson claimed that the most important pronouncement for him and his later work was the line "Perfection is not an aim" (qtd. in Walker 1974, 27). He would echo it months later in the Royal Court's dictum, The Right to Fail.

Anderson's contribution to the first program was *O Dreamland*, shot three years before in the seaside resort of Margate. It was a strangely bittersweet excursion into a garish and hollow world, an amusement park cluttered with waxwork exhibitions, animal displays, and food canteens. Its specific milieu prefigures the setting of Richardson's later film version of *The Entertainer*.

Lindsay Anderson assisted Lorenza Mazzetti in making *Together*, which at fifty minutes was the longest of the three films. It was a simple portrait of the lives of two deaf-mute dockworkers living in the East End of London and the tensions their afflictions caused between them and the community around them. Richardson admired its sympathetic observation of the characters, "how they wash after work, how they wander through a market—and this wonder envelopes too their whole setting, so that the poor streets, the bomb sites, the warehouses take on an almost mysterious beauty of their own" (1956, 17).

Richardson's film was *Momma Don't Allow*, co-directed with Reisz, a twenty-two-minute film shot at a jazz club in Wood Green, a working-class district in north London. Reisz recalls it cost only a hundred pounds and was shot in 16mm. during six Saturday evenings: "We went to [the club] for several months with still cameras so people would get used to us. Later, during the actual shooting, we did a 'fly-on-the-wall' treatment and then cobbled together some sort of continuity" (Reisz interview, 1997). An early sequence crosscuts between the musicians' rehearsal and three young people getting off work and preparing to go out for the evening. They arrive and begin to dance at the rapidly filling club, populated by a variety of students, typists, dental assistants, shop girls, and butcher boys. A little later, two upper-class couples arrive in an expensive automobile.

After removing the hood ornament, they enter the club. They are amused at the abandoned energy of the dancers, but their own attempts to join in seem awkward and self-conscious. Eventually, the rich couples leave and the band belts out a song called "Momma Don't Allow." While class distinctions separating the "teddy boys" and the slumming socialites are pointedly noted, the tone is kept muted and relatively dispassionate.

The technique of the three films seemed clumsy in comparison to establishment cinema. The cameras were mostly hand held, the images grainy and underexposed, the sound recorded on location. Frequently, the filmmakers worked with nonsynch sound or with wild tracks recorded on location and later edited to available footage. The results were sometimes awkward; but more often they contributed to a vital, sharp-etched evocation of scene. As Gavin Lambert wrote in his seminal essay in *Sight and Sound* about the first Free Cinema program, they were films of protest and of a "rigorous, difficult and austere kind of compassion." He continued: "No doubt of it, this is the world in which we live. In seizing upon these aspects—the anonymity of urban life, the aimless lonely figures swallowed up in the greater loneliness of the crowd, the pleasures hideous and mechanical or imaginatively aspiring—these film-makers compel above all the shock of recognition" (1956, 174).

Five more Free Cinema programs followed, presenting not only films from British filmmakers but also from several French directors representing the emerging *nouvelle vague*, including Truffaut, Franju, and Agnes Varda. Other filmmakers represented included Lionel Rogosin, Alain Tanner, and Norman McLaren. However, they reached only a limited audience. Because public exhibition of their films was excluded from the commercial circuits of cinemas, they were mostly shown only in art houses and film societies. Moreover, when Ford withdrew its support, the movement lost a crucial sponsor. In a note appended to the last program in March 1959, Anderson admitted that the aims of the group, although as yet unfulfilled, remained vigorous and unbowed: "In making these films and presenting these programmes, we have tried to make a stand for independent, creative film-making in a world where the pressures of conformism and commercialism are becoming more personal every day. We will not abandon these convictions, nor the attempt to put them into action. Free Cinema is dead. Long live Free Cinema" (qtd. in Walker 1974, 34).

Free Cinema proved, if nothing else, that young, relatively inexperienced filmmakers could work outside the commercial set-up. Abroad,

Free Cinema was interpreted as the shot across the bow heralding a British "New Wave." Meanwhile, Anderson, Reisz, and Richardson forged personal and professional relationships that would extend far beyond Free Cinema. Anderson joined Richardson at the Royal Court and went on to direct many plays there before making his first feature film, *This Sporting Life* in 1963. And Reisz's first feature, *Saturday Night and Sunday Morning* (1960) was produced by Richardson.

AT THE ROYAL COURT THEATER

Hardly had he finished *Momma Don't Allow* than Richardson returned to the world of theater and continued his tutelage under the extraordinary George Devine. Tony had first met Devine during a BBC production of Chekhov's *Curtain Down* in 1952. Devine, eighteen years Tony's senior, admired his protege's youthful "fire, intelligence, and energy" (Doty and Harbin 1990, 34). Tony, in turn, was in awe of Devine's impressive record of achievement, including classical revivals in the 1930s and the management of the prewar London Theatre Studio and the post-war Young Vic, two seminal theatrical ventures. What Tony liked best about Devine was "his openness to new personalities and a total unconcern for his own seniority" (Richardson 1993, 84). He also displayed a comprehensive knowledge of the physical realization of a play. It was another of those inevitabilities in Richardson's career that he and Devine would team up and make plans to form a theatre of their own.

It should be remembered that at this time there was not yet a Royal Shakespeare Company or a National Theater. No new theatre had been built in Britain since the war. Theatrical architecture perpetuated class divisions and artistic conventions, preserving the proscenium-frame stage as the essential platform for drama. The lord chamberlain's censorship paralyzed the freedom of the dramatist. In general, writes Richard Findlater in his history of the Royal Court, it was a time when the London stage was "dominated by the long-run system [and] was moving closer to the hit-or-bust pattern of Broadway, where a play had to be an instant box office success or it would be an instant casualty, probably never to be seen again" (1981, 11). Convinced they had backing from the wife of a wealthy business man, they settled on the Royal Court.

Devine and Richardson had begun looking for a theater house in 1952. They had explored the possibilities of two West End theatres, the

Royalty and the Kingsway, before negotiating a three-year lease of the Royal Court in 1953. The small theater of five hundred seats was located on the eastern side of Sloane Square, between Knightsbridge and Chelsea, in the southwest sector of London. Michael Hallifax, the general stage manager from 1956 through 1959 recalls that the Chelsea area at the time was just a backwater, "a very barren area with absolutely no passing trade because nobody walked in Chelsea. No one ever seemed to go anywhere, and if he did, he went to the tube and scuttled down or came out and disappeared as quickly as possible" (Doty and Harbin 1990, 197).

The structure itself had been erected in 1888. It had been especially noted as the site for the 1904 through 1907 regime of actor-author-director Harley Granville Barker, whose short-run productions included work by Galsworthy, Ibsen, Maeterlinck, and Shaw (eleven of his thirty-two plays were staged). But before Devine and Richardson could mount a production, their promised financial support vanished and they were left in the cold. Disappointed, Richardson left for several months for his first trip to America.

After his return from America and subsequent work directing several successful television shows, Richardson reunited with Devine in the dream to establish their own "art theater." They joined forces with Ronald Duncan, ardent disciple of T. S. Eliot, late of a theater enterprise in Devon; Oscar Lewenstein, former manager of the Embassy Theatre in Hampstead (and famed for his recent production of Brecht's *The Threepenny Opera*); Neville Blond, a wealthy Manchester textile magnate with government connections; and Jocelyn Herbert, who had been a member of the prewar London Theatre Studio. Together, they formed the nucleus of the English Stage Company. After rejecting Blond's recommendation that they settle in the old Kingsway Theater, they sought out their original choice, the Royal Court, at half the Kingsway's cost.

The abandoned old building was in a frightful state. Renovation began in November. The house curtain and proscenium borders were removed, giving greater height to the stage. The interior was repainted. A permanent surround was installed. Its lack of workshops, a green room, adequate dressing-room space, the shallow wing space, and rudimentary storage areas made it a poor candidate for repertory. Adjustments would have to be made. Initial financial support included small subsidies from the Arts Council, Chelsea Borough Council, the neighboring Peter Jones department store, and the council members' initial investment. Budgeting was tight; approximately £2,000 were allotted for each production.

The ESC declared itself open to new writers and to the production of new plays. Its credo, The Right to Fail, was a variant of the Free Cinema's motto, Perfection Is Not an Aim. Richardson dealt with hundreds of script submissions per week, scanning their first pages only: "This method helps you quickly dispatch tragedies in rhyming couplets, melodramas from the 1890s, musical operettas from the 1930s, and suchlike, which all the world and your neighbor have had secreted in their back drawer for years" (1993, 102). Many of them were written by clergymen's wives, and almost every post brought in something about Mary Queen of Scots, Queen Victoria, or Lady Jane Grey. Another popular subject was surviving atomic holocaust. Out of it all came the discovery of only one major new talent, John Osborne, about whom more will follow presently.

The plan for the first season was to perform five plays in repertory. *The Mulberry Bush*, adapted from his novel by Angus Wilson (his first and last play), opened on April 2, 1956. Arthur Miller's *The Crucible* opened a week later. Next was Tony's first show, John Osborne's *Look Back in Anger*, which opened on May 8, 1956. Then came a program of two plays produced by Ronald Duncan, *Don Juan in Hell* and *The Death of Satan*. The fifth and last production was Nigel Dennis' *Cards of Identity* (adapted from his novel), directed by Richardson.

The second season brought changes. The repertory system was scrapped. New directors, such as Lindsay Anderson and William Gaskill were brought in. The first production, opening on October 31, 1956, was Brecht's *The Good Woman of Setzuan*, a virtual copy of the Berliner Ensemble production. Next came a revival of *The Country Wife* with Joan Plowright, directed by Devine. It was the ESC's first big hit (Laurence Harvey would take it to Broadway the following November). Tony directed *The Member of the Wedding* in February 1957. He also directed John Osborne's next play, *The Entertainer*, which premiered on April 10, 1957, and ran for thirty-six performances. (It later played six months at the Palace in London—with Joan Plowright replacing Dorothy Tutin—and six months on Broadway, opening at the Royale Theatre on February 12, 1958.)

Meanwhile, as Richardson recalled, the ESC was "already recognized as like nothing anyone had seen in England for decades—a venue already attracting the attention of every new creative spirit. And even some sense of a different kind of actor—more physical, less dependent on the traditional skills of verbal inflection, timing, and twirling cloaks, and without a so-called gentleman's accent" (1993, 106–107). It was a breakthrough of the Continental art theatre tradition. Radiating out from its example within the next few years were the establishment of the National Theatre and the transformation of the Royal Shakespeare Company, both of which were organized and guided by Royal Court artists. Emerging from its productions were new dramatists and writers such as Arnold Wesker, John Arden, Keith Waterhouse and Willis Hall, Alun Owen, Shelagh Delaney, Harold Pinter, Robert Bolt, Kingsley Amis, John Braine, Alan Sillitoe, David Mercer, Howard Barker, Sam Shepard, and David Hare (Doty and Harbin 1990, 207–8).

FROM STAGE TO SCREEN: *LOOK BACK IN ANGER*

The discovery of twenty-seven-year old John Osborne and his play *Look Back in Anger* has become something of a legend in the history of contemporary English theater. Devine and Richardson had placed a notice in *The Stage* announcing a search for new writers. Among the hundreds of submissions that arrived in the post was John Osborne's play, *Look Back in Anger*. At the time Osborne was a virtual unknown, a struggling actor and untried playwright living humbly in Chiswick on a barge in Cubitt's Yacht Basin with a companion, actor Anthony Creighton. He had finished the play in June 1955, and by the following August it had been rejected by every theatrical management and play agent Osborne could find listed in the *Writers' and Artists' Yearbook*. "It was like being grasped at the upper arm by a testy policeman and told to move on" (Osborne 1991, 4). That all changed when George Devine went out to Osborne's barge, the *M/Y Egret*, and told Osborne he was interested in staging the play. Devine offered Osborne £25 from the English Stage Company for a year's option on the play, with a £50 renewal clause. He also contracted him as an actor, understudy, and play reader.

"Both George and Tony were completely unknown quantities to me," recalled Osborne, "and, of course, I was to them. We were all out there in an unknown world. Nobody knew at all what anyone's real intentions were. For them to support people like myself, as they did, was a great act of faith, and they both expressed that faith openly" (1991, 21). Mutual first impressions were memorable. Richardson remembered that John was poor but had real style: "Tall and lean, with crinkled, wavy hair, full lips and a broad face, with deep-set, almost Slavic eyes, he was sensual and fragile" (Richardson 1993, 100). Osborne in turn recorded that

Richardson was a "loping creature who looked about seven feet tall" and "had the authoritative stoop of a gangler who is born to mastery." Osborne continues: "[I]n what was to become one of the most imitated voices in his profession, Richardson said, 'I think *Look Back in Anger* is the best play written since the war.' He announced himself as its director like a confiding toastmaster" (1991, 12).

Why did Richardson take to the play? Alexander Walker says that he shared with Jimmy Porter a kind of shame. He, like Jimmy, felt

> eternally damned for being simply lower middle-class. He couldn't even boast of coming from the working class. Yet, unlike Jimmy, he didn't have the masochistic consolation of having gone to a 'red brick,' i.e. provincial, university. Being one of the privileged forti-fied Richardson's 'secret shame,' as he ironically referred to it, that in getting this far he had availed himself of the school system which he despised on ideological grounds and accused of stifling individu-ality, of choking off passion, and of creating people who were 'too intelligent. . . . In compensation—perhaps in expiation—he put a high price on the display of passion, on not hiding one's emotions but, rather, flaunting them. (1974, 67)

According to Osborne, the play grew out of a general malaise in the country. "The country was tired, not merely from the sacrifice of two back-breaking wars but from the defeat and misery between them. . . . [T]he leaping hare of the Victorian imagination had begun to imitate the tortoise even before 1914, but in that summer of 1955 it was still easy enough to identify what we regarded as a permanent Establishment" (1991, 3).

Rehearsals for *Look Back* quickly revealed what was to be a standard technique of Richardson, what Osborne calls a "divide and rule" approach: "He controlled an iron conspiracy in which no one dared speak to anyone else out of his presence. George [Devine] and I were mutually intimidated and isolated from each other by this simple ploy for months" (1991, 19).

The play ran for 151 performances. The cast included Kenneth Haigh as Jimmy Porter, Mary Ure (who later married Osborne) as Alison, Alan Bates as Cliff, and Helena Hughes as Helena. Its second run at the Royal Court (104 performances) opened on March 11, 1957, with the core cast intact. In July the Court took it to the International Youth Festival in Moscow. In New York it opened on October 1, 1957, at the Lyceum Theatre with Haigh as Porter, Bates as Lewis, Ure as Alison, and Vivienne Drummond as Helena. It was chosen Best Foreign Play of the season by the New York Drama Critics' Circle. Today, it is difficult to overestimate the tremendous influence its success had on the Court and on contemporary British drama in general.

Nonetheless, the first reviews of *Look Back* were generally poor. *The Evening Standard* declared it "sets up a wailing wall for the latest post-generation of the under-thirties. It aims at being a despairing cry but achieves only the stature of a self-pitying snivel" (Richardson 1993, 104). Osborne was dismayed, but Richardson only said, "But what on earth did you expect? You didn't *expect* them to *like* it, did you?" (Osborne 1991, 21).

But help came from several quarters. Out-and-out raves were written by two key Sunday critics, Harold Hobson in the *Sunday Times* and Kenneth Tynan in the *Observer*. Tynan's review is dated May 13, 1956:

> *Look Back in Anger* presents post-war youth as it really is. . . . To have done this at all would be a signal achievement; to have done it in a first play is a minor miracle. All the qualities are there, qualities one had despaired of ever seeing on the stage—the drift towards anarchy, the instinctive leftishness, the automatic rejection of 'official' attitudes, the surrealist sense of humor . . . the casual promiscuity, the sense of lacking a crusade worth fighting for and, underlying all these, the determination that no one who dies shall go unmourned. . . . I doubt if I could love anyone who did not wish to see *Look Back in Anger*. (Osborne 1991, 22)

Fueling additional public interest was the concoction by ESC's publicist, George Fearon, of the notorious phrase *angry young man*. Osborne says Fearon meant it disparagingly; but it caught on immediately (1991, 20). Finally, on October 16, the BBC presented a twenty-five-minute excerpt on television. Richardson recalled that all this attention "made us the theatre of the moment, the place where it was happening, take it or leave it, love it or hate it" (1993, 105).

The character of Jimmy Porter gave form and voice to the anger, impotence, isolation, and helplessness of his generation. He demands to be at once embraced and rejected. He was recognizable to intellectuals and liberals who supported the Campaign for Nuclear Disarmament and whose political orthodoxy was shattered by the Suez Crisis and the Rus-

sian invasion of Hungary. He was also a product of the postwar Education Act, which opened high schools and universities to those working-
class children of limited aspirations who formerly had been limited to
menial jobs. According to Alexander Walker, they, like Jimmy, had developed an "articulate contempt for its outworn institutions and class-bound
attitudes, but saw no means of changing and replacing them. *Look Back
in Anger* didn't provide the means, but it gave their rage its release" (1974,
42). Indeed, it seemed at times that for people like Jimmy there were no
more causes at all: "I suppose people of our generation aren't able to die
for good causes any longer," he says in the play. "We had all that done for
us, in the thirties and forties, when we were still kids. There aren't any
good, brave causes left" (Osborne 1956, 68).

Indeed, the term *angry young man* itself proved to have enormous
commercial appeal. Not just limited to a particular class or generation of
disaffected youth, it could apply to any strident rejection of the system,
particularly if those doing the shouting did so in a working-class accent.
Journalists, critics, radio and television producers all paid the expression
lip service. "The fact that the world of communications was itself relatively classless," wrote Walker, "—where those who worked in it were
concerned, if not the sectional interests they appealed to for their living—
assisted the speed with which the excitement was diffused through every
level of society between 1956 and 1959" (1974, 42).

The three-act, one-set play is set in a dreary Midland town of the
fifties. Squeezed into a tiny one-room flat is Jimmy Porter, a tall, slender
man of twenty-five, his long-suffering wife of three years, Alison; and
Jimmy's mate and business partner, Cliff Lewis. Although Jimmy has
attended a university and is obviously well educated, he has drifted
through a succession of temporary jobs—journalism, advertising, selling
vacuum cleaners—finally settling into running a market stall. In the first
act, while Alison does the ironing, Jimmy and Cliff read the Sunday
papers, unleashing a fusillade of scorn at the politics and social doings of
the day, from religious news to the bomb. "God, how I hate Sundays!"
exclaims Jimmy. "It's always so depressing, always the same. We never
seem to get any farther, do we? Always the same ritual. Reading the
papers, drinking tea, ironing. A few more hours, and another week gone.
Our youth is slipping away" (11). Jimmy's litany of irritations grows
apace. He resents the class distance he feels from his wife's upper-class
family. "[Her] Mummy and Daddy turn pale, and face the east every time
they remember she's married to me," he confesses to Cliff sardonically.

More attacks are directed at Alison's brother Nigel—a prime example, he jeers, of the kind of politician "who seeks sanctuary in his own stupidity" (16)—and finally at Alison herself, whom he dubs "the Lady Pusillani-mous," taunting her for her timidity, cowardice, and clumsiness. He reserves special scorn for her voracious sexual appetites, which are like the python that "devours me whole every time, as if I were some over-large rabbit" (30). His volley of invective is interrupted when her ironing board is accidentally overturned, the hot iron burning her arm. "I'm wondering how much longer I can go on watching you two tearing the insides out of each other," declares the usually stolid, reticent Cliff. "It looks pretty ugly sometime" (22–23). Act 1 concludes with two revelations: Alison con-fides in Cliff that she's pregnant but that she's afraid to tell Jimmy for fear of his unpredictable reaction. And, to Jimmy's consternation, news arrives that Alison's friend, Helena Charles, an actress, is coming for an indefi-nite stay.

Act 2, scene 1 transpires two weeks later. Helena has moved in. By contrast to Alison, notes the stage directions, Helena has a kind of elegant and imperious authority about her which "makes most men who meet her anxious, not only to please but impress, as if she were the gracious repre-sentative of visiting royalty" (31). It is evident that she intensely dislikes Jimmy and will fight to defend Alison from his continuing tirades. Jimmy hates her right back, calling her a "saint in Dior's clothing" (44), attack-ing her aloof indifference to "ugly problems of the twentieth century" (45).

The two antagonists warily circle around each other, looking for an advantage. But it is not until Jimmy launches a particularly vicious verbal assault on Alison's mother, whom he calls "an old bitch" and whom he wishes were dead (43), that Helena lashes out and threatens to slap him:

JIMMY: I hope you won't make the mistake of thinking for one moment that I'm a gentleman.

HELENA: I'm not very likely to do that.

JIMMY (bringing his face close to hers): I've no public school scru-ples about hitting girls. If you slap my face—by God, I'll lay you out! (45)

Moments later, in a rare moment of self-confession, he explains to Helena the source of some of his bitterness: As a frightened, bewildered ten-year-old boy, he had been the only one in his family to care for his dying father, who had returned home from the war in Spain. The rest of the family had kept their distance, waiting for him to die: "The family sent him a cheque every month," continues Jimmy, "and hoped he'd get on with it, quietly, without too much vulgar fuss" (46). Jimmy had maintained the deathwatch, surrounded by "the despair and the bitterness, the sweet, sickly smell of a dying man" (46). From this experience, concluded Jimmy, he learned at an early age "what it was to be angry—angry and helpless" (46–47).

Minutes later Jimmy gets the news that a dear friend, Ma Tanner—who years ago kindly staked him to his market stall—is dying. He rushes offstage to attend her. Helena takes advantage of the opportunity to contact Alison's father, Colonel Redfern, to come and take the dispirited Alison back home with him.

In Scene 2, a key dialogue exchange between Alison and her father reveals the circumstances of her marriage to Jimmy and explains her parents' antagonism toward him. The Colonel, retired from many years of military service in India, recalls that at the time of the marriage he and Mrs. Redfern could not understand how someone with Jimmy's education would be content with working at a market stall. His brash irreverence and seeming instability, moreover, had offended Redfern's strict and rigid Edwardian values. Thus, the Redferns took Jimmy's proposal to marry their daughter as a flagrant affront to their class: "[Mrs. Redfern] seemed to have made up her mind that if he was going to marry you, he must be a criminal, at the very least" (52). Furthermore, he admits his bewilderment at the hostilies surfacing in Alison's marriage: "I always believed that people married each other because they were in love. That always seemed a good enough reason to me. But apparently, that's too simple for young people nowadays. They have to talk about challenges and revenge. I just can't believe that love between men and women is really like that" (54). Alison replies, "You're hurt because everything is changed. Jimmy is hurt because everything is the same. And neither of you can face it. Something's gone wrong somewhere, hasn't it?" (55).

Alison, her father, and Cliff leave the apartment. Only Helena remains to tell the returning Jimmy that Alison is leaving him. She also reveals that Alison is going to have his baby. In perhaps the most savage speech of the play, Jimmy lashes out, stung by the recent death of Mrs. Tanner and provoked by this new betrayal at home: "Did you honestly expect me to go soggy at the knees," he says, "and collapse with remorse?

Listen, if you'll stop breathing your female wisdom all over me, I'll tell you something: I don't care. I don't care if she's going to have a baby. I don't care if it has two heads! Do I disgust you? Well, go on—slap my face" (59). Helena strikes him, and the two stand apart a moment in mutual horror. Then, as the curtain falls, suddenly (but perhaps not unexpectedly), the two fall into a passionate embrace.

Act 3 transpires several months later. The curtain's rise reveals a carbon-copy tableau of the first act, although it is Helena who now is leaning over the ironing board while Jimmy and Cliff scan the Sunday newspapers. Clearly, since Alison's departure, Helena has made herself at home. Again, the day's headlines draw hoots and jeers from Jimmy and Cliff. After a time, Helena leaves the room, and Cliff takes the opportunity to declare his intentions to leave the apartment and the market-stall business. "The sweet-stall's all right," he says with pointed irony, "but I think I'd like to try something else. You're highly educated, and it suits you, but I need something a bit better" (67). Jimmy agrees to the proposition and falls into a subdued mood. He tells Helena that he's thinking of giving up the stall and going away with her. But her delight quickly fades when Alison knocks on the door.

Scene 2 consists of an extended exchange between Alison and Helena. After relating the news of her miscarriage, Alison confesses that she has done "something foolish and rather vulgar" in returning to the apartment. "Whatever it was—hysteria or just macabre curiosity, I'd certainly no intention of making any kind of breach between you and Jimmy." Stung by the news and Alison's unexpected reappearance, Helena replies that she's racked with guilt over her actions. "By everything I have ever believed in, or wanted, what I have been doing is wrong and evil," she says. "I didn't know about the baby. It was such a shock. It's like a judgement on us" (72–73). Alison rejects that, explaining that perhaps neither of them is right for Jimmy: "He wants something quite different from us. What it is exactly I don't know—a kind of cross between a mother and a Greek courtesan, a henchwoman, a mixture of Cleopatra and Boswell" (73).

Helena confronts Jimmy with her decision to leave him, reaffirming at the same time her love for him. "I shall never love anyone as I have loved you," she moans. "But I can't go on. I can't take part—in all this suffering. I can't!" (75). In one of the most famous speeches in the play—purportedly the speech that convinced George Devine to stage the play—Jimmy replies that "everyone wants to escape from the pain of being alive"

(75). He continues: "It's no good trying to fool yourself about love. You can't fall into it like a soft job, without dirtying up your hands. It takes muscle and guts. And if you can't bear the thought—of messing up your nice, clean soul—you'd better give up the whole idea of life, and become a saint—because you'll never make it as a human being. It's either this world or the next" (75).

In the final tableau, after Helena has left, Alison collapses at Jimmy's feet. He bends down and takes her into his arms. As if in a semitrance, they lapse one more time into their childish game about the "bears and the squirrels": "There are cruel steel traps lying about everywhere," he intones, "just waiting for rather mad, slightly satanic, and very timid little animals." She replies sweetly, "Poor squirrels!" And he adds, softly, "Oh, poor, poor bears!" (77).

Richardson says that from the first he had wanted to film the play. According to Osborne, the relatively untried movie director got the assignment primarily because Osborne insisted on it: "This was based not on blind loyalty but on my untutored faith in his flair and his being the only possible commander to lead Woodfall's opening assault on the suburban vapidity of British film-making" (1991, 107). Richardson gamely took up the gauntlet, declaring in a 1959 article—in terms echoing his Free Cinema days—that with this film he intended nothing less than the revitalization of English cinema: "I should certainly like British films to be different from what many of them have been in the past. I don't know if *Look Back in Anger* will have this effect . . . but that's what I'd like it to have. It is absolutely vital to get into British films the same sort of impact and sense of life that, what you can loosely call the Angry Young Man cult, has had in the theatre and literary worlds. It is a desperate need" (1959, 9). He acknowledged that the pressures within British society in general and cinema in particular would be great, since he was tilting his lance at "all that is most staid and bound and stoic in British life" and at the "censorship and the timidity of many British producers" (1959, 32).

Enter producer Harry Saltzman, a Quebec-born American and an entrepreneur in vaudeville, circuses, advertising, and television. He could make money work, he could make deals, and he was incredibly persuasive. Naturally, he and Richardson took to one another at once. Saltzman interested Associated British-Pathe, a British distribution company in which Warner Brothers had a part interest, in financing the film. His determination to cast Richard Burton as Jimmy was, in Osborne's recollection, "a calculated move on his part to reverse the tide of [Burton's]

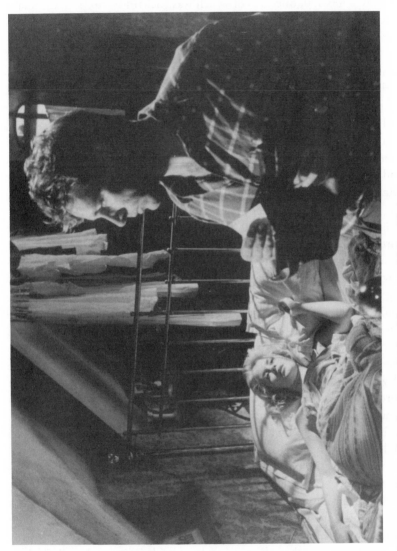

FIGURE 3.1. *Look Back in Anger* (Richard Burton and Mary Ure)

career [since] his most recent films, which had concentrated in Cinemascope on his splendid knees beneath Roman kilts, had failed to establish his surety as an international star" (1991, 107). The final budget came to roughly $500,000, one-fifth of which was Richard Burton's salary. Claire Bloom, the only other "name" actor, received about $20,000. Richardson received no fee for his direction.

The production company was dubbed "Woodfall," after a street off King's Road where Osborne and Ure had rented a little house. At Kenneth Tynan's suggestion, Nigel Kneale, a former associate of Richardson's at the BBC, was brought in to work on the script (Osborne purportedly had little confidence as yet in his screenwriting abilities); Oswald Morris, best known at the time for his work with John Huston (*Moulin Rouge* and *Moby Dick*), was assigned cinematographer (Dennis Coop the operator), and Ralph Brinton the art direction. Mary Ure was the only cast member retained from the original play.

The time of the shoot was, as Richardson describes it, one prolonged party centered around Saltzman's rented home in the fashionable part of Chelsea, Lowdnes Cottage. "We never questioned it—how it happened; who paid—Harry was totally in charge of the business side. Anyway, it was all part of the magic of movies, and all our friends were sharing it" (1993, 126). Shooting began in the autumn of 1958 at Elstree studios, where a set was constructed, consisting of a street market standing against a background of shop fronts. Although Tony realized the story's power stemmed from the sense that the characters were trapped in the attic's restrictive confines, he was in agreement with Kneale that the play should be "opened up" and much of its action transpire outside the Porter flat. Locations in Stratford East, Deptford Market, and Dalston Junction all figured in the shooting. He was making, he said at the time, an important discovery about the filmmaking process: "Miracles happen on location which you could never ever conceive of or imagine when you are writing the script," he said. "Life is always more daring and extravagant than art" (1959, 9).

Richardson's intentions and method are immediately apparent; and it is astonishing how quickly and naturally he adapts to the film medium in this, his first feature assignment. The film sprints nimbly out of the blocks. It opens with a blare of jazz by the Chris Barber Jazz Band (featured earlier in *Momma Don't Allow*) and a flurry of tight closeups of banjos, horns, and dancing feet and then follows Jimmy down the night streets, a solitary figure blowing a trumpet riff of his own. He climbs the stairs to his flat and silently regards the sleeping form of Alison. He bends over her and awakens her with a kiss, first tentative, then passionate. Fadeout.

This prologue functions not only to bring a whiff of the smoky clubs and the rain-streaked streets into Jimmy's cramped flat, but to bring Jimmy's poetic, even tender sensibilities to the fore. In terms of character development, it is the exact reverse of Osborne's play, which first presented Jimmy's angry snarl and only later revealed the wounded vulnerability beneath.

After settling into an extended scene in the Porter flat the next morning—a virtually exact copy of the play's opening tableau—the film abruptly shifts the scene to the street market. Richardson's documentary background is evident in his lingering glances at the early-morning preparations of the stall owners and the faces of the passersby on the street. It is here that Ma Tanner arrives, come to see Jimmy. Her scenes, which derive from a handful of lines of dialogue in the play (and which were added to the screenplay by Osborne himself), not only provide a welcome opportunity to see a great actress, Edith Evans, at work but also function to establish Jimmy's essentially sympathetic nature to working-class virtues. She and Jimmy share a drink at a pub and then go together to visit her husband's grave. It is an affecting scene, shot on location at Kensal Rise. "We had lots of fun," Ma soliloquizes about her life with her husband, as Jimmy tends the grave; "him and me; being alive. You know— just being alive. That's enough for an old girl like me. Chewing the cud and have a nip of what you fancy." Later, in another added scene, when Jimmy flies to Ma's bedside after her stroke, only to find her inarticulate and gasping desperately in a vain attempt to communicate, he cries out, "Hell, hell, HELL." (Director Richardson, in a Hitchcockian sound edit, cuts from his scream to the cries of children playing in the streeet outside.) Jimmy's impotent rage and frustration in this terrifying scene are as affecting as in any other moment in the picture.

More added scenes reinforce the viewer's sympathy for Jimmy and provide better understanding of his rages. In the marketplace the attempts of an Indian trader named Kapoor to open a stall are thwarted by Hurst the market manager (Donald Pleasance). Jimmy is outraged both at the failure of the other stall owners to defend Kapoor against what is obviously an act of racist bigotry and at Kapoor's mistake in expecting enlightened treatment in England in the first place. In another scene, backstage at a theater during a rehearsal of Helena's play, a piece of Edwardian parlor claptrap, *The Forgotten Heart*, he explodes in contempt: "The bloke who wrote that was never in a woman's bedroom; not even his mother's when she found out the truth about him." And when he and Helena later go to a movie, a Korda-esque patriotic saga of English colonialism in India, he hoots at the British Lancers on their charging horses, to the outrage of a nearby patron (who looks suspiciously like J. B. Priestley, that English literary monument to outdated traditions and sentiments with whom Richardson had worked years before at the BBC).

Many of the play's memorable speeches are taken out of the context of Jimmy's flat and redistributed into a variety of locales. For example, Jimmy's soliloquy on Colonel Redfern's "long days in the sun," which originally appeared in act 1, appears midway through the film during a jazz club scene. Some of Colonel Redfern's lines, in turn, are transplanted to the brief scene wherein Alison and her parents converse while sitting on lawn chairs at her father's country estate. Alison's fleeting suggestion that she end her pregnancy with an abortion (also from act 1) transpires with her doctor (George Devine in a cameo appearance) in his examining room. Jimmy's savage confrontation with Helena ("I have no public school scruples about hitting girls.") occurs in her theater dressing room after he's made a mockery of her play. And the concluding scenes in the train station provide the opportunity for a succession of several of the play's key dialogue exchanges, including Jimmy's affectionate farewell to Cliff (Cliff: "My feet hurt"; Jimmy: "Try washing your socks") and Jimmy's reconciliation with Alison (her soliloquy about the pain of her miscarriage and his reference to their game of "bears and squirrels"). These last moments are played out in a powerful two-shot closeup, their profiles silhouetted in sharp relief against the swirling steam of the trains.

John Osborne was on record as resisting such attempts to open up the play. "It seemed to me [Richardson and Kneale] were ripping out its obsessive, personal heart," he later wrote. "I protested without much authority. Indeed, the final effect of the film is a softer-edged, more sympathetic portrait free of the claustrophobic confines of the Porter apartment (1991, 108). Critic Penelope Houston agreed, writing that the movie softened Jimmy's character from the harder-edged spleen of the stage original and functioned to universalize the character (1958–1959, 31–32).

Even when some scenes are played out intact in their original apartment settings, the effect is still rendered in cinematic terms. Note the canny way the shot composition of the first Sunday morning tableau is exactly repeated in the later scene corresponding to the opening of act 3—only now it is Helena, not Allison, who occupies the foreground, the figures of the two men reading their newspapers visible beyond her shoulder in the background. And at the end of act 2, scene 2, when Helena slaps Jimmy, only to fall hungrily into his arms, the scene is played out in a powerful, uncut two-shot closeup, his face brooding into the camera, her face turned slightly toward a three-quarter profile.

The film was released with an "X" certificate. Just prior to the formation of Woodfall Films, censorship had become extremely restrictive in England. Relations between the film industry and the Censorship Board had been near the breaking point when a new man, John Trevelyan, was appointed as the board's executive secretary. Until his retirement in 1970, he encouraged an atmosphere for a more mature cinema, especially if it could be proven to boost box-office receipts. However, the "X" rating that was available for such pictures was a potential kiss of death. Then, as later in Hollywood, it signaled a prurient entertainment to audiences and potential box-office disaster to exhibitors. But Jack Clayton's *Room at the Top*, released in January 1959, one of the first working-class films to emerge from Britain at the time, and *Look Back in Anger*, released a few months later, proved that the "X" curse could be broken, that a quality film containing material not deemed fit for "family viewing" could still do well at the boxoffice. Among the relatively few excisions demanded of *Look Back* were the words *Christ*, *bitch*, and *bastard*.

Look Back in Anger opened in June 1959. A few film critics reacted in terms similar to those who saw the play three years earlier. "[Jimmy Porter] inveighs against his surroundings, his spouse, her middle-class relatives and a civilisation that has made him an outsider. It is hard to imagine any civilisation that would make him an insider" (Betts 1973, 276). Others, such as Isabel Quigly, writing in the *Spectator*, thought the film, which postdated the play by three years, had already been outdated: "What makes it seem diluted is that Jimmy no longer turns up as a surprise. At the tail of a fashion he once set, he now comes with a manner, a voice, opinions and grudges we all know too well. . . . Indeed, the angry young man, cosseted till his anger looks like petulance, has become a stock figure of our society, with its cult of the misfit, even of the gaolbird who publishes mis-spelt articles in the literary or glossy magazines" (Betts 1973, 276).

Writing in *Time and Tide*, Charles MacLaren agreed: "Customers unfamiliar with John Osborne's play may find it hard to figure out what made the original angry young man so angry" (Walker 1974, 58). Although there is no question that Burton's performance is sharp and strong (the misogyny is especially razor-edged), it is perhaps a bit *too* strong. Here's someone wholly capable, unlike Jimmy, of handling almost any adversity. It also could be argued that the thirty-eight-year-old actor looks too old for the part. Saltzman later admitted that casting Burton had been "a monumental miscalculation." He had been available because he owed Warners a film on a "play him or pay him" basis: "If he did *Look Back in Anger* at least they'd get a picture out of their deal; if he didn't, they still have to pay him $125,000. He did it—but it made nonsense of the text" (Walker 1974, 58).

FROM STAGE TO SCREEN: *THE ENTERTAINER*

John Osborne began writing *The Entertainer* before the premiere of *Look Back in Anger*. Although the British music-hall tradition was in its last gasp, Osborne was able to visit a few surviving halls in and around London, the Chelsea Palace, the Met in Edgware Road, and the Collins in Islington. The play's title came when he heard a Bunk Johnson recording of Scot Joplin's "The Entertainer." There was some apprehension about the lead character of Archie Rice. As Osborne says, "If [people] had been baffled that an educated young man, even an ungrateful graduate of a white-tile university, should *choose* to work at a market sweet-stall, they were mystified by Archie. What could possibly be interesting to the civilized sensibility in the spectacle of a third-rate comic writhing in a dying profession?" (1991, 39).

Olivier had come to the Royal Court the year before to see *Look Back*. "Larry" was the undisputed king of the British theatre, an international stage and screen star, an acclaimed director, with his own theatre, the St. James, and a powerful producing company. Richardson remembered he was not exactly a ham, but "a performer, a vulgarian, someone who lives and dies for acting" (1993, 111–12). On a later visit Olivier met Osborne and was subsequently sent the first act of *The Entertainer*. He took to the play immediately, although he first considered taking on the part of Billy, Archie's father. Osborne notes: "Sir Laurence was suddenly 'available' and eager in the way of prized actors who come into season with occasional surprising suddenness and have to be accommodated while the bloodstock is raring" (1991, 36). He accepted the play before it

FIGURE 3.2. *The Entertainer* (Laurence Olivier as Archie Rice)

was even finished, decided he would switch from the role of Billy to that of Archie, and accepted Tony to direct it. "My rhythm of work had become a bit deadly," Olivier recalled, "I was going mad, desperately searching for something suddenly fresh and thrillingly exciting. What I felt to be my image was boring me to death. . . . And now, suddenly, this miracle was happening. . . . In many ways it showed the worst side of me, and that felt good too: something like a confession, a welcome and beneficial expulsion of filth" (Findlater 1981, 40–42). Richardson was delighted. "For the Court to have the king join us on our terms was a great triumph" (1993, 112). However, the Court board rejected the idea at first. No sooner was that resolved than Olivier insisted on casting Vivien Leigh in the role of Archie's pathetic wife, Phoebe. That preposterous idea was also resolved, but only with great tact.

In addition to Olivier, the cast of the Rice family included George Relph as Billie, Dorothy Tutin as Jean, Brenda de Banzie as Phoebe, Richard Pasco as Frank, and Aubrey Dexter as William. Stanley Meadows appeared as Graham. Olivier took to the role readily enough. "At last," wrote Richardson, "after all the regal years, he'd cast off his mantle, been let out of school, and he capered and preened as the hoofer he really was" (1993, 113).

The play is set in 1956 in the backstreets of an English coastal resort—an area, as Osborne notes in his scene description, "full of dirty blank spaces, high black walls, a gas holder, a tall chimney, a main road that shakes with dust and lorries" (Osborne n.d., 9). Most of the action transpires in the living room of Archie Rice, a down-and-out vaudevillian. A series of arguments, peppered by recriminations and denials, punctuated by much drinking and the occasional singing of a ditty, reveals the bitter schisms that divide the family: The debt-ridden Archie is estranged from his wife, and he spends his nights performing in a sleazy nudie club. His alcoholic wife, Phoebe, is resentful of his philandering, distrustful of his misbegotten money-making schemes, and emotionally spent after the years of trying to keep the family together. His stepdaughter Jean is a disillusioned idealist who once taught art to the disadvantaged and protested government policies in Trafalgar Square. His son Frank has served jail time for resisting military conscription and now plays piano in a jazz club. Another son, Mick, has joined the army and has gone away to the Suez conflict. And Archie's father, Billy, a retired vaudevillian, is lost in his newspaper and his memories of the long-vanished, elegant, chivalrous good old days.

Their voices lift up in an elegy for postwar England. Billy bemoans the death of the music hall tradition: "It was all over, finished, dead when I got out of it" (15). Phoebe looks back on a lifetime of failed hopes, crushed under the heel of constant drudgery: "You want a bit of life before it's all over. It takes the gilt off if you know you've got to go on and on till they carry you out in a box" (33). Jean and Frank give voice to a younger generation whose initiatives and opportunities are stunted by the welfare state: "Why do people like us sit here," asks Jean, "and just lap it all up, why do boys die, or stoke boilers, why do we pick up these things, what are we hoping to get out of it?" (67). The absence of their brother Mick is mute testimony to the useless slaughter of too many young men as a result of English empire building. Surveying this familial blight, Archie ruthlessly comments, "We don't get on with anything. We don't ever succeed in anything. We're a *nuisance*, we do nothing but make a God almighty fuss about anything we ever do" (46). Better to hide everything under a mask of normalcy and "pretend we're a happy, respectable, decent family" (49). It is a mask not unlike the painted façade he presents across the footlights to the theater audiences: "You see this face, you see this face, this face can split open with warmth and humanity . . . [but] I'm dead behind these eyes. I'm dead, just like the whole inert, shoddy lot out there. It doesn't matter because I don't feel a thing, and neither do they. We're just as dead as each other" (62).

Any attempts to improve the lot of these people are doomed. When Jean learns of the death of her brother Mick, she abandons plans to marry and decides to remain with her mother. Archie's plans to finance a new show with money from his mistress' parents are thwarted when they learn he's a married man. Billy, who was to come out of retirement and appear in his son's production, collapses and dies. And the opportunity for the family to relocate to Canada, bankrolled by Archie's brother, William, comes to naught. At the end, Archie is alone in a spotlight, singing his theme song, the anthem of resignation and futility:

> Why should I care?
> Why should I let it touch me,
> Why shouldn't I sit down and try
> To let it pass over me.

His final words are addressed to the audience: "You've been a good audience. Very good. A very *good* audience. Let me know where you're working tomorrow night—and I'll come and see *you*" (77).

The action plays out on a divided stage, scenes alternating between the Rice living room upstage—a relatively naturalistic set—and the stylized music hall set downstage where Archie performs his "turns" and monologues. In Alan Tagg's original Royal Court design, the front curtain was replaced by a music-hall advertisement cloth, fake red-plush stage boxes were installed, and an electrically operated numerical indicator signaled each "turn." Thus, the Royal Court audience serves double duty as Archie's music-hall audience.

Richardson claims Olivier's performance was seminal: "He transcended himself and, as with *Henry V*, became the embodiment of a national mood. *Henry V* had been made during the last great moment of heroism for the British: Archie was the future, the decline, the sourness, the ashes of old glory, where Britain was heading" (1993, 115).

The film version of *The Entertainer*, claims Richardson, was more difficult to translate to screen than *Look Back in Anger*. In hindsight, he complained that the "totally realistic medium" of film was ill-suited to the metaphoric resonances of Archie and his third-rate routines (1993, 137). On stage, argues Colin Young in a 1960 interview with Richardson, the music-hall routines had commented in Brechtian fashion on Archie's sensibility and, by extension, his world. However, the concrete specificity of the screen emphasized the failures of a particular man, "a character existing at a specific seaside town, doing particular numbers [that] no longer have this double significance—they are just the sort of numbers that this dead-beat, third-rate music hall artist would have" (1960, 14). Richardson was content to delineate the particular man rather than the universal symbol: "Our only entry to him is through understanding his own vulnerability and squalor so deeply that we can empathize with the individual without extending the character to thoughts about society. The detail of the performance was what had to count, not the leaps to beyond" (1993, 137–38).

The results, complained critic Douglas McVay in 1962, affirmed the problems inherent in Richardson's approach to adaptation, which "muffled [Osborne's] theatrical devices in the interests of cinema 'realism'" (19). And John Russell Taylor agreed, contending it was "totally misconceived" because it "tries to transplant the least realistic sections unchanged into a setting of documentary realism" (1966, 45).

The Entertainer was financed partly by British Lion, partly by Walter Reed, and partly by the National Film Finance Corporation. It cost about $400,000. Olivier, Osborne, and Richardson all took deferments against the cost. The casting of Olivier as Archie, according to Osborne, and Plowright as Jean was not a foregone conclusion. Among the other contenders for Archie were Eddie Constantine and James Cagney; and for Jean, Geraldine McEwan (who had succeed Plowright during the Palace production). Osborne claims it was the suggestion of the costume designer, Jocelyn Rickards, that tipped the balance in favor of Plowright, who had already appeared at the Court in *The Country Wife* and was currently engaged in an affair with Olivier (1991, 147). Brenda de Banzie came over from the original play. Roger Livesey appeared as Billy, Alan Bates as Frank, and Albert Finney as Mick.

The script by Osborne and Kneale burst the confines of the Rice apartment and moved the action to the seaside locations at Morecambe, "a failed popular resort with decaying piers and crumbling theatres, the second-class sister to the livelier, more raucous, still-popular Blackpool" (Richardson 1993, 138). Tony had spent dreary wartime holidays there with his parents, "hating the concrete pavements, the mean boarding-houses, the vulgarity of the restaurants and shows" (1993, 138). Gone is the scaffolding device of the music-hall turns; rather, they are more naturally interpolated into the essentially linear narrative.

The sketchy character development and reported action of the play are elaborately amplified. An extended flashback early in the story fleshes out Jean's work in an art school, her relationship with Graham, and her farewell to Mick as he leaves for the Suez (her political protests are briefly alluded to but not depicted). Numerous scenes are added to fill out the roles of Frank (he now works backstage with Archie) and Billy (who sings a "British Navy" song at his club, walks with Jean at the amusement park, and takes his "comeback" play to London). Archie's extramarital affair, meanwhile—an incident only briefly alluded to in the play—is interwoven throughout most of the film, beginning with his emceeing of the "Miss Great Britain" beauty pageant, his seduction of a contestant (Tina Lapford, played by Anne Field) with promises of stardom, his persuasion of her parents to underwrite his new show, and his ultimate defeat when his true marital status is revealed.

Several of composer John Addison's original songs remain, including Archie's comic turns, " The Old Church Bell Won't Ring Tonight, as the Vicar's Dropped a Clanger," and "Now I'm Just an Ordinary Bloke." Archie's signature song, "Why Do I Care?" which attracted little attention during the original stage production, is heard everywhere, either as a leitmotif on the soundtrack (over the opening credits, during Jean's flashback, and during Billy's comeback scene) or as a performed stage routine (after Archie's hopes for a new show are dashed and after Mick's funeral).

Although Olivier's first appearance as Archie is startling, almost cartoonish—with his grease-painted mask, dark-limned eyes, sharp nose, and slash of a mouth—he soon emerges as an entirely more sympathetic character than in Osborne's original. His savage tongue is, for the most part, tempered. He no longer works in a sleazy nudie club but gets top billing—"Television and Radio's Sauciest Comic" blares the billboard next to a cut-out caricature of his face—in a rather ornate resort theater. Indeed, his final performance is played out to a large audience. He seduces the beauty pageant contestant in a rueful, almost apologetic fashion. His relations with his family, particularly Jean and Frank, are affectionate, if restrained. And his appearance off stage is rather natty, especially in the nautical hat, white slacks, and blazer he wears during the pageant sequence.

However, some of Archie's edge comes through in the portions that are retained from two of his key speeches in episode no. 8—the "dead eyes" and the "negress" soliloquies. In the first, Archie and Jean are alone in the empty theater, and he declaims the words softly but coldly, face framed in a chilling closeup. It is a memorable moment, as commentator Douglas McVay notes: "As Olivier pronounces this sentence in the deserted auditorium, his trapped, ageing face stripped of the buffoon's gay cosmetic veneer, we witness a reversal of a legendary histrionic ambition. We witness Hamlet playing the clown" (1962, 19). In the second, after receiving the news of Mick's death, he staggers across the stage in medium-long shot, singing hoarsely: "Oh, lord, I don't care where they bury my body, no I don't care where they bury my body, 'cos my soul's going to live with God!" It, too, is an effective moment although, according to Richardson, not as effective as when Olivier enacted it on stage: "It was the most thrilling single moment I've ever had in the theatre" (1993, 114).

"LIFE WAITS OUTSIDE"

Richardson claims *The Entertainer* was a key film in his development (1993, 138). In its restlessly moving camera, skewed angles, powerful closeups, flashbacks, and detailed, naturalistic surfaces, it bears scarcely a trace of its theatrical origins. Implicit is his growing aversion to shooting in studio interiors: "Their artificial conditions produced artificiality in acting and image (which for me has been the greatest criticism of all the American studio films of the 1930s and 1940s, for which I have never had and will never have either admiration or reverence), and that I would never be happy shooting except in the open air or inside real locations" (1993, 138).

The Free Cinema manifesto, including the dicta that "perfection is not an aim" and "no film can be too personal," was coming into its own. In a 1960 interview he declared,

> For the sort of realistic films I want to make, by improvising one's way out of the impossibilities of real conditions you get something on the screen that is more true, somehow, than something contrived on a set. . . . I think a real set forces you to come to a simple sort of relationship with the people, to make a direct statement with the camera more than anything else. . . . For once inside a studio you start taking walls out, you start thinking 'Wouldn't it be fun if we tracked from here to there, pan round there?' and—you know—do a lot of fancy stuff. One is getting in fact less of the human reality. (qtd. in Young 1960, 13)

Indeed, with *Look Back in Anger* and *The Entertainer*, Tony was just limbering up. In the films to come, as Alexander Walker notes, Richardson would prefer "the freshness of the sketch compared with the worked-over deadness of the finished painting." Further, "Anything that irons out the natural truth of what he responds to is anathema to him" (1974, 64).

Richardson had come a long way from the roaring broadsides and brave manifestos of the Free Cinema years. But he had hardly begun. And he knew it. His memoirs of these years affirm his lifelong conviction that no matter what he was doing or where he was doing it, something else always lay just beyond his reach. In his own words, it was the sense that "life waited outside." The recurring phrase becomes a metaphor for the destiny he always knew awaited him beyond the isolation of his youthful home at Shipley; the barrack-room austerity of the Harrogate boarding school; the class consciousness at Oxford; the outworn traditions of the proscenium stage; and, now, the restrictive conventions of the British studio cinema.

Free Cinema, the Royal Court, and his blossoming film career were breaching those barriers. But so much of life still waited outside. And "outside," in every sense of the word, metaphoric, realistic, artistic, was where he always wanted to go. With that long, loping stride and quixotic temperament, one knew he had to get there.

WORKS CITED

Alpert, Hollis. "Britain's Angry Young Director." *Saturday Review* 24 (December 1960): 48–49.

Betts, Ernest. *The Film Business: A History of British Cinema, 1896–1972.* London and New York: Pitman Publishing Corporation, 1973.

Doty, Gresdna A., and Billy J. Harbin, eds. *Inside the Royal Court Theatre, 1956–1981.* Baton Rouge: Louisiana State University Press, 1990.

Findlater, Richard. *At the Royal Court.* Derbyshire: Amber Lane Press, 1981.

Gomez, Joseph. "*The Entertainer:* From Play to Film." *Film Heritage* 8 (1973): 19–26.

Houston, Penelope. "*Look Back in Anger.*" *Sight and Sound* 28.1 (Winter 1958–1959): 31–32.

Lambert, Gavin. "Free Cinema." *Sight and Sound* 25 (Spring 1956): 173–77.

McVay, Douglas. "Hamlet to Clown." *Films and Filming* 8:12 (1962): 16–19.

Osborne, John. *Almost a Gentleman: An Autobiography, 1955–1966.* Vol. II. London: Faber and Faber, 1991.

———. *The Entertainer.* London and New York: Samuel French, n.d.

———. *Look Back in Anger.* London and New York: Samuel French, 1956.

Reisz, Karel. Interview with John C. Tibbetts and James M. Welsh, London, 19 January 1997.

Richardson, Tony. "A Free Hand." *Sight and Sound* 28.2 (Spring 1959): 64.

———. " London Letter." *Film Culture* 2.2 (1956): 16–17.

———. *The Long Distance Runner: A Memoir.* New York: William Morrow and Company, Inc., 1993.

———. " The Man behind an Angry-Young-Man." *Films and Filming* 5 (February 1959): 9, 32.

Taylor, John Russell. *Anger and After*. Harmondsworth, England: Penguin Books, 1966.

Walker, Alexander. *Hollywood U.K.* New York: Stein and Day, 1974.

Young, Colin. "Tony Richardson: An Interview in Los Angeles." *Film Quarterly* 13.4 (Summer 1960): 10–15.

CHAPTER FOUR

"Greatest Pleasures": A Taste of Honey *(1961) and* The Loneliness of the Long Distance Runner *(1962)*

WILLIAM L. HORNE

. . . I love making all films, but *Loneliness*, like *A Taste of Honey*, was one of the greatest pleasures to make.

—Tony Richardson,
Long Distance Runner. A Memoir, 153

On the day that Tony Richardson died in 1991, members of his family were surprised to discover a complete manuscript of his autobiography hidden in a cupboard in his Los Angeles home. When this work was finally published in 1993, the title of the chapter covering the years 1961 and 1962 proved highly significant: "O Wonderful, Wonderful, and Most Wonderful Wonderful" (Richardson 151). Clearly, at the time, the play *As You Like It* loomed large for Richardson given Vanessa Redgrave's triumphant performances as Rosalind and the fact that she was playing this part when they got married in April of 1962. However, this euphoria also characterizes the most rewarding period of his professional life. In the summer of 1961, his collaboration with John Osborne reached its apotheosis in the premiere of the play *Luther*; indeed, in the second volume of his autobiography, *Almost a Gentleman*, the playwright recalls the spontaneous excitement that he felt watching the spectacle unfold on the stage of the Royal Court: "My head buzzed with the physical demonstration of my rehabilitated imagination. Not only did it work, it palpably took flight" (Osborne 1991, 188). For Richardson, a monumental performance by Albert Finney was made all the more glorious by a newly discovered synthesis of cast and crew: "*Luther* was one of those extraordinary moments of hardhat-type theatre where the crew—John and I, Jocelyn as designer, Jock as Gregorian chant-master, Albert and George in the cast, and other old friends like Peter Bull and John Moffatt—were united in drilling and hammering the blocks of theatrical masonry together" (Richardson 1993, 153).

Yet it was in the two films that Richardson made in 1961 and 1962 that he found his greatest professional satisfaction. He describes his work on *A Taste of Honey* as "an experience without problems": "Once Rita had been found, everything went wonderfully—a lovefest with both crew and actors—and I felt free and happy making a film for the first time without constraints of any kind." For a confirmed cineaste it was a "consummation/Devoutly to be wished" and it continued into 1962: "*Loneliness* followed with practically the same team and the same spirit" (Richardson 1993, 153). There is much evidence to suggest that of all his accomplishments, the directing of feature films was his primary pride and joy. Despite his presidency of the Oxford University Dramatic Society, when he left Wadham he joined the first group of graduate trainees at the BBC. This served as nothing less than an apprenticeship in the visual media. He may have been responsible for a television version of *Othello*, which attracted the largest British audience up to that time, but he also worked on documentary programs and even on lowly variety shows. What could have been more valuable for a future career in the cinema? In a revealing interview with Tony Richardson and Lindsay Anderson at the Royal Court Theatre in 1962, Robert Rubens asked him how he became involved in the theatre in general and in the founding of the Royal Court in particular. Having mentioned his interest in amateur theatricals and his involvement with Oxford dramatic societies, he provides unequivocal evidence of his motives: "Immediately after Oxford I went into television, doing various odd productions on the side, but I was always thinking of the cinema" (Rubens 1962, 6).

This is not to minimize in any way Richardson's indispensable contributions to the theatre. His efforts, together with those of George Devine, in the establishment of the English Stage Company, were essential in the development of a new movement in the theatre. Indeed, along with Joan Littlewood's Theatre Workshop at the Stratford East, the Royal Court served as a crucial catalyst for the emergence of a drama more lively, more authentic, and more relevant than the traditional fare of insipid drawing-room comedy. In his obituary for the *Independent*, Irving Wardle argues that the importance of Richardson's contribution "has received only grudging recognition": "[H]e was the driving force behind the company in its early years" (1991, 49). Moreover, it was he who discovered and directed the play that came to epitomize the whole dramatic movement: John Osborne's *Look Back in Anger*. An old Oxford friend, Anthony Curtis, writing in the *Financial Times*, recalled that during a visit to his top-floor flat in Chiswick, he was served "with tea by Tony who told me 'I've discovered the best play written since the war'" (1991, 41). During this period, his energy was immense and his efforts frenetic but he succeeded in refining his directing skills, particularly his ability to elicit the very best performances from actors, whether it was an unknown young actor, such as Alan Bates in *Look Back in Anger*, or a celebrated theatrical knight, such as Lawrence Olivier in *The Entertainer*. The author of both of these plays, John Osborne, best expressed Richardson's gift for stimulating the creative energies of those with whom he worked. In the second volume of his autobiography, which has become infamous for the sheer nastiness of its vituperative attacks on friends and relatives alike, he confesses, "No one has inflamed my creative passions more tantalizingly than Tony, nor savaged my moral sensibilities so cruelly. Whatever wayward impulse of torment he inflicted, his gangling, whiplash courage, struggling within that contorted figure, was awesomely moving and, at the last, unimpeachable" (Osborne 1991, 194).

If critics were grudging in their acknowledgment of Richardson's seminal contribution to the English theatre, they have been even less accommodating in their assessment of his career as a film director. Indeed, there always has been an undercurrent of automatic disdain for his efforts. It is hardly surprising that he had an extremely low regard for critics; in a public letter in 1968 announcing his refusal to invite them to attend the premiere of his film *The Charge of the Light Brigade*, he described them as "acidulated intellectual eunuchs hugging their prejudices like feather boas." Critical disregard reached its apotheosis in a number of his obituary notices, which lamented what seemed to be viewed as nothing less than "an expense of spirit in a waste of shame." Sheridan Morley's article in the *Daily Mail* was entitled "Tragedy of the genius with a talent for self-destruction." Apart from the offensive message of such a characterization of someone who has died of AIDS, the thesis of the obituary is as follows: "As a man, he has been dead less than two days: as a director, he had been effectively and critically dead for almost 20 years" (1991, 51). In the *Evening Standard*, Alexander Walker's article was every bit as incendiary; it was entitled "Secret Shame of an Angry Young Man" (1991, 11). It was left to Vanessa Redgrave in a couple of angry letters to counter what she refers to as Morley's " Little Englander view" (1991, 26) and Walker's mixture of "a little fact with a lot of fiction" (1991, 53). Part of this critical indifference has doubtless resulted from an automatic hatred for California and all that it symbolizes in English culture. In a compelling celebration of his longtime friend, published in *Sight and Sound*, Gavin Lambert reached the same conclusion: "One of the more peculiar ethical hang-ups of the English is that an Englishman may expatriate himself to France or Italy without selling his soul to the devil, but if he transplants himself to California he's hell-bent for corruption" (1993, 30). But it was also Richardson's sheer eclecticism that ever militated against him. From Orson Welles to Kenneth Branagh, long knives await those who falter in the pursuit of multiple goals.

If committed theatre critics too often saw his film work as a secondary activity involving the pursuit of mammon rather than the muse, partisan film critics regarded him as a literary hack locked to words at the expense of images. In his book *Creativity and Constraint in the British Film Industry*, Duncan Petrie devotes some seven pages to articulating the notion that so-called "verbal primacy" has served as a corrupting influence in the British film industry: "While a good script is obviously important, the main elements of film-making are images and sounds. Words are only the starting point" (1991, 165). Such an idea is founded upon a fundamental misreading of the nature of the screenplay and its relationship to the film; surely it is not merely a written version of the dialog but a performance text indicating how the elements of cinema will be employed. Richardson was no literary or theatrical hack recording stage performances on film; he was a committed exponent of the cinema who thoroughly understood the history and traditions of the medium. Soon after he arrived in London in 1953, he met the future filmmakers who had founded and edited the film magazine *Sequence*. Lindsay Anderson,

Gavin Lambert, and Karel Reisz. He rapidly became an active member of the group, contributing articles of film criticism to *Sequence*'s successor, *Sight and Sound*. The parallel to the French *nouvelle vague* is readily apparent. Like the group at *Cahiers du Cinema*, they sought to attack what was tired and injurious in the national cinema and identify strengths to be used as the basis for a newly enlivened art. In his autobiography, Richardson recalls the intensity and euphoria of the experience:

> All our writing was important not so much in itself but as an indication of what we hoped to achieve. There was a big difference between the two worlds of the theatre and the movies. In theatre you worked within the structures that already existed, even if you rejected their establishment context; in the movies, as far as we were concerned, you worked as you liked. The dialectic of the cinema was more intense, the passions more divisive, the morality more keen, and often puritanical and often finicky (as would later be true of the young theatre writers). In theatre circles you swapped anecdotes; in the movie world you fought about what you liked and attacked the falseness of the current product. It was intellectual in the best sense, passionate, idiosyncratic, and crazy. (1993a, 94)

"Bliss was it in that dawn to be alive,/But to be young was very heaven."

Before long, Richardson worked with Karel Reisz to make his first film, *Momma Don't Allow*; it was shown as part of the first Free Cinema program at the National Film Theatre in February 1956. A key contributor to both *A Taste of Honey* and *The Loneliness of the Long Distance Runner*, Walter Lassally served as the photographer. The principles espoused by these incipient filmmakers were very much related to those that inspired both the English Stage Company and Woodfall Films when it was established in 1958 by Tony Richardson and John Osborne. In his book, *The History of World Cinema*, David Robinson quotes from the program notes for the first Free Cinema screening; Lindsay Anderson explains the reason why this work is characterized as "free" rather than "experimental":

> It is neither introverted nor esoteric. Nor is the concern primarily with technique. These films are free in the sense that their statements are entirely personal. Though their moods and subjects differ, the concern of each of them is with some aspect of life as it is

lived in this country today. . . . Implicit in our attitudes is a belief in freedom, in the importance of people and in the significance of the everyday (1973, 294)

Enamored of certain aspects of the Grierson tradition in the British film, particularly the "poetic realism" of Humphrey Jennings, these filmmakers sought to put serious portraits of ordinary working people on the screen. At the Royal Court and at Joan Littlewood's Theatre Workshop, the same approach was being applied to the stage. When Woodfall Films was created, part of its mission was to counter the rank conservatism of middle-class studio products with more authentic and personal explorations of contemporary life. In his memoirs, Richardson emphasizes the felt need to empower independent filmmakers: "As with the Court, the concept of Woodfall had not been just to showcase John's and my talents but to use what clout we developed to create opportunities for others to create their own movies (as Francis Ford Coppola and Steven Spielberg were to do in America)" (Richardson 1993a, 140–41). His partner in the enterprise, John Osborne, has recorded his insistence that it be Richardson who serve as the first director in the pursuit of such a goal: "This was based not on blind loyalty but on my untutored faith in his flair and his being the only possible commander to lead Woodfall's opening assault on the suburban vapidity of British filmmaking" (1991, 107).

There are many valuable qualities to the first few films made by the new company, *Look Back in Anger*, *The Entertainer*, and *Saturday Night and Sunday Morning*, but it is in *A Taste of Honey* and *The Loneliness of the Long Distance Runner* that the promise of the Free Cinema movement and Woodfall Films reached its apotheosis. One can argue legitimately that these two films represent an authentic British equivalent to the French *nouvelle vague*. This is not a notion that has been widely accepted by cinema historians, and it is necessary to examine and evaluate the reasons for this attitude. The fundamental ambivalence is nicely summed up by a chapter title in George Perry's book *The Great British Picture Show:* "Nouvelle Vague or Deja Vu?" (218). He proceeds to accuse Richardson of "fashionable borrowings from French prototypes . . . incorporated almost like nervous tics" (219). It is certainly true that there are occasional techniques used in these two films that mirror devices used in *Les Quatre Cents Coups* or *A Bout de Souffle*, and some are misused. In *The Loneliness of the Long Distance Runner*, when Colin and Mike emerge from the bakery that they have robbed, they are seen running down the street in fast motion;

it is a distortion of filmic time that is no less unfortunate than Richard Attenborough's similar artistic misjudgment in *Chaplin*. Nevertheless, the notion that such occasional mannerisms "have consistently marred Richardson's skill as a director" (219) is surely both unfair and mistaken. Such mannered and dated techniques are abundant in French film of the period, but they are not used to devalue the integrity of the directors. One cannot help but feel that Richardson's major crime is not being European enough. In his book *Fires over England*, Ken Russell laments the fact that he would probably fare better with British critics if he were called Russellini: "They may forgive Fellini his excesses, but I am chastised for being too theatrical" (1993, 82). This approach is clearly manifest in John Russell Taylor's book *Cinema Eye, Cinema Ear* (1964), with its secondary title "Some Key Film-Makers of the Sixties"; it explores the works of Fellini, Antonioni, Buñuel, Bresson, Bergman, Hitchcock, Truffaut, Godard, and Resnais. While no one would question the quality of the work of any of these directors, there is an unfortunate canonical tone to the book. Indeed, he singles out Richardson for daring to use some of the cinematic devices used by Truffaut:

> But the evidence of films like Tony Richardson's *The Loneliness of the Long Distance Runner* and *Tom Jones*, for instance, suggests very clearly that only Truffaut can fully control Truffaut's style; with him it is natural, felt, and his extreme eclecticism in his choice of sources does not prevent the result from achieving the coherence of one man's highly personal taste. When anyone else tries to achieve the same effect with the same materials the result is just a ragbag of remembered bits from other men's work. (209)

To paraphrase Alexander Pope, as far as Taylor is concerned, in a film by Truffaut "all discord" is "harmony misunderstood" because "whatever IS, is RIGHT"! Yet it is clear that more than a few *nouvelle vague* and other European films of the sixties were considerably overrated at the time. Andrew Sarris was not entirely misguided when he wrote of "audiences weary of the dreary ennui (not to mention Antoniennui) of much of today's plotless film-making" (1970, 100).

Both *A Taste of Honey* and *The Loneliness of the Long Distance Runner* have been compared to *Les Quatres Cents Coups*. This is a useful enterprise since all three films deal with youthful loners on the edges of polite society. In fact, in a telling postscript to a letter that he sent to Helen Scott in April 1963, François Truffaut wrote: "The only point which I forgot to answer: yes, I saw *A Taste of Honey* at Cannes and I liked it a lot. It was at my insistence that the girl who plays the leading role got a prize" (216). Indeed, both of these Woodfall films compare very favorably with *Les Quatres Cents Coups*. And yet in an essay entitled "The Last New Wave: Modernism in the British Films of the Thatcher Era," Peter Wollen once again articulates the old shibboleths about the inadequacies of the so-called angry young men films of 1959 through 1963 and their failure to pass muster as an authentic British New Wave: "Yet surely to call these films New Wave is both inappropriate and misleading. First, the idea of a New Wave was intimately linked to the project of directorial "authorship." A good case can be made for Lindsay Anderson as a bilious but authentic "auteur" . . . but nobody has made a serious claim for the auteurist credentials of Reisz, Richardson, Schlesinger and others" (1993, 37). There is an eminently serious claim to be made for Richardson as an auteur.

Part of the irresistible allure of the cinema to him was the possibility of being the primary creative force and having complete control over the work. In an article that he wrote for *Granta* in 1962, he argues forcefully that "the impress of the director's personality upon his material constitutes his style." It is a point of view which he had already articulated in his earlier contributions to *Sight and Sound*, but in this piece it is as fiercely auteurist as any manifesto from the *Cahiers du Cinema* of the time or from Andrew Sarris. Richardson makes effective use of detailed examples from the works of Hitchcock, Bergman, Preminger, Mann, and John Sturges. The last of these is viewed as a failed director because he does not preserve an organic relationship between form and content: "Sturges presents his director's credentials at the expense of the action" (Richardson 1962, 122). It is nothing less than a restatement of the classic distinction from *La Politique* between the journeyman *metteur-en-scene* and the true *auteur*. This notion is duly confirmed in the article's concluding paragraph: "Both Mann's composition and Preminger's 'evidence' represent the personal signature which each of these directors brings to his films. Throughout their work they establish their presence through recurring patterns of expression or recurring ideas. And this is true of any good director" (122).

Clearly, Tony Richardson aspired to the role of *auteur*, even if that interpretation of the cinema leaves a great deal to be desired. After all, film is nothing if not a collaborative enterprise, in which the director's role may be of primary significance but not to the exclusion of many other important contributions. In fact, he acknowledged as much in his autobiography when he remarked, in an aside, that "the substitution of director for writer was one of the excesses of the so-called *auteur* theory at its height (Richardson 1993a, 159). In fact, when Renoir argued that it is the *auteur* who is the main creative force behind a film, he clearly meant the writer. Nevertheless, it is apparent from his statements over the years that Richardson has always relished the control inherent in the directing of films. In an interview with Derek Prouse in 1965 he was nothing less than ecstatic about his future in the cinema: "I feel I just want to go on working in the cinema always. The director in the cinema is a real creative force, while in the theatre he's just an interpreter of the text." It was a sentiment to which he returned in his memoirs when he commented on John Osborne's failure to appreciate the need to rewrite and revise movie scripts: "He regards a script once finished as the script of the play, with the director being responsible for staging the author's vision in the most effective way he can. But in movies the director's is the final sensibility. Every choice, every decision, has to be filtered through him, and he converts them all into images the way a writer converts his experience into words" (Richardson 1993a, 159). In his complete control over all aspects of production and in his articulation of a fiercely independent filmmaking process, Richardson's work on *A Taste of Honey* and *The Loneliness of the Long Distance Runner* was the true zenith of his directing career.

Wollen also argues that "the idea of a New Wave involved putting film first and not subordinating it to literature or theatre" (1993, 37). The old prejudice about words rather than images surfaces once again. Yet surely there is no difference in quality *per se* between films that are adaptations and films that are made from so-called original scripts. Truly creative adaptations, such as *A Taste of Honey* or *The Loneliness of the Long Distance Runner* are not mere interpretations of the original but new works in a new medium. Wollen goes on to argue that Woodfall Films compounded its failure to be truly cinematic by employing the original authors of novels and plays to write the screenplays. He argues that the ultimate travesty is the film *Billy Liar* "written by Keith Waterhouse and Willis Hall based on their own play of Waterhouse's novel! This film of an adaptation of an adaptation is about as far from Truffaut's ideal of auteurism as you can get" (37). What a truly peculiar criterion for film excellence, that it should have sprung, like the goddess Athene, fully armed from the forehead of Zeus.

Richardson worked closely with the authors of the play and the novella in preparing the scripts for *A Taste of Honey* and *The Loneliness of the Long Distance Runner*. In the case of the former work, he was only too well aware of the inherent dangers of attempting to make a film out of a play. Indeed, in an article that he wrote for the magazine *Films and Filming* in 1961, he addressed the issue directly:

> I don't really think of *A Taste of Honey* as being from a play I directed, because I prepared the script and conceived the film before I directed the play. In fact when I was first going to do the film I didn't intend to direct the play and it was only because of problems in setting the production up that I did the play on Broadway. I hope this is not influenced as much by the theatre as the other films I've done. I don't really want to do another film that uses a play as basic material because the theatre and the film work quite differently. Once you've done a thing in the theatre it is terribly difficult to look at it as freshly as one should. (1961, 41)

Richardson and Delaney are jointly credited with writing the script for *A Taste of Honey*. On *The Loneliness of the Long Distance Runner*, Alan Sillitoe, who had already worked as a screenwriter for Woodfall in adapting his novel *Saturday Night and Sunday Morning*, was given sole credit for the screenplay. However, in his autobiography, *Life without Armour*, he points out that the first draft of the script based on *Saturday Night and Sunday Morning* was far too long, so "during the next few months the script was honed down to a ninety-minute maximum under his (Karel Reisz['s]) careful and talented scrutiny" (1995, 259). Subsequently, he met with the opposite problem in developing the screenplay for *The Loneliness of the Long Distance Runner*. "Being a story and not a novel, the first draft was much too short, and new material had to be added to bring it to the usual length of ninety minutes" (272). It is certain that Richardson played a crucial role in this process.

Wollen's third criterion for denying New Wave credentials to these films is the most obtuse and obscure of them all. They are not "modernist" enough, unlike the works of the *nouvelle vague*. "The films of Resnais and Godard, even when adaptations, placed themselves clearly in a modernist tradition, as did Truffaut's crucial *Jules et Jim* (1962). Resnais, to take the most obvious example, collaborated with writers like Robbe-Grillet and Duras. The *Cahiers* group followed the path blazed by the

Nouveau Roman" (1993, 38). It is true that *Jules et Jim* is a stunning piece of work, but surely it is not particularly avant-garde and is not the true New Wave supposed to involve "putting film first and not subordinating it to literature?" (37). However, the more destructive part of Wollen's argument is the related contention that the vaunted realism of these British films is no more than a cheap subterfuge to promote a jingoistic nationalism: "Yet in Britain filmmakers fetishized the second-rate novels of regionalists, realists, and reactionaries" (38). Nothing could be further from the truth when one examines Richardson's *A Taste of Honey* and *The Loneliness of the Long Distance Runner*. Both films were made in the manner envisaged by the Free Cinema group and the founders of the Woodfall Company.

These works were to firmly reject the traditional studio model of the so-called wellmade film in favor of location shooting. As John Schlesinger put it, in 1963, the studio tends to create a factory atmosphere and "you are forced to blueprint the work in advance." Nor does the studio necessarily provide the technical crew with more freedom: "whereas skilled technicians working on location do have a very real freedom. This, as I see it, is why the Woodfall people prefer to work away from a studio" (Manvell 1969, 70). However, this movement out of the studio was not simply designed to encourage spontaneity or to create a new look; it was also integrally related to content. Like Wordsworth in the preface to *Lyrical Ballads*, the filmmaker was committed to making use of real language and everyday situations. As Vanessa Redgrave contends in her autobiography: "Tony was the first English filmmaker to shoot feature films on real locations, rather than in a studio. He was the first to show England as it was, from top to bottom" (1994, 114). The brilliant photography of Walter Lassally on both films contributed a great deal to the impact of the movement out of the studio; he made highly effective use of lightweight cameras, such as the Arriflex, fully exploiting their portability and maneuverability. One thinks particularly of the hand-held shots of the landscape through which Colin runs, a resonant interpretation of his state of mind; one also recalls the brilliant low-light close-ups of Jo's face in *A Taste of Honey*.

Tony Richardson knew firsthand the vagaries of studio work. His miserable experience shooting *Sanctuary* in Hollywood in 1960 remained a lifelong exemplum of the consequences of forfeiting one's directorial independence: "It is a totally impossible creative set-up: even after the film is made so much mutilation goes on, and it becomes the product of many different people" (1961, 7). His fellow member of the Free Cinema group Gavin Lambert was also working at Fox at the time: "I . . . witnessed his losing battle with the regimentation and bureaucracy of a major studio. The experience left him vowing never to make another movie shackled to a sound stage, executive censorship, contract screenwriters and players and he never did" (1993, 30). In his autobiography, Richardson reveals that his involvement with *Sanctuary* was indirectly related to his desire to film *A Taste of Honey*. A phone call from Daryl Zanuck invited him to Paris to discuss the possibility of directing a film based on Faulkner's *Sanctuary* and *Requiem for a Nun*:

> My real motive was either financing for *A Taste of Honey* or at least money to secure the rights completely. Zanuck did express interest in *A Taste of Honey*, read it and offered to do it—"Anyway ya like, young fella—only one condition: a happy ending." "It has a happy ending—Jo is happy waiting for her baby to be born." (The father in the play is a black sailor.) "That's the point—the baby's gotta die, and the Mother and girl go off to a better life." I said no, thank you. *Requiem* was different. (Richardson 1991a, 142)

The latter decision was one that he would live to regret.

If there are clear parallels between Richardson's films of 1961 and 1962 and the early works of Truffaut and Godard, there are also clear connections to Italian neorealism. In March of 1961, when the *Times* announced that production on *A Taste of Honey* would soon begin, the article was headed "The Flight from Make-believe: Neo-realism in Film of Delaney Play":

> It will be shot on location in Manchester and London, and Mr. Richardson intends to use it as the occasion for an experiment in "neo-realism" more complete and far-reaching than has yet been attempted in a major British feature film: there will be no studio work at all, and the whole film, interiors as well as exteriors, will be shot in surroundings corresponding exactly to those depicted in the play.

Six weeks later, when the *Times* covered the beginning of the shooting of the interiors for the film, at No. 74, Fulham Road, which had been rented for twenty pounds a week from the Chelsea Borough Council, the writer points out that this was taking place in a derelict house and not on a studio soundstage: "Five years ago this would have been unthinkable for a British film-maker, even if directors were doing it every day in Italy." The author goes on to emphasize the beneficial consequence of this attempt to seek out authenticity provided that "the film-maker is lucky enough to find a story which has some claim to being a truthful reflection of life as it is lived now" (April 24, 1961). This is surely not far removed from the "found story," which is at the heart of Italian neorealism. Despite the fact that both of Richardson's films are adaptations, they have characteristics of the found story. Both deal with fairly minor incidents in everyday life. Surely, the streets of Nottingham and Salford are not so far removed from those of Rome or Milan, and all of these films center firmly on attendant lords rather than on Hamlet. Moreover, neorealist films were always more conventional and less spontaneous than the movement's theorists led one to believe. The clear connection was not lost on some of the more sensitive reviewers, such as Felix Barker in the *Evening News*: "He is, as he will admit, influenced by the Italian neo-realists and helped tremendously by his cameraman, Walter Lassally. He has now done for Manchester what Visconti or Antonioni have done for Milan" (1961). The comparison is made more significant by Richardson's deliberate use of relatively unknown actors for leading roles. It is true that both Rita Tushingham and Tom Courtenay had a little prior stage experience and the latter appeared in the film *Private Potter* shortly before he played the part of Colin. Nevertheless, both these actors were unknown to the general public, and it was a huge leap of faith to place them in such crucial roles. The selection of Courtenay was a relatively painless matter; Richardson met him at a party, knew he was right for the role despite the fact that he had just completed drama school, and offered him the part then and there.

It was much more difficult to find the right actress to play the part of Jo in *A Taste of Honey*. In April 1961, Thomas Wiseman claimed in the *Evening Standard* that Hollywood moguls had been enthusiastic about the project "provided that Mr. Richardson could get Audrey Hepburn to play the girl" (1961). Needless to say, this idea was summarily rejected. According to the *Daily Express*, it was a story in the *Express* indicating that Osborne, Delaney, and Richardson were looking for "an ugly unknown actress to play Jo" that caused Rita Tushingham to apply for the role. Subsequently, she informed the *Express*, "When I read your story I thought I'd never stand a chance but my brother said 'Go on Rita, have a go, you're ugly enough!'" (April 27, 1960). Her nicely self-deprecating humor has remained an endearing characteristic: having always been known affectionately within the industry as "Tush," she has remarked in interviews on her shock when she discovered on a trip to the United States that this expression "was Yiddish for arse." In his memoirs, Tony Richardson revealed in some detail the process whereby he selected Tushingham:

> But there was no Jo. All the actresses who had played it in the theater were far too old for film. We started an immense search. It was very thorough: first photos, then interviews, then readings or improvisation, and finally a full-scale film test. I saw well over two thousand girls. I'd short-listed the best and still felt unconvinced. Out of nowhere, a young girl called Rita Tushingham turned up from Liverpool, with her mother. She wasn't very prepossessing. The only experience she'd had was being the hind legs of a donkey in a local pantomime. (1993b 152)

Out of kindness, he let Rita audition but found her much too abrasive to consider her seriously. However, during the final tests, haunted by "that little hedgehog from Liverpool," he sent for her: "How right I had been initially—she was hopeless! Next day came the dailies. . . . "It's hardly worth running the last girl—she's so hopeless." Five seconds later a close-up of Rita with her all-speaking eyes was on the screen, and the search was over" (152). Richardson had chosen a seventeen-year-old novice to play the crucial role in his film, but the process renders further proof of his integrity as a man of the cinema: there is a complete recognition of the quintessential power in film of close-up images of the face. Indeed, much of the overall impact of the film stems from the mesmerizing shots of Rita Tushingham's eyes. Not surprisingly, however, as John Osborne records, Richardson's decision did not please the accountants: "As with Albert Finney, the money-men went into a frenzy: 'Jeez you can't put that up over the marquee.' Film financiers have an illiterate belief in the power of words. But we had some fun out of their useful publicity: 'Kitchen Sink men discover their Ugly Duckling'" (1991, 154). Naturally, the popular press loved this hook on which to hang their stories, but some of their comments must have been hurtful to the actress. For instance, Leonard Mosley in the *Daily Express* likened her to "Donald Duck's sister" and added that "her backside waddles when she walks—but not, repeat not, in the manner of Miss Marilyn Monroe" (1961); meanwhile, Alexander Walker's description of her in the *Evening Standard* was even more bizarre:

FIGURE 4.1. *A Taste of Honey* (Rita Tushingham on walkway)

"A crow's nest of hair, a ski-tip nose, a mouth you could fit a saucer into—a cup and saucer when it is open—and eyes that have a mongrel dogginess in their depths" (1961).

With Richardson's help, she gave a brilliant performance in the film, one that was almost universally applauded by the reviewers and led to coveted acting awards from the Cannes Film Festival and the British Film Academy. In a *Time* report in 1962, she acknowledged the crucial role played by her director in the interpretation of her character:

> She learned quickly from Director Richardson. "He helped me over the hard bits," she says. "One of the hardest was learning to have the baby kick me. That's pretty hard to do if you've never had a baby. Learning to walk like a pregnant woman was not easy either. I didn't exactly go around staring at them, but whenever I saw one I'd try to notice how they walk." (June 8, 1962)

Richardson was clearly pleased with her work early in the production process, since according to Patricia Lewis in the *Daily Express*, "after a few days shooting he signed her to a six-picture contract worth £30,000" (1961). He recognized, as he had in her film test, that unique quality of screen presence that cannot be learned and is one of the unexplained mysteries of the motion picture. In an interview with Julian Holland of the *Evening News*, he summed it up: "'She explodes on the screen,' he said. 'She has that haunting quality that all the great ones possess—Marilyn Monroe, Elizabeth Taylor. You see them on the screen and you recognize them instantly—it's something that shines through every role they portray'" (1961). But it was also her sheer lack of experience that added to her value in his eyes. As far back as Oxford, he had sought out untried actors to bring fresh vitality to his projects. According to Felix Barker in the *Evening News* "He chose a girl on an Oxford bus for a university play because he claimed he could not find enough innocence among the available undergraduate actresses" (1961). As he polished his skills as a film director, this notion became an integral part of his directing philosophy: "I like working with people who are doing their first film and with people who haven't been used thousands of times. . . . Newcomers are more spontaneous and fresh, and I don't think they are necessarily unprofessional. For instance, Rita Tushingham is thoroughly professional and picked up what professional technique you need to know in the first few days" (Richardson 1961, 41). In Tushingham's comments on her acting techniques in *A Taste of Honey*, there is a palpable reflection of Richardson's methods; during an interview in the *Daily Express*, she explained to Patricia Lewis that she approached the role without prior knowledge of the work of Shelagh Delaney: "It helped not having seen the play because I didn't model myself on anyone. I knew that Jo must seem unloved yet wanting to be loved and the rest came when we went on location to Manchester" (1961). For Richardson, location shooting helps to engender a compelling authenticity: it also stimulates actors to produce their best work. Ideally, as happens in *A Taste of Honey*, the characters and their environment become so completely and seamlessly integrated that the audience feels no sense of separation between the two.

Richardson was greatly helped by the team which, as the producer, he was responsible for bringing together. The art director sought out suitable settings to articulate the director's vision: "Ralph Brinton, tireless in his late sixties, scoured the back streets, the canals, the smokestacks, the docks of Salford—where Shelagh Delaney, who had collaborated on the script, had come from—for locations. An old paint store that was part of the Royal Court workshop was adapted for one of the apartments" (Richardson 1993a, 152). Walter Lassally played a key role as director of photography as did Desmond Davis as camera operator:

> I reassembled all the key people from my old team. Walter Lassally, who had photographed *Momma Don't Allow* for Karel and me, joined as cinematographer. He was an important figure in England, being the first of our lighting cameramen (as distinct from what was happening in France with the *nouvelle vague*) to be able to work in what was becoming known as the Free Cinema style—a minimum of equipment, real locations, and a natural, unmade-up look. A young, adventurous crew was headed by a remarkable, sensitive operator, Desmond Davis. (Richardson 1993a, 151)

Richardson goes on to point out the considerable difference between Britain and the United States in the role of the camera operator. Whereas the director of photography in England controls the overall look of the film, it is the operator who "works directly with the director in laying out the details of the shot—the composition, the movements of the dolly, the laying of tracks" (Richardson 151). Together, these men created a stunning but coherent visual style, which works very well with the dissolves that Richardson uses as a consistent device throughout. As Duncan Petrie points out in his book *Creativity and Constraint in the British Film Industry:*

Richardson was particularly pleased with the production process of *A Taste of Honey* in terms of the freedom the shooting style afforded him. Lassally used three different kinds of film stock on the film including the high speed Ilford HPS (400 ASA) stock which, as he explains, was previously considered suitable only for newsreels and documentaries. This enabled Lassally to shoot at very low levels of light including one close-up shot in a cave lit by one solitary candle—fifteen years before Stanley Kubrick's celebrated use of candle-light in *Barry Lyndon.* (1991, 38)

Dilys Powell in the *Sunday Times* spoke of Lassally's "sensitive desolate images" (1961) and Nina Hibbin in the *Daily Worker* argued that "the camera searches out grimly and bleakly the crumbling exteriors of the Manchester slums with their broken-down buildings humped up each side of a dirty backwater canal" (1961).

And yet this is far from the "grimy grittiness" or "gritty griminess" that often has been used to characterize the regional films of the period. In fact there is often a distinctly lyrical quality to the cinematography here. It is not that it is merely decorative, for it provides an authentic and believable environment for the characters. It effectively realizes Richardson's vision, which is never a doctrinaire portrait of the indignities and deprivations of industrial working-class life, but a portrait of individuals who experience loneliness and loss but are also capable of great warmth and romance. John Addison's music is effectively built around children's songs, which are a key motif of the play: they add a further lyrical quality to the work. In fact , there are moments in the film when the children singing and the stunning beauty of the images remind one of the René Clair of *Sous les Toits de Paris* or *A Nous La Liberté.* Richardson was much criticized by some for his use of children singing throughout the film. Albert Hunt, writing for *Universities and New Left Review* was particularly outraged by this practice:

> These festivals and expeditions are continually accompanied with a counterpoint of child-song. Whenever Richardson takes the camera out of doors, streets, graveyards, fields and hills seem to be filled with picturesquely dirty children playing singing games. Nowhere is Richardson's tendency towards abstraction more irritatingly apparent. The children are not included because they are interesting and alive. They are atmospheric props, part of the pseudo-poetic blur. (1961, 8)

The children and their songs are far from being mere props. Sometimes they function as a chorus obliquely commenting on the lives of the major participants. As Jo and Geoff walk by the canal we hear the children sing:

> On a hill there lives a lady
> Where she is I do not know.
> All she wants is gold and silver
> And a fine young man, you know.

Above all, however, the children and their traditional songs add a delicate sense of context and continuity: "Generations have trod, have trod, have trod . . ."

On the day that the production team began shooting the first scene of *A Taste of Honey*, Rita Tushingham celebrated her nineteenth birthday. The drama on which the film is based was written by Shelagh Delaney at the tender age of eighteen. It is a brilliant first play, but it suffers from a lot of the problems that one would expect from a relatively immature work. Its structure is arbitrary at best and capricious at worst. Characters are slight, and actions are improbable. One also feels that a number of elements are self-consciously devised to shock. As Eve Perrick nicely remarks in an article in the *Daily Mail*: "But did the love-her-and-leave-her-pregnant sailor have to be coloured? And did her protector have to be a homosexual? And did the man that mum ran off with have to have one eye?" (1961). According to her own account of the genesis of the play, Delaney had been less than impressed when attending the Terence Rattigan *Variations on a Theme* and had decided that she could do better. She promptly wrote *A Taste of Honey*, and the work was accepted by Joan Littlewood to be presented as part of the Theatre Workshop at the Stratford East. In the process, the text was substantially modified. Indeed, even the ending was changed. Having been allowed to read the original script by Joan Littlewood, John Russell Taylor comments on the differences in his book *Anger and After*.

> But the most far-reaching changes are those concerning Peter's character and the end of the play. . . . In the second act, however (in which, incidentally, his marriage to Helen seems to be working out quite satisfactorily), he reveals a child-loving heart of gold beneath the cynical exterior when, in an extraordinary scene just before he and Helen visit Jo, he suggests that they should take on the baby, and Jo, too, if she will come! (1962, 135)

At the end of the original version of the play, Helen comes to take Jo home to Peter's house after the birth. While Geoff is out, Jo goes to the hospital to have the baby, Helen and Geoff discuss the situation, and, finally, Geoff accepts the fact that Jo will leave and is left holding the doll as the play ends. The modified Littlewood text provides a very different resolution, with Helen leaving Peter and returning to her old flat where Jo is now living with Geoff. There is a verbal exchange between Helen and Geoff, who ultimately withdraws from the battle. The end of the play focuses on the renewed and still problematic relationship between Jo and her mother. In a sense, the film version makes use of both versions as stimuli for the inevitable radical transformation inherent in the movement from one medium into a very different one.

Joan Littlewood changed the play in other ways. Part of the Theatre Workshop method was what Taylor characterizes as "a sort of magnified realism, in which everything is like life but somehow larger than life" (1962, 132). This involved speaking certain lines directly to the audience. For instance, a few minutes from the final curtain there is this interchange:

HELEN: Where's my hat?

JO: On your head.

HELEN: Oh yes . . . I don't know what's to be done with you, I don't really. (*To the audience.*) I ask you, what would you do? (Delaney 1959, 87)

The effect seems both mannered and self-consciously avant-garde. It is joined by another rather annoying idiosyncrasy, the use of music and dance to effect scene changes. For instance, in act 1, scene 2 the transition between the scene involving Jo and her boyfriend and Jo's arrival home is handled in typically mannered fashion:

JO: (*as she goes*): I love you.

BOY: Why?

JO: Because you're daft.

(*He waves good-bye, turns and sings to the audience, and goes. Helen dances on to the music, lies down and reads an evening paper. Jo dances on dreamily.*)

HELEN: You're a bit late coming home from school aren't you? (26)

As Richardson points out, this technique of "mixing working-class drama with pub vitality and vaudeville songs" can be effective in staging plays such as Brendan Behan's *The Hostage*, but "her technique had worked less well on *A Taste of Honey*, where it made the play seem coarse and forcedly jolly" (Richardson 141). These devices clashed violently with the naturalistic tone of much of the dialog.

In writing the screenplay, Richardson and Delaney rightly abandoned Littlewood's self-reflexive tics in favor of a complete naturalism. Far from merely opening up a stage play, they transform the piece into a work for the cinema. Tony Richardson was only too well aware of the inherent dangers of filming plays: "[J]ust photographing an existing stage production—however successful—is bad cinema, and usually the acting is not adjusted for the screen" (Richardson 260). Key structural changes are introduced that preserve essential characteristics of the characters and their interaction but increase their credibility. Thus, we discover the manner in which Jo meets her black sailor boyfriend: he volunteers to carry her suitcases as she and Helen get off the bus to move into their new flat. In his book on the new British drama, John Russell Taylor bitterly lamented the changes made to the play in the making of the film:

> Here the treatment is uncompromisingly realistic and exterior, and consequently the script-writers find themselves trapped into devoting an excessive amount of time to useless illustration and explanation. . . . In the process, the special quality the play has of just letting things happen, one after the other (like in a dream) disappears and modifications clearly intended to strengthen the material succeed, paradoxically enough, only in making it seem thinner and more contrived. (1962, 134)

It is truly an odd perspective that accuses the film of undermining the play's capacity for "just letting it happen." It betrays one of the most frequent prejudices against adaptation: it is condemned because it is not the original work.

In the best tradition of creative adaptation, the screenwriters use the text of the play, not as an end in itself but as a stimulus to find solutions to the new problems of a very different medium. For instance, early in act 2 of the play, Geoff comments on the size of Jo's flat:

GEOFF: Ee, this place is enormous, isn't it?

JO: I know. I've got to work all day in a shoe shop and all night in a bar to pay for it. But it's mine. All mine. (Delaney 1959, 47)

This hint is used to create a fully realized film scene in which Jo is shown on her first day in the shoe shop. Having experienced the frustration of dealing with a woman who tried everything on but bought nothing, Geoff comes into the shop and provides her first sale. Later they are seen meeting by accident watching the parade, which leads to fairground and flat. The relationship becomes far more authentic and believable because we have seen its origins and its development.

But the process of stimulus and creation is more complex. In the play, Jo says that the flat is "mine. All mine." And yet on the stage this is the very same flat into which Jo and Helen enter at the beginning of the play. Indeed, when Helen comes to visit her now pregnant daughter in act 2, she emphasizes the fact:

HELEN: All right, all right. This place hasn't changed much, has it? Still the same old miserable hole. Well, where's the lady in question? (Delaney 1959, 59)

In the screenplay, Delaney and Richardson pointedly emphasize that after her mother abandons her to get married, Jo leaves school, gets a job, and finds a place of her own. We see her inspecting her new flat and paying her hard-earned "thirty bob" advance rent. This is highly significant, not just because it adds further to our sense of the authenticity of Jo's world, but because it subtly changes the relationship between Helen and her daughter and Geoff. However irresponsible she appears in the play, she retains some residual territorial rights to her former home; in the screenplay she has none. Because of this crucial change, the nature of the final confrontation between Helen and Geoff is significantly changed.

A number of the reviewers suggested that Murray Melvin as Geoff almost steals the sympathy of the audience away from Jo at the end of the film. In the *Evening Standard*, Alexander Walker implies that this was an unintended consequence of the respective skills of Tushingham and Melvin: "To be fair, she is brilliantly directed by Tony Richardson. But even he, I think, can't quite stop Mr. Murray Melvin from stealing the last scene from the girl by the length of his long plantagenet nose" (1961). In similar fashion, the reviewer in the *Guardian* suggests that "Mr. Melvin plays his supremely difficult, equivocal role with such shrewd, gently humorous pathos that he, indeed, does nearly upset the general dramatic balance" (Sept. 16, 1961). Both critics are absolutely right about the impact of Melvin's performance, but they are wrong in suggesting that it is somehow gratuitous. For it is clearly part of the film's complex restructuring. We see Geoff, much more than in the play, engaged in all the little everyday tasks that manifest in action a deep and abiding love for another person: cleaning, sewing, cooking, baking, making baby clothes, taking care of Jo's physical and psychological health. In the play he says rather sadly, "[Y]ou need somebody to love you while you're looking for someone to love" (Delaney 1959, 76). The line is also used in the film, but we also see him live the sentiment in all the little everyday details. In the play, Geoff suddenly pulls a life-sized doll from his pack so that Jo can "practise a few holds on it over the weekend" (74–75). In the film, this engenders a brilliant little scene in which Geoff braves the latent hostility of the antenatal clinic to get help for Jo. In the play, it often seems as if Geoff's homosexuality is merely a device to make the work seem less conventional; in the film, it is an essential part of the narrative structure. For both Jo and Geoff are social outsiders; they provide each other with the strength and support to overcome their isolation.

The inspired changes in structure devised by Richardson and Delaney reach their culmination in the concluding scene. The initial text of the play had focused on Geoff left with nothing but the doll. In the final version, Jo tells Helen that the baby may be black and leaves temporarily to get a drink. The last few seconds involve Jo reciting a nursery rhyme that Geoff had recited to her earlier in the play. The film brilliantly combines both of these notions and adds resonance and complexity. We see a series of images that suggest the sense of loss experienced by both characters and the inevitability of it all. Once more, the original text serves as a stimulus in the process of creation. In her last conversation with Jo, Helen hears the children singing outside and is led to reminisce about the lost joys of childhood:

HELEN: Are you all right now? There we are. (*Children sing outside.*) Can you hear those children singing over there on the croft, Jo?

JO: Yes, you can always hear them on still days.

HELEN: You know when I was young we used to play all day long at this time of the year; in the summer we had singing games and in the spring we played with tops and hoops, and then in the autumn there was the Fifth of November, then we used to have bonfires in the street, and gingerbread and all that. (Delaney 1959, 85)

The Fifth of November, Guy Fawkes Day, provides a telling cinematic context in which to end the film. The celebration of the discovery of Guy Fawkes and his fellow plotters before they blew up Parliament has ever been an exciting childhood festival in England. Effigies of Guy are burned on bonfires, and fireworks of all varieties are ignited. What could provide more potent images for the end of a film that deals with the absence and loss of childhood than a recurring childhood festival with extremely sinister origins?

After Helen leaves to get her drink, we see Jo's gradual recognition that Geoff has moved out. It is confirmed by her realization that his prized portrait for which she posed is no longer hiding the large hole in the wall. All in the same shot, she checks under his pillow to discover that his few possessions are gone, and then she sees his note on top of the cake that he baked for her. Its words are similar to the ones that, in the play, he speaks to a sleeping Jo, and yet their context radically changes their effect. In the film, we see a close-up of the note as Jo sees it: "Tr'ra Jo, Good luck, Geoff." It is commonplace, simple, and moving and we feel the loss along with Jo, who gently and tearfully murmurs, "You clown, Geoff, you clown." In the play, the dramatist cannot resist the urge to provide the audience with a cheap aphorism:

GEOFF: Yes, the one thing civilisation couldn't do anything about—women. Goodbye Jo, and good luck. (*He goes.*) (Delaney 1959, 84)

It is mildly amusing, but it wholly undermines the resonance of Geoff's valediction. In the closing scene of the film, Tony Richardson makes brilliant use of the capabilities of the cinema. The burning of the man on the bonfire, along with the fireworks, establishes a resonant context for the final break between Geoff and Jo. We see her coming down the steps obviously looking for Geoff, from his perspective as he hides in the shadows. A momentary, involuntary movement toward her is checked by the sudden reappearance of her mother, who articulates the only words of the final scene, when she falls back upon the universal mantra of the English—"I'll make you a cup of tea"—and goes up the stairs. We see the powerful emotions in Geoff's face as he turns and walks away. The final image of the film shows Jo lighting her firework from that of a child and watching it sparkle. It is a highly telling image for it contains a sense of hope, of new life and vitality, of a baby soon to be born, and yet it also resonates with an indefinable sense of loss. It is cinema of the first order, and it is not surprising that Delaney and Richardson won the British Film Academy Award for the best sceenplay of 1961.

In the following year, work was begun on *The Loneliness of the Long Distance Runner*. According to Derek Hill in *Scene*, the film was originally intended to be Lindsay Anderson's first feature; in fact he "had been working on a preliminary draft when Richardson advised him that he planned to direct the film himself" (1962). After some considerable difficulties finding a publisher, once Alan Sillitoe's short story was in print it met with an enthusiastic reception including the prestigious Hawthornden Prize. Since Woodfall had achieved something of a breakthrough with *Saturday Night and Sunday Morning*, it was natural that the company should seek out another work from the same author. In August 1960, Sillitoe was paid £6,000 as an advance for the screen rights; the author was contracted to write the screenplay, work on which was scheduled to begin in 1961. Like many writers of fiction, Alan Sillitoe has remained rather equivocal about his involvement in film and not a little suspicious of the relationship between words on the page and images on the screen. According to his autobiography, he was not surprised by Harry Saltzman's contention that his novel *Saturday Night and Sunday Morning* seemed to have been written with film in mind "since I must have seen as many films as I had read books" (1995, 256). He goes on to praise Reitz and to acknowledge the fact that it is unreasonable to want "the film to be exactly the one set going in my mind's eye" (266); however, he continues to express profound misgivings about the process:

I was also weirdly perturbed at having set off the whole complex mechanism of a movie in the first place, and though in the end my unease remains a mystery, such sensations were to come back with my next film, and return even more fully some years later when a story was dramatized for BBC television, reinforcing my belief that the novel is merely a blueprint, while the film made out of it is something different. Such reality was a peculiar form of art because it left little to the viewer's imagination, giving nothing to do except supinely watch. (266)

Such an attitude is a direct consequence of a profound loss of control by the author of the printed work, even if he does serve as the screenwriter. Nevertheless, it is completely misguided, for a novel cannot be a blueprint for a film; it can only serve as a stimulus to the creation of a work in a wholly different medium. Moreover, the notion that film leaves little to the imagination and only involves supine observation is palpable nonsense.

If Sillitoe suffered from a loss of control, Richardson reveled in the power of the director. When asked by Marcel Martin in *Lettres Francaises* what problems he encountered in adapting Sillitoe's short story for the screen, he replied that there had been very few problems because the story had been written in a cinematic way and the collaboration with the author had been easy and productive: "Très peu de problèmes, car l'histoire est écrite en termes cinématographiques et ma collaboration avec l'auteur a été aisée et féconde (1965). Sillitoe does not address his work with Richardson directly in his autobiography but his comments about the process of adaptation are most revealing: "My temperament was not suited for work which depended on a certain amount of consultation" (Sillitoe 1995, 258). In September 1962, before the film was released, *Films and Filming* published a fascinating extract from the screenplay that clearly reveals the dominance of Richardson in the process of interpreting the screenplay on film. The segment is far more wordy than the film. Scenes are radically cut down, and some are completely eliminated. For example, a sequence in which the governor, the chief officer and Fenton seek out Stacey's escape route does not appear in the film. The most significant difference, however, involves the scripting of a segment in which Colin sallies forth on a training run. The images are matched by substantial voice-over sequences. The words are taken from key parts of the short story:

> COLIN (*narration: off*): It's a good life if you don't weaken and give in to the coppers and Borstal bosses and the rest of them bastard faced In-laws. They're stupid because they can't see as much into the likes of me as I can see into the likes of them. And I'll win in the end—even if I am in jail—because I'll have more fun and fire out of my life than ever that half dead gangrened governor. Be honest like me. It's like saying be dead. But I'm alive, not dead. If he ran 10 yards he'd drop dead. If he got 10 yards into what goes on in my guts he'd drop dead as well—with surprise. Because I'm alive . . .

Colin runs down a slope, slithers and finally collapses, half laughing at the bottom. He looks up at the sky and at the tops of the trees as though for a minute the whole world has turned over. And we hear his voice crying triumphantly "Alive, alive, alive." DISSOLVE

In this extract, the screenplay articulates a notion that plays a major role in Smith's thought patterns in the short story: the dichotomy between "In-laws" or conventional law-abiding citizens and "Out-laws " who inhabit the Borstals and the prisons. It also deals with his idiosyncratic definition of honesty. With the help of the brilliant camera work of Walter Lassally, Tony Richardson makes full use of the ecstasy of Colin's physical fulfillment, but he abandons Sillitoe's voice-over narration. The only place in which he makes use of this technique is in the running sequence before the opening titles when Colin provides a brief definition of the title.

As with so many other films based on novels, the writer's intrinsic suspicion of adaptation was endorsed by critics who disliked the film. In a substantial article in *Sight and Sound*, Peter Harcourt launched a vicious attack on the film and on the competence of Tony Richardson. The first half of the piece is full of praise for the subtle joys of Sillitoe's literary achievement; the story is seen as more a brilliant universal parable than an examination of social discontent: "[I]f in the breathless sweep of the long sentences there is the enactment of the breathlessness of the runner himself, there is also in the imagery a certain ambiguity, a quality simultaneously of beauty and of threat which gives the passage (and so the story) a wider range of reference than just to life today in Britain" (1962–63, 16–17). In the second half of his piece, Harcourt argues that the film fails miserably to live up to the promise of the novel:

> [I]t is the sad and central failing of Tony Richardson's film that none of the suggestiveness of the original story has been allowed to survive. In the process of adaptation, the best elements in the original, elements that are inseparable from Alan Sillitoe's words, indeed the living breath of the story itself—all this has been lost; while the element of spite, just a part of the story, seems to be the basic impulse from which the film has been conceived. (18)

But what could be more absurd than to condemn a film because it is not a novel! Of course it is different from the short story; film is a different medium! Harcourt reaches the ultimate absurdity by bemoaning the fact that the cinema destroys ambiguity with explicit images: "Indeed, the fact that the society he inhabits is never clearly visualised increases our sense of the boy's isolation. In Tony Richardson's film, however, we are forced to see it all" (18). Such a reductive view of film adaptation is founded upon the mistaken notion that it is the obligation of the filmmaker to attempt to be "faithful" to the printed work. Not only is this insupportable but it is also truly impossible. There is also a pronounced elitism to this prejudice that literature is automatically more serious and more profound than the cinema. Indeed, in an essay published in *Literature /Film Quarterly*, Eugene Quirk explains the differences between the short story and the film as an inevitable consequence of the need to talk down to the film audience: "Thus I will argue that the politics of mass-media art and the necessity to comfortably appeal to the audience of that art (especially in the light of the need to recoup the vast economic investments required of a film producer) both coalesce to force Sillitoe to radically alter his initial artistic reaction" (1981, 162). Once again a reductive perspective is founded upon the notion that a faithful transcription is possible but inevitably compromised by the inferiority of the medium and the limitations of its participants.

Analysis of the short story from which the film is adapted allows us to examine key elements in the creative process, for the literary work serves as a stimulus to the screenwriter and the director. Despite the difference in form, Sillitoe's ideas remain integral to the finished film even in relatively minor ways. There remain clear elements of the autobiographical. The context of the flashbacks in the dank streets of industrial Nottingham preserve the indelible locale of his youth. In *Life without Armour*, he writes of his father's cancer of the palate and of his death in 1959, when the only mourners at his funeral are "his long-suffering wife and five children" (Sillitoe 258). When Sillitoe created a name for the elitist public school that provides the Borstal with its athletic challenge in the film, he picked "Ranleigh," which is one letter removed from the Raleigh bicycle factory in Nottingham where he gained his first experience of industrial labor at the age of fourteen. Tony Richardson brought his own concerns to the project as well. He attended a minor public school during its wartime evacuation to the Lake District. His hatred for this institution has been well documented. Indeed, a connection to his work on *The Loneliness of the Long Distance Runner* was drawn in obituaries such as the one in the *Daily Telegraph*: "Richardson was very much a loner at school, although he became senior prefect. The spirit of his experience at Ashville, along with the Windermere background was reflected in *The Loneliness of the Long Distance Runner*" (1991). In his autobiography, Richardson began his chapter on the joys of Oxford with the contention that "it's impossible to write anything bad enough about English public schools" (66). He shared with Sillitoe a hatred for the English class system but also a loathing for the trite labels, such as "angry young man" repeatedly applied to them by the popular press.

There are radical formal differences between the short story and the screenplay/film. Sillitoe's novella is a first-person account that takes place after Smith has been released from the Borstal and after he has completed a new and more substantial theft. The film begins with Colin's arrival at the institution and makes use of his training runs to launch into multiple flashbacks, which explain the sequence of events that led to his arrest and confinement. If Sillitoe's major concern in the short story is to express the nihilistic world view of his antihero, as a dramatic form, the film emphasizes structure and conflict. Far from being the arbitrary act of the novella, the bakery job is triggered in the film by a direct confrontation between Colin and his mother's lover, after which Colin's mother tells him to get out and not to come back until he has some money. Stacey, the runner who is replaced by Colin in the good graces of the governor, allows Richardson to stage a battle between the two boys that anticipates the final confrontation between the Ruxton Towers and Ranleigh. The character of Stacey also allows the filmmakers to provide dramatic evidence of the failure of the governor to remain true to the principles that he articulates and to reveal the latent brutality of the system. In the short story, the readers are well aware throughout the work that Smith is planning to lose the race: "The pot-bellied pop-eyed bastard gets pleased at this: 'Good show. I know you'll get us that cup,' he says. And I swear under my breath: 'Like boggery, I will.' No, I won't get them that cup, even though the stupid tash-twitching bastard has all his hopes in me" (1965, 13). In the film, the audience does not find out that Colin will deliberately lose until the end of the race itself, thus preserving the dramatic conflict.

An interesting example of the way in which the story serves as a stimulus in the creation of the film is provided by the scene between Colin and the new housemaster at the Borstal. In Sillitoe's work, the narrator explains his feelings as he engages in the robbery of the bakery: "I didn't think about anything at all, as usual, because I never do when I'm busy, when I'm draining pipes, looting sacks, yaling locks, lifting latches. . . . That's what the four-eyed white-smocked bloke with the note-book couldn't understand when he asked me questions for days and days after I got to Borstal" (1965, 26). This brief suggestion led to a brilliant, funny, well-observed scene in the film in which the new housemaster seeks to apply his cut-price psychological theories to his newest miscreant. A number of reviewers attacked this sequence as a prime example of the inadequacy of Richardson when compared to Truffaut. According to Dwight MacDonald, it reveals the difference between an artisan and an artist: "Truffaut had an inspiration: he doesn't show the interviewer; all we have is her voice, calm and self-assured. . . . Richardson's version is not inspired, or clever: his camera just swings back and forth" (1969, 390). Yet Richardson's scene is brilliantly modulated to encompass, with a gentle comic touch, some of the key concerns of the film. The slightly too friendly housemaster daringly offers a cigarette to his subject. Small gestures are employed to capture the well-meaning ineptitude of the newly trained, socially aware officer, who is every bit as uncomprehending as the older traditionalists.

The English class system plays a considerable part in both the short story and the film. Both Sillitoe and Richardson were anxious to be part of the movement to focus the arts on those who traditionally had been ignored. Sillitoe published an essay in the *Times Literary Supplement* that argued that "writers were appearing who would counter and ultimately stifle the stereotypes issued by films, radio and television" (1995, 267). In his introduction to the British edition of Richardson's autobiography, Lindsay Anderson points out that a prime motive for moving to the United States was "the cramping confines of the English class system, which he always loathed" (Richardson 1993a, xvi). There is an inevitable class component to a narrative set in a Borstal, for these institutions were designed to reform young criminals between the ages of fifteen and twenty-one. Named after a prison in Kent, Borstals rapidly acquired a pejorative aura. In 1983, they were officially renamed "Youth Custody Centers," and, as a result of the Criminal Justice Act of 1988, they became "Young Offender Institutions." There is a clear, if muted, element of class revenge in Sillitoe's story: "I only want a bit of my own back on the In-laws and Potbellies by letting them sit up there on their big posh seats and watch me lose this race" (1965, 45). More interesting, however, is the notion that Smith, the working-class nihilist, is physically superior to members of the upper class. He refers to them and to the governor as "pot-bellies," ugly and unfit: "They're training me up fine for the big sports day when all the pig-faced snotty-nosed dukes and ladies—who can't add two and two together and would mess themselves like loonies if they didn't have slavies to beck-and-call—come and make speeches to us about sports being just the thing to get us leading an honest life" (8). Despite the amoral nature of Sillitoe's Smith, one thinks of J. M. Barrie's *The Admirable Crichton* and the survival of the fittest.

The nature of class conflict is very different in the film for it is both less explicit and more insidious. The film picks up the governor's trite exhortation to newly arrived inmates, "If you play ball with us, we'll play ball with you" (1965, 9) and transforms it into the summation of institutional philosophy. For the governor seeks to combine the famous aphorism of Juvenal, "Mens sana in corpore sano," with the ethos of Tom Brown's Rugby and apply the result to the reform school. In his first scene, Michael Redgrave nicely articulates this philosophy to new arrivals:

> If you play ball with us, we'll play ball with you. We want you to work hard and play hard. Good athletics, sports, inter-house competition. We believe in all that. Come in. (*Stacey enters.*) We're divided into houses. Now none of you is proud of being here, but there's no reason why you shouldn't be proud of your house. Stacey here is proud of being the leader of Drake House.

There is profound comedy to this earnest, well-meaning but essentially absurd assertion of patrician values. In the short story, the cross-country race involves a competition among sister Borstal institutions, whereas in the film the battle pits Colin's Ruxton Towers against an elite local public school. When the sports day arrives, Richardson relishes the sequences in which we see the governor interacting with his peers on the Ranleigh Board of Governors. This is just the sort of conjunction of class and sport that upset Tony Richardson. Indeed, in the introduction to the American version of his autobiography, Joan Didion recalls his passionate defense of John McEnroe for throwing down his racket at Wimbledon: it reflected "his essential loathing of the English class system and attendant sporting rituals" (Richardson 1993a, 15). The final confrontation between the urban loner, Colin Smith, and the polished, if uncomfortable, public school athletes has cultural origins beyond Sillitoe's story. In his brilliant essay on boys' weeklies, George Orwell pointed to the irony that young minors were reading comic papers about aristocratic youths in the hallowed halls of Greyfriars School. By the late 1950s, a paper, *The Rover,*

FIGURE 4.2. *Loneliness of the Long Distance Runner* (Tom Courtenay)

FIGURE 4.3. *Loneliness of the Long Distance Runner* (Tom Courtenay and others)

provided weekly installments in a story entitled "Alf: The Tough of the Track." This serial documented the exploits of a working-class hero who, despite a lack of money and equipment, ran barefoot and regularly beat "the toffs" at their aristocratic sport running. When Richardson presents us with his Ranleigh team, clad in expensive white track suits and contrasted with the Borstal boys in their basic dark shorts and tee-shirts, it is very much in that tradition. Indeed, the contrast is further accentuated by the physical differences between the tall, fair-haired James Fox, as the runner whom Colin overtakes, and Tom Courtenay, small, dark, and wiry. As Hollis Alpert suggests in his piece in *Saturday Review*, he "is the least likely looking movie star since Ernest Borgnine" (1962).

Richardson makes effective use of the comic possibilities of the class conflict. A good many ponderous reviewers completely missed this aspect of the work. So, Leonard Mosley in the *Daily Express* bemoans the fact that "this film is not so much a dirge for the Establishment as a lament for a layabout" (1962). Yet there is nicely effective humor in the interaction of the inmates of Ranleigh and Ruxton Towers. The bemusement of the Borstal boys that anyone would end up paying to be subject to corporal punishment leads to a nicely ironic needling: "Sure you don't want to lock up your gear?" (Film). Richardson's comedy is all the more effective here for being gentle and unforced. In other parts of the film, he sometimes lacks such a sure touch. The speeded-up sequences are a case in point. The way in which the appearance of the muscular Roach causes a rapid speeding up in the undressing of the boys after their arrival at the Borstal is wholly misconceived since it undermines the integrity of the dramatic reality by gratuitously distorting space and time. In his review in *Films and Filming*, Peter Baker argues: "The family characters (notably Avis Bunnage as the mother) and the establishment figures often lean too much towards caricature: there is a danger at times of our laughing at them instead of with them" (1962, 32). But it is Richardson's gentle comedy that gives the film its staying power for it rises above other British New Wave films of the period precisely because it does not take itself or its characters too seriously. In the *Spectator*, Isabel Quigley called the film "an illustrated guide to current fashion, with every attitude and every statement perfectly predictable and conventional" (1962). Yet it resolutely refuses to be doctrinaire. With the sole exception of the "screws" who beat up Stacey, there are no villains in the work, but only well-meaning individuals who are unable or unwilling to comprehend other ways of viewing the world.

The class division is ever present in accent, in vocabulary, and in attitude. However, at its best, this submerged conflict also embraces the age divide. Nowhere does Richardson make better use of this than in the concert for the boys. We see the earnest leaders of the Borstal presenting performers who have no possible relevance to the world of the boys: an expert in birdcalls is followed by deadly dull musicians. It forms a nicely observed metaphor for the incomprehension inherent in the chasms of class and age. It is at this point that Richardson introduces the only diegetic rendition of Hubert Parry's setting of Blake's *Jerusalem*, which forms a leitmotif throughout the work When the film first appeared, John Addison's repeated use of variation on this theme was much criticized: "And then there is the sound-track, ponderously satirizing with its playing of "Jerusalem," the gulf that exists between the ideals of the poem and the reality of this band of underprivileged youths cooped up in Borstal" (*Times* 1962). The use of the hymn does point to the gulf between the life of these boys and the notion of Jerusalem, but it also functions in a much more complex way. If this has become a second national anthem, the kind of piece that is played along with "Rule Britannia" at the last night of the proms at the Albert Hall, it is truly ironic that the intent of the original poem was so different from its current use:

> And was Jerusalem builded here
> Among these dark Satanic mills?

There is effective double irony in the fact that a poem so subversive to the Establishment has been adopted as a middle-class anthem. But there is further resonance to the use of this hymn. The best known verse is the last one:

> I will not cease from mental fight,
> Nor shall my sword sleep in my hand,
> Till we have built Jerusalem,
> In England's green and pleasant land.

In the film, Colin clearly finds his salvation in the "green and pleasant land" of his solitary runs. They afford him the chance to analyze and reflect on his life, but he also achieves a degree of balance and harmony that he achieves elsewhere only in his brief romantic idyll on the beaches and in the sandhills of Skegness.

Richardson's film is a flawed work. Its great strength is that it goes beyond contemporary social comment to examine the struggle for personal identity. The Colin of the film is a much more complex and sympathetic character than the Smith of the short story. Yet the director clearly misjudges some of his sequences. The most widely condemned technique involves the overuse of montage editing at the final race. Alexander Walker in the *Evening Standard* was typical in his response: "All I could have wished dropped from the film are the arty, machine-gun blasts of flashbacks that riddle Colin with bitter memories in the last 100 yards" (1962). Other reviewers argued that this technique betrayed an infirmity of purpose, even a failure to trust his actors, as suggested by David Robinson in the *Financial Times*: "but at the end Courtenay's playing of the equivocal feelings that lose the race is accurate and explicit enough not to need the elaborate montage with which it is glossed" (1962). The earlier montage sequences during the final race are more muted and more effective. As a response to the stimulus provided by the short story, they establish a connection between Colin's action and the death of his father. However, the final montage is much too explicit. As a consequence, it seems to suggest a direct explanation for the refusal to run the race. In his autobiography, Richardson reveals his attraction to montage when working with Karel Reisz on *Momma Don't Allow*: "I veered from wanting to expand our hint at dramatic situations involving individuals outside the group to using ideas of montage as abstract as a music video. (Alone of the group, I was a keen Eisenstein fan) (Richardson 1993a, 94). And, indeed, the final montage of *The Loneliness of the Long Distance Runner* gives one exactly that feeling of intellectual constriction that renders the Eisenstein of *Strike* so annoyingly heavy-handed.

At the other end of the spectrum is one of the most brilliant and telling scenes in the film when Colin burns the one-pound note. In the short story, Smith's attitude to his father's death benefits is very different: "Now I believe, and my mum must have thought the same, that a wad of crisp blue-black fivers aint a sight of good unless they're flying out of your hand into some shopkeeper's till" (Sillitoe 1965, 20). In the film, Colin is shown as an observer in the process of spending the money. Richardson nicely uses this sequence as a muted comment on the tawdry consequences of a consumer popular culture. When Colin's mother proffers the pound note, he tries to refuse it, to no avail. His subsequent retreat from the beer and television, the bread and circuses of the TV politicians that he subsequently lampoons, is a potent gesture of personal defiance. Alone with a picture of his father, he slowly burns the note. It is Richardson's most potent use of the power of the cinema, and it brings to mind Monroe Stahr in *The Last Tycoon*, demonstrating to the obtuse Boxley the sheer power and resonance of simple images. For this is no simple gesture. It is a symbol of intellectual independence and of power over the social and material realities of the world, but it is also a defiant gesture of self-assertion. And there is no explication provided; Richardson allows the images to resonate for themselves.

A number of reviewers found the central character of the film to be bound up in the clichés of the new British cinema: "There is much that is all too recognizable. We have already witnessed the dingy family background, the parental misunderstanding and youthful resentment, the stark irreverent language, the general air of cynical defeatism" (1962). The critic for the *Guardian* proceeds to suggest that Colin Smith is even over the edge of socialist realist cinema because he "is not just a puzzled young rebel, he is also an apprentice in burglary" (1962). Yet Colin is far beyond *Time*'s inept characterization of him as "too palpably prolier-than-thou" (1962). As Tom Courtenay wrote in an article published in *Films and Filming*: "The Runner, though, is not just a 'hard case.' Some of his thoughts, particularly in the way he thinks, are very romantic" (1962, 10). He uses native cunning to survive, but he is clearly both thoughtful and sensitive. His reaction to the death of his father and his involvement with Audrey confirm this. In the short story, the only mention of women is talk of "latching on to a couple of tarts that would give us all they were good for" (1965, 37). In the film, it is apparent that Colin has much deeper feelings for Audrey. In an interview published in *Cinémato*, Tony Richardson explained the reasons why he preferred *The Loneliness of the Long Distance Runner* over the other films that he had made: "De tous les films que j'ai réalisés, c'est celui que je préfère. Jamais je n'ai livré autant de moi-meme sur l'écran. Le héros est vraiment mon fils spirituel : un révolté, comme dans mes autres films. Mais qu'on ne s'y trompe pas : plus que la contestation sociale, c'est toujours le cas personnel qui m'intéresse" (1965). It is a potent summation of Tony Richardson's philosophy of filmmaking, and if Colin is his "spiritual son," it is because he so evidently seeks to achieve a unique personal identity. In a recent piece in *Sight and Sound*, Frank Deasy argues perceptively that "the centre of the film is his aching to transcend, for life to be something greater" (1995, 33). In her analysis of the film in the *Sunday Times*, Dilys Powell accurately points to this personal element that raises the film above others of similar genre:

And it is in his most fightable moods that one feels most sharply for him. That seems to me the unique achievement of the film. The rebel against the world (I don't mean the psychological, James Dean rebel; I mean the social outlaw) has become familiar on screen: familiar, but not, to me at any rate, welcome. "The Loneliness of the Long Distance Runner" makes him a sympathetic figure. For the first time in the cinema one is persuaded to experience his defiance. It is not a matter of pity. One looks at the hopeless layabout of "Accatone" and pities him. One looks at Colin Smith and understands him. (1962)

Since *A Taste of Honey* and *The Loneliness of the Long Distance Runner* were made, like Tony Richardson himself, these works have not been afforded the respect that they deserve. It was mainly to these two films that obituary writers were referring when they spoke of Richardson's "gritty working class realism" (*Scotsman*, Nov. 16, 1991) and said that "Richardson's films had broken new ground bringing a gritty realism to the British screen" (*Times*, Nov. 16, 1991). It is true that these films placed a new emphasis on the creative use of location shooting to achieve true authenticity; they also reinforced the notion that fine films could be made that deal with common people in everyday situations. But they did much more than this. In these two works, Richardson achieved a genuine synthesis of all the aesthetic concerns that he had brought to the Free Cinema group, to the Royal Court, and to Woodfall Films. Part of the reason for this was the degree of control that he was able to exercise over these projects. When interviewed in 1962, he told Robert Muller: "At this point I feel equally divided between film and theatre, though if I had to make the choice, I'd choose movies, because they're a director's medium. In films I can say something that is absolutely my own—what I feel about the world and about people" (1962). Reaching such an apotheosis required the kind of independence and power that he achieved at Woodfall in 1961 and 1962. Ironically, he sometimes bemoaned the need to deal with the everyday worries of the business: "Working as a producer is something I don't like because I am really interested in being a director" (1961, 41). It is clear that his frenetic activity contributed to an insidious lack of critical respect for his work. Yet he was very successful in the early years at Woodfall at developing a solid base for independent work. In reviewing *A Taste of Honey* in the *Evening News*, Julian Holland calculated, with some amazement, that the production budget of £125,000 was "only one-twenty-fifth the original estimate for *Cleopatra*" (1961). Richardson provided a solid base from which to encourage many actors, artists, and technicians to commit themselves to a new British cinema. It is significant that when Sir John Gielgud wrote to the *Times* in 1991 to express his sorrow, he placed a great deal of emphasis on his friend's role as a catalyst: "He was the first to encourage me in that field and to persuade me to overcome my former dislike of filming" (1991).

The great European auteur directors of the 1960s developed and nurtured their own cadres of artists and technicians with whom they worked again and again. One thinks of Bergman and Sven Nykvist, Fellini and Nina Rota, Truffaut and Raoul Coutard, or Buñuel and Jean-Claude Carrière. In his career as a director, Tony Richardson came closest to this ideal in the two films of 1961 and 1962. With Walter Lassally as innovative director of photography backed up by Desmond Davis as camera operator, he could rely on a complete and sensitive visual interpretation of his intentions. Other key contributors remained in place for both productions: Anthony Gibbs as editor, John Addison as composer and arranger, Ralph Brinton and Ted Marshall in art direction and production design, Leigh Aman as production supervisor, Michael Holden as assistant producer, Rita Davison in continuity, and Don Challis as sound editor. The consequence of this teamwork was that Richardson was able to create tightly integrated works that truly reflected his vision.

His careful casting and his intuitive ability to elicit the very best performances out of his actors also contributed a great deal to the success of these works. The confidence to follow his instincts and make use of inexperienced actors paid dividends in achieving fresh and dynamic performances. Clearly, the use of both Rita Tushingham and Tom Courtney were triumphs, but this ability extended to minor roles as well. For instance, it was Richardson who gave James Fox his first part as the public school runner who finally wins the race, despite the fact that his friend, agent Robin Fox, was bitterly against it: "We only had one quarrel, when he forbade me to offer his son 'Willie' James Fox a small role in *The Loneliness of the Long Distance Runner*, saying that his son had no talent and that for him to quit his job in a bank would be to disrupt his life" (Richardson 1993, 251). But Richardson was also very good at nurturing experienced actors. Murray Melvin, who played the role of Geoff in the first West End production of *A Taste of Honey* in 1958 gives a luminous cinematic performance of the character. Dora Bryan, who had become typecast as a comedienne in dozens of farces and "Carry On" films is used very effectively in the film. The program notes for the screening at the Cannes Film Festival reveal that there were those who seriously questioned the director's wisdom in using the actress: "When doubters confronted director Tony Richardson, he threw them aside with a terse: 'I think she's perfect for the role and I'm directing the picture.' He was right, but he must also be credited with nicely controlling Bryan's performance so that it does not go over the edge into self-parody.

The most important aspect of Richardson's vision in these two film is not their location shooting or their examination of working-class life in the industrial hinterlands of Britain. It is that they deal sensitively with the inner lives of ordinary individuals. Much to the chagrin of certain critics, there is very little of a purely political nature to these portraits. Hard though life is in the streets of Salford or Nottingham, there is no attempt to argue that Jo or Colin is merely a blameless victim suffering the consequences of "dark satanic mills." This would be far too simplistic. Besides, Richardson is not interested in creating doctrinaire socialist realism. His characters are authentic individuals who find themselves isolated on the margins of society and attempt to deal with this reality. In an article that he wrote for *The Listener* in 1968, he summed up the aims of "Free Cinema": "[T]he films should be free of commercial pressures. But they should also be free of what were then called 'well-made' techniques: they should be an attempt to introduce a much more poetic and humanistic approach, both into making short films and into making feature films" (Tony, May 2, 1968). These two works can be described as "poetic and humanistic." Indeed, it is this that distinguishes them from a good many other works of film, fiction, and theater of the same period. They are never preachy or dogmatic in the way of *Look Back in Anger* or *Room at the Top* or even, on occasion, the play *A Taste of Honey.* A number of the reviewers praised the film *A Taste of Honey* for providing such a sensitive portrait of a gay person, though, in the manner of 1961, some of the admiration was none too subtle in its prejudice: "Murray Melvin plays the boy without one hint of pansy effeminacy" (Walker, *Evening Standard,* Sept. 14, 1961). One cannot help but feel that Tony Richardson's bisexuality, which was not publicly known until many years later, helped him to direct this character and that of Jo with delicacy and tact. For surely such a secret must make one very much aware of the isolating effect of feeling oneself to be different. Obviously, this is a very sensitive matter, but Gavin Lambert was quite right when he suggested in his piece for *Sight and Sound* that ignoring it does an insidious form of violence to his memory. He points out that this aspect of his life is absent from his memoirs: "There is no mention of the bisexuality that was surely a key factor in his life. This part of himself he left hidden, like the typescript, in a closet. I dislike the premise of 'outing,' with its implication of revealing a guilty secret, but to ignore this aspect of Tony's life not only falsifies him, but slurs his memory by lining oneself up with those who regard the secret as guilty" (Lambert 1993, 33). It is clearly fallacious to judge a work according to the life of its creator, but both *A Taste of Honey* and *The Loneliness of the Long Distance Runner* are fine films because they are the product of a director who is firmly committed to articulating a personal vision. In this sense, Richardson's direction of Jo and Geoff and Colin Smith benefits from an intuitive sympathy for the social outsider.

The general critical attitude toward these films has remained largely negative. A good index of this is the books listing available movies. In a 1989 edition of *The Time Out Film Guide*, the entry for *A Taste of Honey* begins, "A perfect example of how the new British Cinema of the late '50s and early '60s has dated and become almost unwatchable" (Milne 1989). *The Critics' Film Guide* is just as vituperative: "It now looks underplotted and unspeakably dreary" (Tookey 1994, 838). Leslie Halliwell (1985) damns *The Loneliness of the Long Distance Runner* with the most insipid of faint praise: "Rather pale study of a social outcast; interesting scenes do not quite form a compelling whole." This has been coupled with a sustained pattern of studied disregard for Richardson's achievements. It is true that he helped to exacerbate some of this critical disdain with his 1966 suit against the *Spectator* for defaming him in their review of *Mademoiselle*. This was further compounded by his very public refusal to admit the critics to a screening of *The Charge of the Light Brigade*. Nevertheless, as James Monaco aptly suggests in his *Movie Guide*: "It was considered chic among cinephiles in the 1960s to denigrate British stage and film director Tony Richardson, but on balance he was responsible for as many important British films in these years as anyone else" (1992, 485). Typical of this automatic response is a review of *The Loneliness of the Long Distance Runner* by Dwight Macdonald:

> If directors may be compared to horses, without offense to either party, I see Antonioni as a thoroughbred flat-racer, Truffaut as a steeplechase jumper soaring lightly over obstacles . . . Tony Richardson I see as a hackney, by which I don't mean "hack," for he is ambitious and serious, but merely the dictionary definition: "a horse for ordinary driving and riding." (1969, 389)

It would be difficult for any self-respecting director to take such criticism with equanimity.

Richardson's films of 1961 and 1962 are living proof that his work has not been valued fairly. *A Taste of Honey* and *The Loneliness of the Long Distance Runner* have aged much better than his more successful film, *Tom Jones*. Ken Russell is quite right when he argues that this latter work has not worn well: "When I saw it again recently, I noticed an air of desperation in the way the hand-held camera panned relentlessly hither and thither in the hope of catching something of interest, at the same time trying to convince us that the pace is fast and furious" (Russell 1993, 85). In the long term, Richardson's reputation as a director should be reevaluated in the light of the two films of 1961 and 1962. There is some encouraging evidence that this is beginning to occur. When he died, for every Michael Billington and Derek Malcolm who reproduced the old canard that "Richardson, who came from the theatre, was never the most natural of film-makers and never managed a coherent style of his own" (*Guardian*, Nov. 16, 1991), there was a Tom Hutchinson who pointed to the probability that his core works will be properly reevaluated: "Outside his time . . . Tony Richardson withered. But he was never a safe director—and for that give praise. I have a feeling his real influence will surface some years ahead" (1991, 93).

But the most telling indication that a proper reexamination of the power and quality of these two works came in an eloquent article by Frank Deasy in the May 1995 issue of *Sight and Sound*. He testifies to the sheer power and influence of *The Loneliness of the Long Distance Runner*, which he credits with being "one of the reasons I write screenplays": "For me, *The Loneliness of the Long Distance Runner* is a deeply spiritual film, reaching far beyond the social realism to which critical consensus usually consigns it. It amazes me how rarely it is mentioned, or anyway mentioned positively, in accounts of British film, or new wave cinema" (33). One can only cheer at the truth of these comments. Deasy's article also cites Visconti's first film, *Ossessione*, as another film that always moves him. At the end of the article, he links these two works which have proven so influential in his life: "Vito Mussolini, the Duce's son, stormed out of *Ossessione*, shouting 'That isn't Italy.' I don't imagine there was much shouting or public brawling in Britain about *The Loneliness of the Long Distance Runner*. I suspect a muted more corrosive whisper was heard: 'That isn't England.' Or else, more destructive still: 'That isn't film-making'" (33). Sooner or later, Tony Richardson's *A Taste of Honey* and *The Loneliness of the Long Distance Runner* will be afforded their rightful places in the pantheon.

WORKS CITED

Books

Delaney, Shelagh. *A Taste of Honey*. New York: Grove Weidenfeld, 1959.

Halliwell, Leslie. *Halliwell's Film Guide*. New York: Scribner's, 1985.

Lassally, Walter. *Itinerant Cameraman*. London: John Murray, 1987.

Manvell, Roger. *New Cinema in Britain*. London: Studio Vista, 1969.

Macdonald, Dwight. *Dwight Macdonald on Movies*. Englewood Cliffs: Prentice Hall, 1969.

Milne, Tom, ed. *The Time Out Film Guide*. London: Longman, 1989.

Monaco, James. *The Movie Guide*. New York: Putnam, 1992.

Osborne, John. *Almost a Gentleman*. London: Faber and Faber, 1991.

Pesiny, George. *The Great British Picture Show*. Boston: Little, Brown and Company, 1985.

Petrie, Duncan J. *Creativity and Constraint in the British Film Industry*. New York: St. Martin's Press, 1991.

Redgrave, Vanessa. *Vanessa Redgrave: An Autobiography*. New York: Random House, 1994.

Richardson, Tony. *The Long Distance Runner. An Autobiography*. New York: Morrow, 1993a.

———. *Long Distance Runner. A Memoir*. London: Faber and Faber, 1993b.

Robinson, David. *The History of World Cinema*. New York: Stein and Day, 1973.

Russell, Ken. *Fires over England*. London: Hutchinson, 1993.

Sarris, Andrew. *Confessions of a Cultist*. New York: Simon and Schuster, 1970.

Sillitoe, Alan. *Life without Armour*. London: Flamingo, 1995.

———. *The Loneliness of the Long Distance Runner*. New York: Knopf, 1965.

Taylor, John Russell. *Anger and After*. London: Methuen, 1962.

———. *Cinema Eye, Cinema Ear*. New York: Hill and Wang, 1964.

Tookey, Christopher. *The Critics' Film Guide*. London: Boxtree, 1994.

Truffaut, François. *François Truffaut: Letters*. Ed. Gilles Jacob and Claude de Givnay. London: Faber and Faber, 1989.

Journals and Essays

Baker, Peter. "Peter Baker sees Courtenay lose and Richardson win the race . . ." *Films and Filming* (November 1962): 32.

Courteney, Tom.(sic) "The Loneliness of the Long Distance Runner." *Films and Filming* (September 1962): 10–13.

Deasy, Frank. "Obsession." *Sight and Sound* (May 1995): 33.

Harcourt, Peter. "I'd rather be like I am: some comments on The Loneliness of the Long Distance Runner." *Sight and Sound* (Winter 1962–63): 16–19.

Lambert, Gavin. "Tony Richardson: An Adventurer." *Sight and Sound* (November 1993): 30–33.

Quirk, Eugene F. "Social Class as Audience: Sillitoe's Story and Screenplay 'The Loneliness of the Long Distance Runner.'" *Literature/Film Quarterly* 9.3 (1981): 161–71.

Richardson, Tony. "Directions." *Granta* 122 (10 November 1962).

———. "Free Cinema." *The Listener* (2 May 1968).

———. "The Two Worlds of the Cinema." *Films and Filming* (June 1961): 7, 41.

Rubens, Robert. "Conversations at the Royal Court Theatre." *Transatlantic Review* 9 (Spring 1962): 5–10.

Wollen, Peter. "The Last Wave: Modernism in the British Films of the Thatcher Era." *British Cinema and Thatcherism.* Ed. Lester Friedman. Minneapolis: University of Minnesota Press, 1993.

Newspaper Articles (in chronological order)

"The Flight from Make-Believe: Neo-Realism of Delaney Play." *Times* (11 March 1961).

Holland, Julian. "Comes True for the Girl in 2000." *Evening News* (15 March 1961).

Thomas Wiseman. "Mr. Richardson Shoots It Rough . . . and Keeps the Bite in That Taste of Honey." *Evening Standard* (7 April 1961).

"Quest for the real Thing: Film Director Flouts Tradition." *Times* (24 April 1961).

"The Padded Waif." *Time* (8 June 1961).

Lewis, Patricia. "Wide-Eyed Appeal in Tush's Violet Gaze." *Daily Express* (7 September 1961).

Barker, Felix. "This puts Richardson at the Top." *Evening News* (14 September 1961).

Perrick, Eve. *Daily Mail* (14 September 1961).

Walker, Alexander. "No Beauty, but My, What a Girl This Is!" *Evening Standard* (14 September 1961).

Mosley, Leonard. "How Do You Like a Girl?" *Daily Express* (15 September 1961).

Hibbin, Nina. "Shelagh's Sweet Miss Better Than Many a Slick Hit." *Daily Worker* (16 September 1961).

Powell, Dilys. *Sunday Times* (17 September 1961).

Muller, Robert. "The Other Half of Osborne and Co . . ." *Daily Express* (11 February 1962).

Alpert, Hollis. *Saturday Review* (22 September 1962).

"Reality with Everything." *Guardian* (25 September 1962).

"A Borstal Boy's Protest." *Times* (26 September 1962).

Mosley, Leonard. *Daily Express* (27 September 1962).

Walker, Alexander. "No Glamour Boy, but My, What a Performance!" *Evening Standard* (27 September 1962).

Hill, Derek. "Defiance and Defeat." *Scene* (28 September 1962).

Quigley, Isabel. *Spectator* (28 September 1962).

Robinson, David. *Financial Times* (28 September 1962).

Powell, Dilys. "Rebel in Our Midst." *Sunday Times* (30 September 1962).

"Borstal Boycott." *Time* (26 October 1962).

Cinémato (13 February 1965).

Martin, Marcel. *Lettres Francaises* (17 February 1965).

Walker, Alexander. "The Secret Shame of an Angry Young Man." *Evening Standard* (15 November 1991).

Billington, Michael, and Derek Malcolm. "Exiled Maker of the Court." *Guardian* (16 November 1991): 25.

Bremmer, Charles. "Film World Mourns Its 'Angry Young Man.'" *Times* (16 November 1991): 20.

Curtis, Anthony. "Tony Richardson." *Financial Times* (16 November 1991): 41.

Morley, Sheridan. "Tragedy of the Genius with a Talent for Self-Destruction." *Daily Mail* (16 November 1991): 51.

Wardle, Irving, and Allen Eyles. "Tony Richardson." *Independent* (16 November 1991): 49.

Gielgud, John. "Tony Richardson." *Times* (22 November 1991): 20.

Redgrave, Vanessa. "Demeaning a Fine Man." *Daily Mail* (26 November 1991): 26.

———. "AIDS Victim Who Inspired Generations of Talent." *Evening Standard* (27 November 1991): 53.

Hutchinson, Tom. *Hampstead and Highgate Express* (29 November 1991): 93.

CHAPTER FIVE

Novelist versus Filmmaker: Richardson's Adaptations of Faulkner's Sanctuary (1961) and Waugh's Loved One (1965)

GENE D. PHILLIPS

If it is true that a novel somehow resists translation to the screen because of the inherent differences between the two media, the fiction of William Faulkner and that of Evelyn Waugh have resisted such adaptation as much as any writer's. Yet Tony Richardson sought to bring a work by each of these novelists to the screen. The *International Dictionary of Films and Filmmakers* affirms that "Richardson's strongest talent is to adapt literary and dramatic works to the screen" (Welsh 1996, 817). As a matter of fact, Richardson succeeded in adapting works of Waugh and Faulkner for film with varying degrees of success.

Let us begin with the movie of Faulkner's *Sanctuary*, which Richardson filmed in 1961. The 1931 novel deals with an irresponsible and immature college girl named Temple Drake, who is taken after a dance to the Old Frenchman's Place—a ramshackle house in the country, which serves as a hangout for bootleggers—by her drunken escort, Gowan Stevens. Gowan wrecks his car en route, but he and Temple make it to the house all the same. There Gowan sobers up and, ashamed of his conduct, returns to town without Temple. She is thus left stranded with the inhabitants of the Old Frenchman's Place, including Popeye, a vicious Memphis racketeer.

Shortly thereafter, Popeye, who is impotent, rapes Temple with a corn cob. He then takes the unresisting Temple with him to the Memphis brothel where he hangs out when he is in town (the big city is always the citadel of sin in Faulkner). Temple stays on at the brothel because of her growing morbid fascination with Popeye's perverted world. Temple does not really repent of her wayward life by the end of the novel. Faulkner brought about the redemption of Temple Drake in *Requiem for a Nun*, the sequel to his earlier novel, which he published in 1951. When Tony Richardson filmed *Sanctuary* a decade later, the plots of *Sanctuary* and its sequel were combined into a single story, allowing the regeneration of Temple to develop as Faulkner had envisioned it.

Requiem for a Nun takes place eight years after the events chronicled in *Sanctuary*. Gowan Stevens has married Temple to make up for his earlier shabby conduct. Nancy Mannigoe, a black woman whom Temple has rescued from a life of prostitution and drug addiction, is Temple's housekeeper. As the story opens, Nancy has smothered Temple's six-month-old daughter to death, and Temple has quite unaccountably asked Gowan's uncle, Gavin Stevens, to defend Nancy. The lawyer later persuades Temple to drive with him to Jackson to see the governor about obtaining a pardon for Nancy, on the grounds of evidence which Temple had withheld at the trial.

In due course actress Ruth Ford turned Faulkner's *Requiem* into a viable stage play.[1] Tony Richardson decided to mount a production of the drama at the Royal Court Theater in London, which opened in November 1957. The British production, starring Ruth Ford as Temple Drake, garnered fairly enthusiastic notices and played to packed houses for the whole of its one-month engagement. Twentieth-Century Fox, which had already purchased the screen rights to *Sanctuary*, decided to make a film that would blend the two works into a single motion picture under the overall title of *Sanctuary*. The film was to be directed by Tony Richardson—a particularly felicitous choice, given the fact that he had directed the successful London production of *Requiem* (as well as a somewhat less successful Broadway production in 1959).

In creating the 1961 wide-screen version of *Sanctuary*, the director, along with screenwriter James Poe, merged the original plot of *Sanctuary* with that of the sequel into a single narrative that elides incidents from the two books in a most inventive fashion. The film opens with a pre-credit sequence that depicts the sentencing of Nancy (Odetta) to the gallows for murder and her muttered prayer, "Thy will be done. Thank you, Lord."

The lawyer, who is called Ira Stevens in the film, visits Temple (Lee Remick) after the trial. Ira (Harry Townes) tells her that he knows that a man was with her on the night of her baby's death and that she can still help Nancy if she will tell the truth. Temple decides to go to the home of the governor (Howard St. John), who happens to be Temple's father in the film.

As Temple recalls, voice over on the soundtrack, that fatal night eight years before, when she was going to the dance with Gowan (Bradford Dillman), we see a younger Temple standing in the doorway of the living room in which the older woman had just begun telling the story. She bids goodnight to her father and goes off to the dance with Gowan. They both get drunk and decide to pay a visit to the Old Frenchman's Place to get more liquor. After the auto accident, they are taken to the Old Frenchman's Place by one of the bootleggers (Strother Martin). Nancy is one of the inhabitants of the place, where she cooks for the bootleggers and takes care of her baby. At this point in the film, Nancy makes a remark that foreshadows her later killing of Temple's baby: making reference to her own infant who is lying in a crib in the kitchen, she muses, "He's sick; been sick all his life—ain't no place to raise a child up." Such an atmosphere of depravity, she feels, can only stunt the development of an infant. Some eight years later Nancy will take steps to see that Temple's child is not exposed to the same sort of environment, as we shall shortly see.

Popeye, who is called Candy Man in the film, is played by Yves Montand, whose native French accent is explained in the movie by making Candy a Cajun from New Orleans. His name, Faulkner critic Pauline Degenfelder notes, suggests the dual underworld meaning of candy: "whiskey," indicating that he is a bootlegger, and "desire," implying his sexual prowess (1976, 555)—for Candy, unlike his novel counterpart, Popeye, is definitely not impotent. Richardson explained that the "in-house studio censor" at Fox would not allow even the suggestion that Candy was impotent and hence had raped Temple with a corn cob (1993, 146).[2]

As a matter of fact, Candy demonstrates his virility unequivocally in the rape scene. He enters the barn where Temple is spending the night and easily overcomes her token resistance, just as the scene shifts to the next morning. Candy informs Temple that he is taking her with him to the city in the car that she came in. In her room at Miss Reba's (where the ubiquitous Nancy works as a maid), Candy promises to protect her and care for her. "I was learning what it was like to be with a real man," Temple comments over the soundtrack. "Next morning I woke to a different world: gin for breakfast, new clothes that Candy had bought for me. That dingy little room at Miss Reba's became my sanctuary of sin and pleasure." As she watches herself in the mirror take a swig of gin, she says to her reflection with undisguised glee, "Jazz Baby, you are low down."

Candy subsequently takes Temple's car on a bootlegging expedition so that he will think of her while he is gone—or so he says. He is, however, pursued by the police in a chase that ends with Candy swerving off the road and crashing in a ditch. He is presumed dead, although his body is not found in the wreckage. (In Faulkner's novel Popeye is executed as a criminal.)

"That's how they found me," Temple adds, voice over, "by tracing the car. It was the return of the innocent from the ranks of the damned. Of course, it was hushed up because the injured party might lose her reputation. And she said to herself, 'Here we are, back home, and that's that.' But she was still screaming under her skin for her lost love." This last remark serves as a preparation for a later event in the film, which represents another interesting departure from Faulkner. As Temple finishes the narration, we are back in the present, where she says to her father, "I let you have your own way, even to marrying Gowan—he felt responsible; he knew the facts."

When Temple again takes up the narrative, we slip back into the past and see her hiring Nancy as a maid and nurse for her two children. Nancy, after all, was her only link with the past. She explains: "Nancy was kind and understanding to me when I needed kindness and understanding."

The importance of Temple's earlier aside, that she still was in love with Candy, becomes clear when he suddenly comes into her life once more. It seems that he escaped from the auto accident in which he was thought to have perished and has been lying low. Thus it is the Popeye character himself with whom Temple is going to run away in the Richardson film, whereas in *Requiem for a Nun*, it is Pete, a racketeer whom Temple had met at Miss Reba's. This plot twist enables Richardson to avoid introducing an important new character so late in the film and also helps to tie *Sanctuary* and *Requiem* more tightly together into a single narrative. With the exception of the substitution of Candy for Pete, however, the events in the film proceed as they do in Faulkner.

Temple confesses to Nancy that she plans to take her baby with her but to leave her four-year-old son with his father. Nancy begs Temple to think of her child. "You can't take it with you when you run off, and you can't leave it here. The baby will wind up in a garbage can or an orphanage." When Temple still insists that she is taking her little gift with her, Nancy folds her hands and whispers, "I've tried everything I know; you can see that" and then goes into the nursery. Temple stands in the foreground of the frame as she tells Candy that she has him to protect her. In the background is the closed door of the nursery. A moment later Temple enters the nursery to get the baby, but the camera stays outside, as if it is recoiling from what has happened within. There is an instant of silence and then Temple's anguished scream.

Nancy smothered the infant with a pillow to keep Temple from taking the baby with her and to save Temple herself from surrendering once more to evil. After she is convicted at the trial, Nancy, the "nun" of the novel's title, is prepared to carry through her sacrifice to the end, in order to expiate her own life of vice.

"The rest you know," Temple concludes to her father, the governor, and Ira. "Candy vanished and Nancy has been sentenced to hang; and all the time she has said nothing but, 'Thank you, Lord.'" When the governor says that there is nothing he can do for Nancy, Ira explains that Temple's painful admissions have not been in vain. "I brought you here to wipe the slate clean, to give you a chance to start again," he says. He suggests that, in owning up before the governor, her father, to her responsibility for the things that have happened, Temple Drake for the first time has earned the right to be known as Mrs. Gowan Stevens, that is, as a genuine wife and mother. She is no longer living a lie, and her penance will be to live out her days with a husband who will soon learn the facts about her sordid past.

Indeed, Ira goes to see Gowan and relays the facts to him. After doing so, Ira says: "Out of what happened tonight could come a new beginning. Free her by standing by her to face the past. Face your own weakness, your own evasions." Gowan responds thoughtfully, "Sure—like the Good Book says, 'The Truth shall make you free.'"

The next scene, in which Richardson and Poe make use of Faulkner's dialogue from *Requiem*, is almost an illustration of that scriptural text. Temple tells Nancy in her death cell that she has confessed everything. Nancy replies, "I gave up this life when I raised my hand against that child. You had to suffer through the telling of it—that's the way we get salvation." "Salvation," repeats Temple. "We're all looking for some place to feel safe, a place to hide. We look for it in such strange places." "Salvation means more than hiding," Nancy continues. "It means facing up to your life, for your children now and those to come. You've got to believe that you are forgiven as I know I am forgiven."

Temple emerges into the sunlight, where she finds Gowan waiting for her. They walk down the street together as the camera pulls back to show Nancy, a serene expression on her face, gazing through her prison bars. Getting all three of them into the same shot marks the most notable use of the wide-screen frame that Richardson makes in the entire picture. The film is photographed in black and white, which is fitting since the use of even the most muted color process would not be in keeping with the stark atmosphere of Faulkner's somber tale. In fact, Richardson found the right note for the film: the dark, brooding atmosphere which he creates around his characters adds powerfully to the film's impact on the viewer.

Moreover, Lee Remick's portrayal of Temple Drake's sexual obsession has the intensity of Renaissance tragedy. In addition, Yves Montand's French accent gives him an exotic quality that helps the filmgoer better understand Temple's abiding attraction for him.

Richardson migrated from Britain to Hollywood to make Sanctuary at Fox because he liked the script, especially its evocation of the 1920s and 1930s. Don Radovich writes in his book on Richardson that the director had been enticed to Hollywood to make the film "by false promises of location filming and control of casting and script. Richardson became mired in a studio-bound production paralyzed by the dictates of censors, produces, and sycophants." Consequently, as things turned out, "Richardson had little choice in casting, and the screenwriter had already been chosen." In addition, "despite a token pre-production visit to Mississippi, Richardson's ideas of location filming were vetoed." Radovich concludes, "The finished film, after still more interference and a final cut made by the studio, was neither a critical nor a popular success" (1995, 16, 107).

Accordingly, after the film was completed, Richardson said, "It is impossible to make anything interesting or good under the conditions imposed by the major studios in America. It is a totally impossible creative setup: even after the film is made, so much mutilation goes on, and it becomes the product of many different people" (1969, 138).

Although Richardson was not happy with the film—and both the critical and popular response to the picture was lukewarm—it has much of the flavor of Faulkner. Indeed, it may be that the unpleasant events chronicled in the movie are too unpalatable for the average filmgoer when they are depicted on the screen. As British filmmaker Ken Russell once said to the author about making his controversial film *The Devils* (1971), when one reads of gory events in a book, "one can sift them through one's imagination and filter out as much of the unpleasantness as one cares to; but you can't do that when you are looking at a film."

All in all, Richardson's film is technically a polished piece of work, which qualifies as an in-depth examination of the psychology of character. However, it contains some slow-paced, talky stretches—one of the major flaws that contemporary cinema critics found with the film when it was released. As a result, the viewers' interest occasionally tends to flag while they watch the movie. It is this author's belief that Richardson's movie is more to be admired than enjoyed.

Although he decided that he did not want to make another film in Hollywood, for the reasons cited above, Richardson did return to America to make a film of Evelyn Waugh's *Loved One* in 1965. When Metro Goldwyn-Mayer invited him to make the film, Richardson accepted the invitation because he had long admired Waugh's 1948 novella about Hollywood. Moreover, this time around Richardson demanded—and received—full artistic autonomy over the production.

The Loved One is a satire of Hollywood, which resulted from Waugh's visit there to negotiate the film rights for *Brideshead Revisited* with MGM. In the end the film was canceled, but the trip to Hollywood inspired him to write a story about the American film capitol. "I found a deep mine of literary gold in the cemetery of Forest Lawn," said Waugh in rounding off his diary account of his Hollywood sojourn, "and I intended to get to work immediately on a novelette staged there" (April 7, 1947).[3] Needless to say, Whispering Glades, the cemetery in *The Loved One*, is closely patterned after Forest Lawn Memorial Park in Los Angeles, which Waugh likened to a necropolis belonging to the age of the Pharaohs.

In writing a novel set in Hollywood, Waugh joined the ranks of distinguished novelists who have embodied their unhappy experiences with Hollywood in their fiction, notably Nathaniel West in *Day of the Locust* and F. Scott Fitzgerald in *The Last Tycoon.*

The first scene of the novel introduces Dennis Barlow, newly arrived from England to pursue a career in Hollywood, under the tutelage of another British expatriate, Sir Francis Hinsely. When Sir Francis is peremptorily fired by the studio, having outlived his usefulness, he promptly goes home and hangs himself. Thus, Waugh introduces the novel's preoccupation with death. Dennis accordingly visits Whispering Glades to arrange for Sir Francis's funeral. He is interested in seeing how the cult of death is practiced there, partly because by this time he has gotten a job at the Happier Hunting Ground, a pet cemetery, in lieu of launching a career in films.

The reduction of the human spirit to the level of that of other animals, implied by the very existence of the pet cemetery, is underscored by the sermons given by the nonsectarian minister who presides over the burial rites at the Happier Hunting Ground. One of his more inspiring efforts begins: "Dog born of bitch hath but a short time to live."

During the course of Dennis's visit to Whispering Glades to arrange for Sir Francis's funeral, Dennis meets and falls in love with Aimée Thanatogenous, an assistant mortician there. Aimée's last name means, in Greek, "child of death." Hence she seems to have been fated to work at Whispering Glades.

For her part, Aimée cannot decide whether to marry Mr. Joyboy, the eccentric chief mortician at Whispering Glades, or Dennis. (She does not know yet that Dennis works in a pet cemetery.) She seeks spiritual advice outside Whispering Glades by having recourse to the Guru Brahmin, whose column appears daily in a local newspaper. Her letters are actually answered by Mr. Slump, who lives in an ever-increasing alcoholic haze; Slump is often irritated when Aimée is not satisfied with the standard advice he dispenses to her. As a matter of fact, Aimée's dependence on Slump's spurious advice is instrumental in bringing about her sad fate at novel's end, as we shall shortly see.

Since *The Loved One* is set in Hollywood, it was fitting that a Hollywood studio would want to film it. In 1964, MGM undertook the project, and onlookers conjectured that the studio would get no further with its attempt to film *The Loved One* than it had with its attempt to adapt *Brideshead Revisited* to the screen. To everyone's surprise, Waugh agreed to let the filming proceed.

"He had initially turned *The Loved One* over to his very good friend Alec Guinness, who was going to star in the film for an independent producer," his late wife Laura explained to me. "When the latter went bankrupt, however, the script was turned over, along with several other properties, to MGM, who proceeded with the film." Guinness then proved unavailable; and when Tony Richardson announced in a newspaper interview the extent of the changes that he was going to make in the novel in order to "update" it, Waugh demanded that the director be replaced.

Richardson recalls in his autobiography that, during the preproduction period, he gave an interview to *The New York Times.* "I talked about bringing *The Loved One* into contemporary reality," the director recalled, and Waugh took his remarks to mean that "the book was out of date." Waugh accordingly bombarded MGM with "a stream of hurt and angry cables" (Richardson 1993, 194). But Waugh's objections to Richardson's directing the film came too late, and the film went into production according to Richardson's specifications.

The "expansion" of the script got decidedly out of hand, admits Terry Southern, one of the collaborators on the screenplay. "The first assembly of the footage," after principal photography had been completed, "was almost five hours long," he remembers; and it had to be trimmed to two hours (1965, 4). In the course of all these revisions, Waugh's original story got mislaid, just as he had feared that it would. "He tried to have his name removed from the screen credits," said Mrs. Waugh, "but it was already too late to do so."

The film of *The Loved One* opens promisingly enough with Robert Morse as the British poet Dennis Barlow arriving at the Los Angeles airport to visit Sir Francis Hinsely (Sir John Gielgud, in an impeccable performance); Sir Francis is one of the colony of Englishmen marooned in Hollywood. As Southern notes, "Sir Francis takes Dennis to the dilapidated and curiously grotesque cottage where he now lives, on the grounds of his former estate—symbolic of his failing status in the film capitol" (1965, 20). Sir Francis and Dennis have breakfast by the cracked, empty swimming pool. "It was like a great acquarium in the old days," Sir Francis muses, "flashing with the limbs of great beauties—all, alas, since departed."

The dinner which Sir Francis and his compatriots give for Dennis is humorously staged, with neat touches such as a waiter hastily replacing a picture of President Lyndon Johnson with a portrait of Queen Elizabeth, while the exiles solemnly toast their lost homeland. The dinner is presided over by Sir Ambrose Abercrombie (Robert Morley), who tells Dennis that the members of the English colony in Hollywood are "ambassadors to

America"; so he exhorts Dennis not to let their side down.

Later, when Sir Francis's job in the studio publicity department is turned over to a witless in-law of a company executive, the old knight stoically collects his things and is stopped by an imperious secretary, who inquires whether or not the painting he is carrying (which he painted himself) is studio property. After this final humiliation, Sir Francis goes home to hang himself over his deserted swimming pool.

On the credit side of the ledger, one must report that Richardson wisely transplants into the film some key sequences from the novel. For example, he includes the burial service for Sir Francis, at which Dennis reads a poem he composed for the occasion. Dennis's grotesque apostrophe to the dead knight concludes, "now 'tis here you lie;/Here pickled in formaldehyde and painted like a whore,/Shrimp-pink incorruptible, not lost or gone before." Not surprisingly, Sir Ambrose is totally chagrined by Dennis's grossly inappropriate poem and tastily points out that Dennis has indeed let the British side down. He adds ruefully that the sooner Dennis clears out of Hollywood and goes back to England, the better off the British in Hollywood will be.

Richardson also incorporates into the movie virtually intact the episode that precipitates Aimée's death. It seems that Slump is very disgruntled about having been fired by his editor when she phones him at a bar, in order to get one last helping of wisdom from her guru. Aimée has just found to her horror that Dennis works at the Happier Hunting Ground; she asks Slump if she should therefore break her engagement. In exasperation, Slump advises her to take the elevator to the top floor of the building across the street, "open a nice window and jump out."

Because Aimée has placed all her confidence in her Guru, she follows Slump's advice and takes her own life: she goes to Joyboy's workroom on the top floor of the mortuary and embalms herself. Living constantly in an atmosphere of death, Aimée has never learned to cope with life; she goes to join the dead, among whom she has learned to feel at home. She thus lives up to her last name, "child of death," by bringing about her own demise.

Once Aimée has committed suicide, Dennis decides to relinquish his job at the Happier Hunting Ground, in favor of blackmailing Mr. Joyboy (Rod Steiger), who fears that Aimée's death will bring scandal to himself and to Whispering Glades. Dennis offers to dispense of Aimée's body and let it be thought that she has gone to England with him—provided that Joyboy pays his first-class passage home. Joyboy agrees, and Dennis sets about arranging to dispose of Aimée's corpse.

Although the episode just described is very faithful to the film's literary source, the same cannot be said for other scenes in the film. Indeed, Richardson and his writers, Terry Southern and Christopher Isherwood, allow the bitingly satirical flavor of the film to turn sour, as their myriad additions to Waugh's original novel range farther and farther afield.

For example, Wilbur Glenworthy (Jonathan Winters), the founder of Whispering Glades Cemetery, who is known as the Blessed Reverend, concocts a plan whereby he can get rid of the ever-increasing number of "stiffs" that are filling up his memorial park; otherwise the total remaining acreage of Whispering Glades will be depleted in a few years. Glenworthy therefore arranges with the directors of the air force Space Program to fire the corpses into perpetual orbit under the aegis of his new slogan, "Resurrection now!"

Other additions to the original story include a sex orgy among the caskets in the mortuary, presided over by a homosexual host (Liberace). The wild party is occasioned by the Blessed Reverend's efforts to lure the air force brass into giving their full support to his space-burial scheme. Another addition involves a scene in which Aimée visits Mr. Joyboy's mother, at a time when she is toying with the idea of marrying Joyboy instead of Dennis. Mr. Joyboy's obscenely fat mother is shown having an orgasm over a series of food commercials on television. William Everson rightly calls this episode "one of the grossest cinematic comedy highlights of all time" (1994, 242). In any case, a single evening with Mr. Joyboy's "mom," to whom her son is totally dedicated, is enough to persuade Aimée not to marry him.

The last major addition to the story occurs at the climax of the film. Dennis decides to take advantage of Glenworthy's space-burial program in order to get rid of Aimée's corpse. Specifically, he arranges to put her corpse into the first coffin to be launched into space. So, Southern comments, "Aimée is fired into space—to soar through the farthest reaches of celestial grandeur in an orbit of eternal grace" (1965, 92). Surely Waugh's ending, whereby Dennis cremates Aimée's body in Whispering Glade's crematorium, is much neater and more in keeping with the thrust of the novel as a whole than the film's elaborate finale. To be precise, Aimée's winding up in the furnace at the pet cemetery implies once again the reduction of the human spirit to the level of that of other animals—a notion that, as noted above, recurs throughout Waugh's novel.

The finished product opened in London only two weeks before Waugh's death in the spring of 1966, but he would never have gone to see the film in any case. Richardson wrote to Waugh at the time, apologizing for the interview in the *New York Times* that had so offended the novelist. "I got a postcard back," Richardson recalled. "He listed all the woes that had fallen on him because of film plans. Besides me, these included that he had only just escaped" the possibility of the film adaptation of *The Loved One* "being directed by a 'Mexican.' The postcard ended, 'and I hope the film will never be shown in Taunton,'" the village near Waugh's country estate.[4] "As far as I know, it hasn't been," the director offered (1993, 194–95).

Most of the reviews of the film were ultimately tributes to Waugh, since they pointed out how his superb satire had been cheapened by the film's bad taste. *Newsweek* is typical:

> In place of the beautifully controlled satiric explosion that Waugh's little volume visited upon an unsuspecting public in 1948, Richardson's blowsy film relies on scatter-gun gagsmanship, much of it derivative, and on camp, some of it dirty. . . . Isn't satire supposed to be offensive? Of course. The crucial difference is that the film version of *The Loved One* fails at satire and therefore never earns the right to be scabrous. ("Candy in Lotusland," 122)

Pauline Kael had little that was positive to say about the movie: "From the look of the film, Richardson shot every plausible idea that came to him, and then, as the footage had no flow, no development, he chopped it up and slapped it together hard. . . . This botched picture is a triumphant disaster—a sinking ship that makes it to port because everybody on board is too giddy to panic" (1991, 440). Furthermore, playwright-screenwriter John Osborne, who was Richardson's frequent collaborator, was compelled to term *The Loved One* "one of the most ill-judged films ever perpetrated" (1991, 247).

Critical opinion of the movie has not improved much over the years. Ken Russell, in his book on the cinema, writes, "Tony lost control when attempting to bring Evelyn Waugh's *Loved One* to the screen. It was too over the top for words" (1994, 85). Furthermore, film journalist Jeff MacGregor cites screenwriter Buck Henry as dubbing the movie "a glorious mess" (1995, 24).

In essence, Waugh's novel succeeds as satire, where the film based so loosely on it fails, precisely because Waugh's personal standard of values provides the norm by which his character's selfish, materialistic view of life and death is judged. Lacking any frame of reference at all, the film fails even to be funny, which the book certainly is.

Radovich cites Donald McCaffrey as one of the few critics who has championed the film in recent years. McCaffrey defends the film against "the purists" who claim that Richardson changed his literary source too much. He goes on to call the film "quality social satire," adding that *The Loved One* is one of the best dark comedies to come out of the 1960s, a work "that will stand the test of time" (1995, 261, 214).[5] For his part, Radovich observes that "over the years, *The Loved One* has developed a strong cult following" among those who see it as an audacious, irreverent film of bad taste and black humor (22, 119).

In summing up Richardson's films of Faulkner's *Sanctuary* and Waugh's *Loved One*, I would offer the following reflection: the director's screen treatment of *Sanctuary*, regardless of its shortcomings, is fundamentally faithful to its literary source. By contrast, his film of *The Loved One* takes far too many liberties with the Waugh original to retain much of its flavor. Nevertheless, both films contain enough memorable moments—moments which I have been at pains to point out—which do justice to their respective literary sources. As such, both films remain worthy of the discriminating moviegoer's serious attention.

NOTES

1. Tony Richardson erroneously states in his autobiography that Faulkner himself composed the stage version of the novel (1993, 155). On the contrary, William Faulkner, in his brief introduction to the published play, clearly states that the novel was adapted for the stage by Ruth Ford (1959, i).

2. For the record, *Sanctuary* was one of the first American films to deal frankly with the subject of rape. See Frank Walsh, *Sin and Censorship: The Catholic Church and the Motion Picture Industry* (New Haven: Yale UP, 1996): 292.

3. For Waugh's account of his sojourn in Hollywood, see his diary entries, edited by Michael Davie.

4. In his postcard, Waugh erroneously refers to the Spanish filmmaker Luis Buñuel as "a Mexican." Buñuel had been slated to direct the film version of *The Loved One* that was to star Alec Guinness.

5. The readers may judge for themselves if the film withstands the test of time, since it is available on videocassette.

WORKS CITED

"Candy in Lotusland." *Newsweek* (18 October 1965): 122.

Davie, Michael, ed. *The Diaries of Evelyn Waugh.* Boston: Little, Brown, 1973.

Degenfelder, Pauline. "Faulkner's *Sanctuary* and *Requiem for a Nun* on the Screen." *American Quarterly* 28 (Winter 1976).

Everson, William. *Hollywood Bedlam: Classic Screwball Comedies.* New York: Carol, 1994.

Faulkner, William. *Requiem for a Nun: A Play.* New York: Random House, 1959.

Kael, Pauline. *5001 Nights at the Movies.* New York: Holt, 1991.

MacGregor, Jeff. "Film View: Terry Southern." *The New York Times* (12 November 1995): 2:24.

Osborne, John. *Almost a Gentleman.* London: Faber and Faber, 1991.

Radovich, Don. *Tony Richardson: A Bio-Bibliography.* Westport, CT: Greenwood Press, 1995.

Richardson, Tony. *The Long Distance Runner: An Autobiography.* New York: Morrow, 1993.

———. "The Two Worlds of the Cinema." *Filmmakers on Filmmaking.* Ed. Harry Geduld. Bloomington: University of Indiana Press, 1969.

Russell, Ken. *The Lion Roars: Ken Russell on Film.* Boston: Faber and Faber, 1994.

Southern, Terry. *The Journal of the Loved One: The Production Log of a Motion Picture.* New York: Random House, 1965.

Welsh, James M. "Tony Richardson." *International Dictionary of Films and Filmmakers,* rev. ed. Ed. Laurie Hillstrom. Detroit: St. James Press, 1996.

CHAPTER SIX

Impossible Dreams:
Mademoiselle *(1966) and*
The Sailor from Gibraltar *(1967)*

REBECCA M. PAULY

In the space of eighteen months, from mid-1965 to the end of 1966, Richardson made two French films that impacted his personal life more than they did the ensemble of his artistic oeuvre. Jean Genet's script for *Mademoiselle* was as protean as its author. The first version documented was in 1951, as *Mademoiselle ou les feux interdits* (both an autobiographical illusion and an allusion to René Clément's 1951 *Les Jeux interdits*, the story of an orphaned Parisian girl taken in by a peasant family). Another version from the same period bore the title *Les rêves interdits ou L'autre versant du rêve*. The 1965 version of *Mademoiselle*, now subtitled *Les Rêves interdits*, was first suggested to Richardson by his producer Oscar Lewenstein, who had found out about Genet's filmscript. That it should have been Lewenstein who brought Richardson and Genet together was ironic, in that Richardson's first contact with Lewenstein some twenty years earlier was over the staging of Henri Montherlant's *The Town Where the Child Is King (La Ville dont le prince est un enfant)*. At the time, Lewenstein had refused to stage the play because "he was so horrified by homosexuality, with which the play dealt, that he could never soil himself by having anything to do with anything which touched on the subject" (Richardson 1993, 98). By 1965, both Lewenstein and Richardson had long and successful careers. Richardson had gone on to direct a number of other French plays, by Giraudoux and Ionesco, and Lewenstein had been on the board of the Royal Court Theatre for twenty years. A Communist, he had arranged a production of *Look Back in Anger* in Moscow in 1957. By the mid-1960s, he was producing films for Richardson's Woodfall production company. Furthermore, on the surface, Genet's script was not a homosexual or homoerotic tale, as were his controversial and even scandalous works from the 1940s. *Mademoiselle* is the story of the relationship between a violent destructive schoolmistress and an erotic but generous and goodhearted itinerant woodcutter in a small village lost in the French countryside. What Lewenstein may or may not have seen under the script's surface thematic of destructiveness, sexual awakening, isolation, humiliation, and sexual frustration was the transposition of Genet's erotic ambivalence rooted in his own childhood into the characters of *Mademoiselle*. However, Genet's personal protean ambiguity presented itself directly to Lewenstein and Richardson when they arrived at his hideout in Norwich and were informed that it was "Monsieur Jeanette" in the hotel room. Genet's only other finished and produced filmscript was on the contrary completely open, the short *Un Chant d'amour*, a work detailing in a lyric voice homosexual love in prison, the primary autobiographical thematic of *Journal du voleur*. The released version of *Un Chant d'amour* was censored and edited by Genet himself, as the original film was explicitly erotic and intended for private homosexual audience viewing. What was less known, if at all, was the fact that Genet worked extensively on a number of filmscripts throughout his writing career, the first of which was *La Révolte des anges noirs* (1947), a biographical narrative based on his childhood. Other scripts, *Le Prisonnier* (1949), *Le Bagne* (1952), *Le Bleu de l'oeil* or *La Nuit venue* (1976–1978) and *Le Langage de la muraille: cent ans jour après jour* (1970s), achieved various states of development but were never filmed and released. (An interesting if slightly irrelevant historic irony: Vanessa Redgrave has been instrumental in bringing to light a previously unpublished and unperformed 1939 play by Tennessee Williams entitled *Not about Nightingales*, a tale of homosexual passion and violence in an American men's prison. The play's debut was set for February 1998 at London's Royal National Theatre.)

Much of Genet's other literary production has cinematic qualities, using flashbacks and nonlinear narrative or allusions to filmgoing experiences, and many of his plays and novels have been adapted to the screen by other writers and directors, notably Rainer Werner Fassbinder, who in 1981 filmed *Querelle* with Jeanne Moreau, from *Querelle de Brest*. Genet's own filmscripts divide into two distinct categories of thematic: the childhood fantasy diegesis and the prison world. The very first script contains in its title the dual elements that would mark Genet's life, political, civil, literary, sexual: revolt and revolution and the saturnian influence of the black angel. One of the greatest ironies of Genet's film career was that the original print of *Un Chant d'amour* was given to the Cinémathèque and was consumed in the fire of 1980.

By 1965, Richardson had been following the explosive energy and innovations of the French *nouvelle vague* for several years. Vanessa Redgrave in her autobiography states that both she and Tony had fallen in love with Jeanne Moreau as Catherine in François Truffaut's 1961 *Jules et Jim*. Prior to undertaking the project of *Mademoiselle*, Richardson had attempted to negotiate the filming of Carson McCullers's *Reflections in a Golden Eye* with Moreau in the lead, to showcase her sexual liberation as a foil for the bisexual character of the major, a role refused by Marlon Brando (who would go on to make the film in 1967 for John Huston with Elizabeth Taylor, Brian Keith, and Julie Harris). When the McCullers project fell through, Richardson settled on *Mademoiselle* instead, although without Brando, who liked the male lead role but was trapped in another commitment. The woodcutter Manou was played rather by a virtually unknown Italian actor, Ettore Manni. The fact that the filmscript was not what it seemed should have been apparent immediately when Genet objected to Jeanne Moreau as Mademoiselle because she was too well-known and too beautiful. This self-reflexive transposition of Genet's own childhood persona called for a more brutish and bestial incarnation of the primal forces that had ravaged his life since 1922.

Genet had been sent from a Paris orphanage in 1911 at age seven months to Alligny-en-Morvan in the Massif Central, to mercenary adoptive parents Monsieur and Madame Charles Régnier, the husband a carpenter whose figure is echoed in the profession of the woodcutter of *Mademoiselle*. Until his adoptive mother's death, Genet was a model student and voracious reader. After this loss at age eleven, his life became a patchwork of alienation, crime, infractions, and sexual exploitation and experimentation. In his own words, he "began to do evil at age fourteen in order to justify his existence."[1] A true "*voyageur sans bagage*," he was at one point a transvestite prostitute for British sailors in Gibraltar, in between stints in the French army in Morocco. In and out of prison up to and through World War II, Genet read widely and worked on several novels, although the first he admitted to were *Un Condamné à mort* and *Notre-Dame-des-fleurs* from the early forties. Thus his real life outpaced the existential characters of his literary mentors Sartre and Cocteau, and his violent and erotic works were published with trepidation and circulated clandestinely throughout the war years. The first staging of a Genet play was *Les Bonnes* in Paris in 1949. In the following years, Genet fought for his sexual, social, civil, and political identity in many theaters. His initiation into film was as an actor in the 1948 unreleased *Ulysses ou les mauvaises rencontres*, directed by Alexandre Astruc (Sartre's film biographer), with Jean Marais (Cocteau's homosexual lover), Simone Signoret, the poet Raymond Queneau, and the painter Christian Bérard.

In 1952 Jean-Paul Sartre changed Genet's life by dispossessing him of his identity in his legendary and extremely inaccurate biography *Saint Genet*. The ensuing existential battle for control of Jean Genet very nearly drove Genet to suicide. During this period, virtually all of his works (*L'Enfant Criminel, Les Bonnes, Les Nègres, Le Balcon, Le Pape, Le Bagne, Les Paravents, La Mort*) have titles with definite articles, declare themselves generic and definitive. The only exception is his first film, the thirty-minute silent work *Un Chant d'amour*, shot in Milly and Saint-Germain. *Mademoiselle*, it is to be recalled, originally bore the title *Les Rêves [Feux] interdits*. Genet began work on it in 1951, reworked it in the spring of 1953, and approached it sporadically over the next several years.

By the time Lewenstein heard about the screenplay and arranged the meeting with Genet, the latter was erratic and despondent over the death of his circus performer lover, for which he carried much guilt. At this time in his life, he had inflicted considerable physical injury to himself and was prone to accidents. His new and present lover was a race car driver. According to Richardson, Genet agreed to come to London and worked on the script punctually for two hours every day, until Richardson made the fatal mistake of complimenting him on his reliability. This assault on his identity was unbearable; Genet disappeared the next day for good. According to Genet's biographers, this was also a fatal blow to the script, which was disfigured permanently by Richardson and David Rudkin. There is disagreement about the English and French reworkings of Genet's script. Michel Cournot wrote the French dialogues for the film; Bernard Frechtman, Genet's friend and agent, is credited with the English subtitles. It was about this time that Genet and Frechtman split for good over money matters. Frechtman later committed suicide.

Thus the Mademoiselle of Genet's memory and imagination, part himself, part his mother, part his father, part his schoolteacher, this kaleidoscopic reconstruction, was handed over to a luminous and very famous persona in the person of Jeanne Moreau, already known for *L'Oeuf*, Peter Brook's Paris production of *Cat on a Hot Tin Roof*, and for her role in his film of Marguerite Duras's *Moderato Cantabile*, but most of all for Truffaut's *Jules et Jim*. Worse yet, Richardson was falling in love with her, not casually as an icon of sexual energy, but profoundly, for the long duration, in an affair that destroyed his marriage to Vanessa Redgrave. The location finally chosen for filming was the hamlet of Le Rat in Corrèze. The film was shot by David Watkin, the ostracized cinematographer who was best known for his work on Richard Lester's *The Knack*. Watkin, according to Richardson, achieved "stunning" effects in black and white. The film was dual-released in French and English and had a mainly French crew. Watkin hired Philippe Brun, Alain Resnais's *opérateur* on *L'Année dernière à Marienbad*, for a voyeuristic fixed-frame effect, which also creates a frozen entrapment of the visual field, with figures moving in and out of frame. Ambient sound adds to the haunted effect, with no externally imposed lyricism of the rhythm or thematic of a musical score to break the intensity of the setting, which itself almost achieves characterial primacy.

Intriguingly, the film, while in French and set in a remote French village with its suffocatingly provincial society, is marked stylistically as much by Hitchcock as by his disciples of the *nouvelle vague*. Philippe Brun's camerawork recalls the claustrophobic world of *Dial M for Murder* or *Psycho* as much as it does the haunted halls of the castle in Resnais and Robbe-Grillet's 1961 *Last Year at Marienbad*. Furthermore, in *Marienbad*, Brun used a lot of traveling shots, introducing cinematographically the thematic of pursuit. It is Hitchcock rather who was the master of obsessive-compulsive psychotic behavior and of the mesmerizing horror generated by the fixed camera, the voyeuristic viewpoint riveted to the spot, fascinated, helpless. Some of the wide-angle shots of the open landscape also recall the work of Jean Renoir, another spiritual father of the New Wave.

The MGM video release version of *Mademoiselle* opens with the ground-level shot of Jeanne Moreau opening the floodgates, unleashing symbolically a devastating force of nature that swamps the world of the provincial agrarian village. (In fact, it could be said that the arrival and installation of the film crew at Le Rat had a similar effect, as they rented all the available real estate for miles around and commandeered the services of the locals for the film and for their own personal needs; they also introduced into the provincial village setting a cast of characters of carnival dimensions, hangers on unconnected to the filming.)

Moreau is referred to later in the film as a "goddess," which she is on multiple levels: as a film icon, as an obscure object of desire, and most important in the context of Genet's psychofantastic landscape of the imagination, as a malevolent force of nature. The flood achieves biblical overtones as well, occurring in the midst of a religious procession of the local relic through the landscape. This newly awakened force of evil disrupts the lives and economy of the villagers and their spiritual focus as well, as they talk of the fires of arson which have been set in the area. Thus fire and water, two of the four primal elements, are unleashed against the humble and stable structure of primitive society. After Mademoiselle is seen ripping a blossoming branch off an apple tree to crown herself and then crushing a nest of quail's eggs, the villagers indulge their xenophobic fears, complaining of the outsiders and foreigners in the village. However, their suspicions gravitate not to the chaste and learned schoolteacher but to the ill-kempt, impoverished itinerant Italian woodcutters, Manou, Antonio (Umberto Orsini), and Manou's son, Bruno (Keith Skinner). The film works throughout on the tension of dramatic irony, as the spectators are privy to Mademoiselle's secret world of hidden matches and fetishized objects of clothing, her fishnet gloves and stiletto high heels. This guise becomes a "travestie," a disguise, a schizoid destructive personality and a transvestite projection of Genet's homoerotic psyche.

Genet's script incorporates numerous classic fabular elements, with Mademoiselle going into the woods where there is a "wolf" as the villager says (of course the wolf is in this fable the woodcutter), and all manner of symbolic snakes, rabbits, fish, and so on. Mademoiselle is seen sleeping in the woods, *Belle au bois dormant,* by the woodcutter. And there are numerous allusions to *Beauty and the Beast,* which combine reworked mythological sources and allusions to Jean Cocteau's 1946 film.

Richardson's *Mademoiselle* also includes allusions to other classic films of the era: De Sica's 1948 *Bicycle Thieves,* with father and son characters named Antonio and Bruno, and Pagnol's 1953 *Manon of the Spring,* whose feral heroine is reflected inverted in Manou, just as Ugolin's pectoral mutilation of love is reflected in the mirror when Mademoiselle ravages her own breasts, in anger and frustration over her savage lust for the woodcutter.

The house of mirrors of the sexual psyche extends to the orphaned son, Bruno, as well, who is tormented by his love for Mademoiselle. Adolescent knight in the derisive armor of his father's trousers, he carries Mademoiselle's handkerchief on him. He follows her as a spying voyeur throughout the film, arousing constant suspicion as to his whereabouts. Berated and rejected by her in front of his classmates, he suffers alienation and isolation throughout the film and at the end must make a moral decision as a keeper of fatal knowledge when he has found the partially burned piece of notebook paper that would condemn Mademoiselle for arson. He lets his father die in her place, beaten to death by the angry villagers, as he betrays him out of jealousy. This criminal adolescent rejecting the father and loving the mother figure recalls directly the figure of Antoine Doinel of Truffaut's 1959 autobiographical *400 Blows*, as do the scenes of anger and humiliation in the classroom. Earlier in the film, in fact, Bruno has tried out his father's chainsaw, against his explicit interdiction. Throughout the film, the chainsaw felling the giant phallic trees is a symbol of castration and Freudian rivalry between father and son. This same rivalry resurfaces in *The Sailor from Gibraltar*, interestingly enough, when the narrator confesses his adolescent desire at age fifteen to murder his father.

The bestiary of animals in *Mademoiselle* includes both domestic and wild creatures, both victims and catalysts. Bruno captures a young hare in his coat and is taking it to Mademoiselle as an offering of his affection (another allusion to *Manon of the Spring*). When he is summarily thrown out of the classroom, he retreats to the woodshed and beats the rabbit to death in humiliated anger and frustration. The shot of the battered rabbit's head is identical to that of the dead father at the end of the film. When Mademoiselle ventures into the woods in search of sexual initiation with the woodcutter, he meets her carrying a corn snake under his shirt (in reality a happy, hungry corn snake that kept the film crew scampering after rats and mice to appease its appetite). As the harmless corn snake entwines around their arms, joining them in a satanic union, Mademoiselle flashes back to her first act of pyromania, a literal "feu de paille" wherein she started the first fire by accident, letting her lit cigarette fall into a haystack as she spied upon Manou, generating a conflagration that consumed the farm and its owner. In this same sequence with the snake, she remembers a classroom history lesson about Gilles de Rais who stole and burned children for Charles VI and his queen Isabeau de Bavière. It was in response to this situation that Jeanne d'Arc fought to crown

Charles VII, Jeanne d'Arc the female transvestite heroine of Jean Genet, heroine burned at the stake.

After a subsequent vilainous act of poisoning the animals' water trough with white arsenic, Mademoiselle is seen in the classroom, presenting a lesson on cities of India, particularly Benares on the Ganges where sacred funeral pyres are launched into the river, the classroom shots crosscut with images of cows lying dead in the barnyard.

In the parade of almost suffocating intertextual allusions to fable and film, there is one scene where Mademoiselle is typing depositions at the police station, using a Remington typewriter. The camera focuses at length on the name several times, just before the townspeople form their vigilante posse and head out into the woods in pursuit of their victim, Manou. Their all-night hunt for him is intercut with the night of love-making between Mademoiselle and Manou, in the woods, in the fields, by the lake. After he tells her that he is leaving for good the next day, she walks back into town in a trancelike, disheveled state and announces to the villagers that he did this to her, thus sacrificing him, the predatory female destroying the male after coupling, the virginal goddess exacting her revenge on the beast—in her male lover, in her own breast.

Richardson achieves ironic closure in the film as the surviving interlopers leave the village seemingly tranquil and intact, with the new schoolmaster making the students recite their multiplication tables. There is no longer any place for the fabular, the fantastic, the epic in the provincial village. Fantasy has another realism of its own; as Gaston Bachelard said, "Le réel, c'est le dessous." (Reality is what is underneath.) The mathematical precision of the provincial village is the antithesis of Mademoiselle previously dictating to the same students "Bientôt nous plongerons dans les froides ténèbres; Adieu vive clarté . . . [de nos étés trop courts!]" (Soon we will plunge into the cold darkness. Farewell bright light . . . [of our too short summers!). This earlier dictated fragment of the first two lines of Baudelaire's poem "Chant d'Automne" from his 1857 Les Fleurs du Mal has a double resonance as cited by Genet in this film, for it is quoted by the protagonists, Jérôme et Alissa, of André Gide's 1909 La Porte Etroite, as they mourn the inevitable end of their summer idyll. (This has further resonance as the homosexual Gide had just died in 1951.) The quote from Baudelaire is thematically significant for the entire filmscript in fact, as the poem goes on to remark the funereal sound of fireplace logs falling on the cobbles of the courtyard. The hollow sound recalls the hammer blows assembling a scaffold and the polar hell of a frozen heart, the poet's mind compared to a tower falling beneath the blows of the battering ram. These lines recall the saturnine verses of both François Villon and Gérard de Nerval and offer considerable Freudian symbolism. Baudelaire goes on to reference the assemblage of a coffin and the imminent departure at the end of summer, with the poet gazing into the green eyes of the love object, exhorting her to love him as a mother, lover, or sister. The poem ends with the poet's head resting against his lover's knee, as he is lost in bitter resignation to the inevitable.

Genet's original script of the forbidden fires and dreams had numerous distinct differences from Richardson's filmed version. Manou and Anton were Polish rather than Italian, and the snake was a *couleuvre*, alluding to a similar scene between Culafroy and Alfredo in *Notre-Dame-des-Fleurs*. What is most important, at the end, Bruno confronts Mademoiselle at the shore of the lake. She takes a fatal backward step and drowns as he watches without making any attempt to rescue her. Genet sold the script several times and was never satisfied with it. He had been unable to create a cinematic equivalent of the scenes of memory and imagination that he carried within him through his life.

THE SAILOR FROM GIBRALTAR

The Sailor from Gibraltar appeared in 1952, while Genet was working on the project of *Mademoiselle ou les Rêves interdits*. It has the same cold war suicidal, nihilistic modernism throughout, buried beneath the surface of its seemingly gratuitously violent and erotic narrative. Both tales also share the internal driving structure of autobiographical elements, which involve an epic itinerary of international eroticism and betrayal, disguised by numerous transpositions and inversions.

The primary intrigue of Marguerite Duras's novel *Le Marin de Gibraltar* involves a first-person male narrator who abandons his girlfriend of two years, his boring job in a bureaucracy, his life in short, in a rebellious gesture of liberation while on a trip to a seaside resort in Italy. In this setting, he finds a beautiful, mysterious, widowed French woman living aboard a luxurious yacht and decides that through fate and sheer will he will join her crew and sail with her in search of adventure. Ostensibly, she is seeking a lost lover (the sailor from Gibraltar) who perpetually evades her pursuit. The narrator becomes in derisive mirror fashion the latest in a string of surrogates of the other whom she so ardently pursues and never finds. This tale contains mirror echoes of Duras's own life experiences of separation from her Chinese lover in Vietnam and her enforced exile to France, as she set sail down the Mekong River aboard an ocean liner bound for the open seas. These experiences she recounts in more autobiographic narrative in her 1984 *L'Amant (The Lover)* and 1991 *L'Amant de la Chine du Nord (The Lover from North China)*, the latter of which was written in response to Jean-Jacques Annaud's film *L'Amant* (narrated by Jeanne Moreau), which Duras saw as a betrayal. There are also numerous intermingled literary antecedents shaping the text: the classical myths of Dionysos, Homeric epic, Coleridge's *Rime of the Ancient Mariner*, French poetry such as Paul Valéry's *Le Cimetière marin* (a topos near Montpellier and Sète) and Arthur Rimbaud's *Le Bateau Ivre*, Stendhalian lyric narrative, and of course the literary fathers acknowledged in the text: Balzac, Hegel, and Hemingway.

Jeanne Moreau had made *The Lovers* in 1958 for Louis Malle and the adaptation of Duras's *Moderato Cantabile* for Peter Brook. Thus, not only was *The Sailor from Gibraltar* her favorite book (according to Richardson), but she had established a screen persona closely interwoven with Durasian thematics. The casting of the film alone reads like a soap opera. The choice of Ian Bannen to play the protagonist, now an Englishman, was a disaster; Richardson claims in his memoirs that he had no warning or knowledge in advance of Bannen's quirky, almost schizophrenic, behavior, behavior that distorted the lead male role and virtually destroyed the film. And, almost unbelievably, Vanessa Redgrave, now spurned in favor of Moreau, volunteered to play the shunned girlfriend, Jacqueline, renamed Sheila, as a barely disguised declaration of her own personal humiliation. Raoul Coutard's cinematography is usually associated with the New Wave and particularly Jean-Luc Godard; his framing and pacing give the film a surrealistic and anguished quality that paralyze the acting and the script, a script that is already a travesty, hastily assembled in order to respond to other contingencies of the filming: availability of the yacht, conditions on the Mediterranean, conflicting offers awaiting the film's cast and crew. Richardson admits in his memoirs that the film was a failure and that he pushed the project to "enchaîner" as they say appropriately in French, to keep working with Jeanne Moreau without a break between *Mademoiselle* and *Sailor from Gibraltar*, a very insecure attempt to possess a woman whom he loved most for her unpredictability and untamable spirit. In fact, the *ménage à trois* of Richardson, Redgrave, and Moreau in this period becomes almost a real-life mirror of

Jules et Jim, containing many of the elements of Roché's and Truffaut's characters and their sexual and moral ambiguities, a melodrama that ended not with a murder-suicide but with Moreau attempting to leave Richardson for a young Greek. All that was missing from the casting of *Sailor from Gibraltar* was for Richardson himself to play the role of the narrator, baptised Alan.

In Duras's text, the sailor from Gibraltar, variously also named Pierrot and Gégé in his uncertain incarnations, is first found drifting at sea in extremis by the yacht *Cypris*. The female protagonist, Anna, the eventual owner of the yacht, began as a server crew member on board after drifting to Marseille from Paris. During the time the sailor spends on the yacht, they fall madly in love and pursue a torrid affair. Due to circumstances as ambiguous as always in Durasian narrative, the sailor fails to return to the ship in Shanghai (like Duras's own lost first love, he is resorbed into the mainland Chinese landscape). Anna marries the aging owner of the yacht who rechristens the vessel *Anna* (which every sailor knows is bad luck). Anna and her fugitive sailor lover are reunited once in Paris for five weeks after a chance meeting (a desultory scene in which he attempts to sell pornographic postcards to the couple she and her husband are with for the evening, a gesture that is transferred oddly to the narrator in the film). Her subsequent abandonment of her aging, wealthy husband leads to his suicide in England. When he dies, she thus inherits the boat and his immense fortune. In turn, she rechristens the yacht *Gibraltar*, in honor of her lover. Throughout the text are scattered transposed allusions to the rock: the Italian town of Rocca (the rock) where the narrator meets Anna; the fugitive sailor, Pierrot (Rocky).

The *Gibraltar* becomes an ironic and derisive echo of the eponymous British colony, a loose canon in ambiguous and uncertain pursuit rather than a sentinel rock. However, politically, the novel and the film thus reflect the left-wing anticolonialist views of all involved, especially Duras, who became a member of the Communist party. The narrator, who comes aboard without possessions as Anna's newest lover, has given up a job of ten years as a bureaucrat in the colonial office inscribing new births and is thus tied by fate to her search through the French colonial world for her missing other. He was also born and raised in a French colony, which in the anglicized film becomes Ceylon (Sri Lanka).

In a series of encounters and pursuits, Duras's text offers both a derisive parody of a maritime epic odyssey and an exercise in futility similar to Samuel Beckett's later *Waiting for Godot*, which appeared in 1956.

There are also references to Samuel Taylor Coleridge's *Rime of the Ancient Mariner* and the image of the albatros. Coleridge's poem contains numerous other thematic elements, which echo through the text, such as the lines quoted by Mechthild Cranston in exergue to an article on the text,

> And is that Woman all her crew?
> Is that a Death? and are there two?
> Is Death that woman's mate?[2]

The elusive sailor is furthermore a fugitive, running from the police, wanted for the murder of the ball-bearing king Nelson Nelson in the casino area of Montmartre. In the painful narrative present of deadend leads and drinking bouts are embedded a series of flashback-style tales of the history of the sailor from Gibraltar recounted by various characters, the story of Anna as told to the narrator in a café, and a series of other secondhand tales, recounted by the Greek Epanimondas, by the crewmembers Bruno and Laurent, and by Epanimondas's friend Louis. The plurality, ambiguity, and unreliability of these multiple, embedded narratives make the work a true *nouveau roman*. But generically the book is much more than the sum of its narratives.

Duras delights throughout her work in constructing an elaborate parody of macho narrative, particularly of Hemingway. Throughout the text are scattered references to the narrator's "American novel" that he will write of their adventure, as well as the expected self-reflexive narrative references characteristic of almost all "nouveau roman" writers. It is significant even if coincidental that *The Sailor from Gibraltar* appeared the same year as *The Old Man and the Sea*. Duras's text incorporates numerous sequences and characters based on earlier Hemingway works, namely his 1935 *Green Hills of Africa* and 1950 *Across the River and into the Trees* (set in Italy) or short stories such as *The Short Happy Life of Francis Macomber, A Clean Well-Lighted Place, The Snows of Kilimanjaro,* or *The Fable of the Good Lion*. At the time the novel appeared, this web of parodic intertextuality was interpreted literally by critics such as Gérard d'Houville, who said of the novel in "Lectures romanesques" (December 15, 1952), "If it did not bear the name of the writer, we could believe [it] to be an excellent French translation of an original Hemingway narrative."[3]

The stakes change in the course of Duras's text; what begins for the narrator as an "acte gratuit" of jumping ship in reverse and for Anna as a passionate pursuit of the lost grail of all-consuming love evolves into a search for innocence in the jungles of the eastern Congo. The hunt for the sailor is equated in the final sequence with that of the endangered and rare kudus, one of which is seen roasting on a spit in camp at the end of the book. Duras openly acknowledges the aleatory plurality of her text, as the narrator says, "Sometimes I have the impression that there are ten stories of the sailor from Gibraltar." The tale of the sailor's incarnation as Gégé, the tough guy of Dahomey, is recounted by a nameless black African schoolteacher friend of Louis who usurps the text and transforms it into an African epic tale. Duras offers a perfect pastiche of African Francophone storytelling. Louis in turn performs the tale of King Béhanzin and the treaty of 1890 (selling out his country to the colonial power) at the farewell dinner before they proceed to Léopoldville. And in a bar in Léopoldville, the text is taken over by a conversation between two white hunters, André Legrand and Henri, then drifts into a long polemic over primitive beasts (the invented "saumuriens" whose name has been singled out as a phonetic inversion of the name of Camus's protagonist Meursault of *The Stranger*) versus modern *homo sapiens*. At this point, a new character is introduced, Jojo from Indochina. Their final destination in the text is the village of Dodo (slang for "sleep" in French, as well as the name of an extinct species). There Anna finds a native woman who is obviously the current companion of the recently fled Gégé and who is fiercely defending her territory and her right to him. Abandoning the deepest jungles and this latest futile pursuit of the asymptotic sailor, Anna and her entourage receive a message from the Caribbean, where the narrator leaves them in suspense, stating in Proustian fashion that he cannot yet speak of their adventure there. It should have been obvious to Richardson that this eminently literary, intertextual, intoxicated romp was ill-suited to cinematic adaptation. In fact, the text reiterates obsessively its search for parentage and identity, its own generic uncertainty. But, as John Irving said in *The World According to Garp*, lust makes even the best men behave out of character, and this was a classic case of fools rushing in.

According to Richardson in his autobiography, Jeanne Moreau had expressed her love of Duras's book even before they began filming *Mademoiselle*. In a mad gesture, attempting to please his new love, Richardson hired on David Mercer in 1965 to work on a filmscript of the Duras text (which had not yet been translated into English; the English translation appeared the same year as Richardson's film). They planned to film *Mademoiselle* and *The Sailor from Gibraltar* back to back and then edit both films back in England. The yacht they rented for the film had to be returned by Christmas to Alexandria, Egypt. The film's ending thus is transposed from Hemingway's Cuba (now Castro's Cuba) to Alexandria, where they had to go anyway to return the boat. It is clear from Richardson's own account that he had no qualms about adapting the text from the beginning. He states in his autobiography years later that the tale went from Italy to Greece to Ethiopia to the jungle, when in fact the odyssey in Duras's text is quite different, as they proceed ever westward, up the Italian coast to the French coast at Sète, then importantly out through the straits of Gibraltar (one is tempted to call Richardson's whole project "the dire straits of Gibraltar") to the open ocean, first to Tangier in Morocco, then down the coast of Africa to Abidjan in the Ivory Coast and then through a fierce storm on to Dahomey (Bénin), then further south to Léopoldville in the Congo, then inland to the eastern Congo, the fabled darkest Africa of Stanley and Livingstone, full of legendary cannibals and headhunters and kudus. This itinerary is redolent of classic epics (of the exiled journey of Dionysus) and the adventure into the unknown of the Renaissance navigators. It also echoes, as I stated earlier, Duras's own odyssey westward by ship away from impossible love when she was exiled as a teenager by her own family from Vietnam to France. What in Duras's narrative is a complex fable of love, suffering, and death, her primary thematic, becomes in the hands of Richardson and his several screenwriters (the released film credits Christopher Isherwood, Don Magner, and Richardson, without David Mercer) an unwitting self-parody, a Chandleresque B-grade black and white film of frozen angst and stifled desire on the waterfront. Although these characters like Duras's fill their dead space with smoking and drinking, their dialogical exchanges culled from the novel and translated literally have none of the oneiric resonance and reflectivity achieved by the text and its "highfalutin French metaphysics" (Richardson 1993, 212). Only the opening credits of the film, which offer an intriguing series of images isolated on a black field, come close to achieving cinematically the complexity of Durasian narrative. Accompanied by haunting music by Antoine Duhamel, the images—of the statue head of a woman, then a teardrop containing a man, then the Parthenon caging a male head, then two nude lovers entwined—serve as screens onto which are projected other images, of water, of the hull of the yacht, and so on. One of these opening images offers the facade of a building from which protrude arms and hands pointing in all directions, recreating the surrealistic effects of the sconces in Jean Cocteau's 1946 *Beauty and the Beast.*

However, with the opening shot of the film, the travesty begins. In Duras's text, the trip in the truck (one of Duras's most original films is entitled *Le Camion, The Truck*) that carries the narrator and his girlfriend from Pisa to Florence initiates the narrator to the glories of Rocca and the "beautiful American woman" with the yacht. Several days later, they expend Herculean amounts of energy just to get to Rocca (it is 1947, and the trains are jammed); they never get on the train. The scenes in Rocca, at the village dance, at the river, and on the beach are filled with intensity, of desire, of baptism, of oppressive heat. The narrator sees the "American" woman first in the dunes and later at the hotel. Thus she is introduced as a mythical siren figure beckoning to the sea. At the hotel, a mass of grapes frames her, marks her as a Dionysian figure (the novel is dedicated to Duras's lover at the time, Dionys Mascolo). Throughout Richardson's film, it is apparent that he and his three screenwriters tried in vain to select moments, objects, gestures that would convey the sensorial and sensual richness and dramatic intensity of Duras's text, but her playful uncertainty of pastiche, parody, and homage is impossible to capture on film. Jeanne Moreau had already interpreted a Duras novel on film, and she carried throughout *Sailor* inside her head the resonance of the French text; it illuminates her performance. Ian Bannen's depressed, diffident reluctance conveys none of the narrator's anger or the energizing empowerment of his insane grasp at freedom, of his death and rebirth at this liminal point of passage where the river meets the sea. There is a profound existential significance to the last scene of part 1 of Duras's text, wherein the narrator walks the length of the beach in the dazzling heat after lunch (again like Camus's *The Stranger*) and falls asleep, to awaken a different man, only this time it is four short knocks on the door of happiness. Ian Bannen never manages to convey that joy, the Joycian epiphany of this newly reborn identity, who like Pirandello's late Mattia Pascal lifts anchor and cuts himself adrift. The narrator's long walk in the midday sun of Arab Africa upon their arrival in Tangier reiterates the allusion to the character of Meursault.

Although Duras's text is certainly not reducible to a parodic intertextual web and affirms on every page its innovative originality, the comparisons are inevitable, primarily because of her own repeated acknowledgement, with Hemingway. And one of the most difficult if not impossible challenges in cinematic history has been to incarnate and interpret the essence of the Hemingway-style hero, whose ideological identity is a conjunction of conflicting energies rather than a unified force. It is the paradoxical dynamic of this nexus that gives his sparse prose its lasting

FIGURE 6.1. *Sailor from Gibraltar* (Orson Welles, Jeanne Moreau)

attraction. The textbook description of his heroes portrays them as "passable combinations of adventure, brutality, drunkenness, sexual aggressiveness hiding deep frustrations, and artificial gaiety obscuring poorly the most desolate sadness, loneliness, and boredom."[4] This is a passable description of Richardson's film, which in no way manages to accommodate the subversive modernism of Duras's text. In spite of the fact that Richardson had two major figures of the French New Wave on his crew, Raoul Coutard and Truffaut's script girl Suzanne Schiffman, his film never achieves the violent energy of Godard's work or the auteur voice of Truffaut's lyric autocinography. It is ambiguous in its uncertainty and cynical in its purpose.

What is much more interesting and truly ironic is the series of events surrounding the production of the film, which mirrored unbelievably events in the diegesis of the film itself, an experience best illustrated on film by Truffaut in *Day for Night* (1973). Richardson has Anna and her *Gibraltar* sail not for Sète but for Greece, for Hydra. The arrival in the Greek port is accompanied by swelling Greek folk music redolent of Michael Cacoyannis's 1964 *Zorba the Greek* or Jules Dassin's 1960 *Never on Sunday*, a film that also pairs a naive tourist and a promiscuous woman. This Greek destination acknowledges the mythical elements of the ship's endless odyssey and ironically mirrors the melodrama that erupted when Richardson introduced a handsome young Greek, Theo Roubanis (a friend of Henry McIlhenny of Philadelphia), into the film and more particularly to Jeanne Moreau. This began a lengthy rivalry for her time and affections, which continued long after the filming had ended, a rivalry that was resolved only when Theo finally married Lady Sarah Churchill, whom he met (where else?) on McIlhenny's yacht. Before he was fired from the film, Theo constituted the real-life incarnation of *The Sailor from Gibraltar*, echoing the "A" (for Athena or adultery or amour) of Epaminondas's tatoo. In the film, Epaminondas has become Noori, interpreted by Zia Mohyeddin. In the film as in the text, the sailor in Hydra proves like Pierrot from Sète to be someone else.

Rather than script the sequences from Tangier or Abidjan or Dahomey, Richardson chose to transpose them to Ethiopia, where a Sydney Greenstreet-style character (played by Orson Welles) complete with fez and djellabah comes on board in the role of Louis to describe the figure whom he claims is her sailor. The incredibly rich sequences of the novel from the café in Léopoldville, with the embedded narratives, dialogues and theater, are lost to the film.[5] And the scenes in the café and the streets in Tangier are transposed to the end of the film to Alexandria, where Anna and the narrator embrace in the street between the passing trams. It is noteworthy that in Duras's text, the narrator's declaration of his love for Anna takes place while they are looking for a cinema.

As in Duras's text, Louis sends Anna and her entourage in pursuit of the fearless, white game hunter Gégé he has heard of from Legrand (in the Congo among the Momboutu), a hunter whom they compare to the legendary prize trophy kudu, already enjoying literary status from Hemingway's tales. They pursue Gégé to Léopoldville, then to a village he has just fled, and finally to the village of Dodo (which indicates, as do the sequences where characters fall asleep, that the whole novel is an oneiric fantasy). Richardson has them proceed rather to Addis Ababa, where they meet Legrand (played by an incorrigibly inebriated Hugh Griffith), who takes them inland, first to the village where the police have just chased off the elusive criminal sailor (hunter become hunted, predator become prey), and finally to the village where they meet the sailor's current paramour, a black African woman. The sequence between Anna and the black woman is rather faithfully recreated in the film, with the identification of the sailor again proven false. What is not recreated is the accidental burning of the *Gibraltar* at the end of Duras's text, which like the fire consuming the kudu creates an epuration and permits the rebirth of the narrative at its conclusion, in a Proustian invagination.

At this point, for a variety of reasons (obligatory destination of Alexandria, impossibility of filming in Castro's Cuba), Richardson and his screenwriters created an entirely new ending for their narrative, an act of cinematic delirium, where the sailor is actually located in a bar, from which he flees after starting a mêlée, like Cocteau's or Marcel Camus's Orpheus, with the narrator in hot pursuit. At this point, the script announces its own self-reflexive individuality, as the narrator muses that the chase was like something out of a "thriller, a mystery, like being in a movie." And when he embraces Anna between the two tram cars in the street afterward, his declaration of love seems to him "like lines from a movie...that's all I can ever say out the thousand things I want to express." In the next scene, they are watching a movie where a man reaches out to embrace a woman at a table in a restaurant, and she vanishes into thin air. The closing scene of the film portrays the crew on the same yacht once again, with Noori announcing that there is another message, this time from Yokohama. The screen irises out to frame in black the disappearing image of the yacht under sail. Richardson himself pursued his elusive love object for several months after the filming was completed.

When that relationship soured, and with the double guilt of a failed marriage and a failed film added to the burden, Richardson indulged in a *fugue* of his own and fled to Tahiti and Bora Bora, mythically sensual destinations, which ironically would perhaps have made a better setting for the film than the various shores of the Mediterranean. At the least it was a complete change of scenery to help him forget the incredible string of errors and disasters that had plagued the project from start to finish.

Originally distributed by United Artists, *The Sailor from Gibraltar* has never been released on video and is available only in film archives such as the Library of Congress.

NOTES

1. Robert Poulet, *Aveux spontanés: conversations avec...* (Paris: Plon, 1963) 111. Paraphrased in Gene Plunka, *The Rites of Passage of Jean Genet* (Cranbury, NJ: Associated University Presses, 1992), 284.

2. Mechthild Cranston, "Rehearsals in Bas Relief: *Le Marin de Gibraltar* of Marguerite Duras," *Studies in Twentieth-Century Literature* 17:2 (1993): 287.

3. Quoted and translated by Cranston, 287.

4. Alfred Cismaru, *Marguerite Duras* (Boston: Twayne, 1971) 17–18, quoted in Cranston, 287.

5. Especially Louis's performance as Béhanzin, the traitorous King of the Realm of Abomey who sold out his country to France in the treaty of 1890. After two years of military campaigns led by Dodds, Dahomey became a protectorate officially in 1894, and Béhanzin was banished to Algiers.

WORKS CITED

Chapier, Henri. "Jeanne Moreau sauve *Mademoiselle* de Tony Richardson du grotesque." *Combat* (13 May 1966).

Child-Olmstead, G. "Transfigurations of the Mother in Jean Genet." *The French Review: Journal of the AATF* 71:1 (October 1997).

Coe, Richard, ed. *The Theater of Jean Genet: A Casebook.* New York: Grove Press, 1970.

Cranston, Mechthild. "Rehearsals in Bas Relief: *Le Marin de Gibraltar* of Marguerite Duras." *Studies in Twentieth-Century Literature* 17:2 (Summer 1993), 287–307.

Eynard, Leupold. "Pour une approche active d'un texte littéraire." *Le Français dans le monde* 220 (October 1988) 62–65.

Fauvel, Maryse. "*Le Marin de Gibraltar* et *Détruire dit-elle* de Duras: Sous le signe de Dionysos." *The French Review: Journal of the AATF* 65:2 (December 1991): 226–35.

Giles, Jane. *The Cinema of Jean Genet: Un chant d'amour.* London: BFI Publications, 1991.

Lambert, Gavin. "Tony Richardson: An Adventurer." *Sight and Sound* 3:11 (November, 1993): 30–33.

Menager, Serge Dominique. "La Légende de Saint Genet du théâtre à la théâtralité." *Australian Journal of French Studies* 32:1 (January-April 1995) 66–76.

Moraly, Jean Bernard. *Jean Genet, la vie écrite.* Paris: La Différence, 1988.

Moraud, Yves. "La Dramaturgie de l'absence dans les théâtres de Marguerite Duras et de J. Genet." *Travaux de Linguistique et de littérature* 19:2 (1981) 201–17.

Radovich, Don. *Tony Richardson: A Bio-Bibliography.* Westport, CT: Greenwood Press, 1995.

Richardson, Tony. *The Long-Distance Runner: An Autobiography.* New York: Morrow, 1993.

Savona, Jeannette. *Jean Genet.* London: Macmillan, 1983.

Schuster, Marilyn. "Reading and Writing as a Woman: The Retold Tales of Marguerite Duras." *The French Review: Journal of the AATF* 58:1 (October 1984) 48–57.

Stewart, Harry. "Capefigue: An Historical Source for Jean Genet's Fantasies." *Romance Notes* 22: 3 (Spring 1982), 254–58.

Thody, Philip. *Jean Genet: A Study of His Novels and Plays.* London: Hamish Hamilton, 1968.

CHAPTER SEVEN

History Revisited:
The Charge of the Light Brigade *(1968)*

LINDA CONSTANZO CAHIR AND STEPHEN CAHIR

> MILITARY GLORY! It was a dream that century after century
> had seized on men's imaginations and set their blood on fire.
> Trumpets, plumes, chargers, the pomp of war, the excitement
> of combat, the exultation of victory—the mixture was intoxi-
> cating indeed. To command great armies, to perform deeds of
> valour, to ride victorious through flower-strewn streets, to be
> heroic, magnificent, famous—such were the visions that danced
> before men's eyes as they turned eagerly to war.
>
> —Cecil Woodham-Smith, *The Reason Why*

In *The Reason Why*, the highly regarded account of Britain's involvement
in the Crimean War, Cecil Woodham-Smith asserts that the sensibilities
that drove England's military leadership in its 1854 campaign against Russia were, at heart, fueled largely by dreams of pomp, manly tumult, and
soldierly display. War, with its intimations of military glory, was believed
to be an aristocratic trade, where leadership was reserved for nobles, who
had been trained, "as no common man was trained, by years of practice in
dangerous sports" (1953, 1). It was the sport of war as the supreme adventure that was the ruling *esprit* behind James Thomas Lord Brundenell, heir

of the sixth Earl of Cardigan; George Charles Lord Bingham, heir of the second Earl of Lucan; and Fitzroy James Henry Somerset, Baron Raglan of Raglan, the three principal military leaders of Britain's campaign in the Crimea in of support Turkey's conflict with Russia.

Thirty-nine years earlier, Russia had been an ally of Britain in the Napoleonic War. In the intervening years, Russia, seeking greater global strength, wanted naval access to the Mediterranean Sea; and, in an aggressive attempt to secure this right of entry, Czar Nicholas had set up a naval base at Sebastopol on the Crimean peninsula, from which, as if placing stepping stones in a lily pond, he planned to enter and secure Constantinople, Russia's intended gateway to the Mediterranean. England remained neutral until, on November 30, 1853, the Russian fleet left Sebastopol and destroyed a Turkish fleet. Russia's aggression, Britain believed, threatened all of Europe. Russia had declared itself a menace to world peace. The image of Russian warships commanding the Mediterranean speared England's rage and incited angry mobs to protest throughout London. War was inevitable.

For the Earl of Cardigan, fifty-seven, and the Earl of Lucan, fifty-four, war in the Crimea was the venture they had most sought. As Woodham-Smith explains, "dreams forty years old were coming true, trumpets were shrilling, squadrons gathering. . . . Military glory beckoned them at last" (1953, 135). Woodham-Smith locates her study of Britain's involvement in the Crimean War largely in the lives and decisions—the blunders and flaws of Cardigan, commander of the Light Brigade, and Lucan, commander of the Cavalry Division, who, as such, was Cardigan's direct military superior. Men of equal noble birth and wealth, Lucan—married to Cardigan's youngest sister—and Cardigan were bitter arch rivals, who had felt deep enmity, each for the other, since youth. Lord Raglan, commander-in-chief of the British Expeditionary Army to the East knew of their deep rancor, yet he appointed them to key interdependent positions anyway even while it was "'notorious in every circle acquainted with them both that the state of feeling which had long since existed between them was likely to lead to unpleasant results'" (137). The two appointments were greeted with "cynical amusement," exacerbated by Cardigan's declaration that "he would operate squarely on his own account: there would be no question of carrying out Lord Lucan's instructions" (137). Woodham-Smith makes evident that Lucan and Cardigan, both "proud, narrow, overbearing, and peremptory," allowed their rivalry, their animosity, their egos, and their inflated sense of military knowledge to contaminate their battlefield conduct. *The Charge of the Light Brigade*, Tony Richardon's 1968 filmic version of Britain's involvement in the Crimean War, acknowledges in the screen credits that his account is based on Woodham-Smith's book.

Preceding Richardson's film are four other versions of the famous charge of the English Light Brigade into the valley of Death, the event which Alfred, Lord Tennyson's poem made legend. The first two were undistinguished silent films (Biograph Studios in 1903 and Thomas Edison Studios in 1912). The third, an early British talkie titled *Balaclava* (1930), was released in the United States in 1931 as *The Jaws of Hell*, taking its American title from a collision of two of Tennyson's lines. The fourth, *The Charge of the Light Brigade* (1936), was directed by Michael Curtiz, starred Errol Flynn and Olivia de Haviland, and held little relation to either Tennyson's popular poetic account, from which the film took its title, or, more surprisingly, to the historical events. Instead of dramatizing the Crimean War and the military incompetence of the British, the movie is a Kiplingesque costume epic, set in India, not the Crimea, and centered on two brothers in love with the same woman and on an Indian potentate secretly plotting against the British. Characterized by Hollywood opulence and action, the movie is fully indifferent to historical accuracy, but, instead, attempts to be Warner Brothers' answer to the success that its competitor, Paramount, had with *The Lives of a Bengal Lancer* (1935).

In his autobiography, *Long Distance Runner*, Richardson mentions that as an eight-year-old boy, he saw this 1936 *Charge of the Light Brigade* in his local movie theater with his "Auntie Ethel." He remembers it. However, the only similarity Warner Brothers' film has to Richardson's film is the title. Used for its "obvious box-office heroics," the movie's title was the only regret Richardson cited about his work (1993, 240). By today's standards, the title is matchless in the resonating irony it suggests. Tennyson's *Charge of the Light Brigade*, informed by Victorian standards of staunch, unquestioning adherence to authority, states quite clearly that the duty of the cavalrymen was to follow blindly their military leaders: "Theirs not to make reply,/Theirs not to reason why,/Theirs but to do and die." For Tennyson, the duty of the common cavalryman, the source of his valor, grandeur, and virtue, was to march headlong—forward— "Into the valley of Death," even while "the soldier knew/Someone had blunder'd." As much a product of 1968 and the spirit of "questioning authority" that the Vietnam War stirred as Tennyson's poem was a prod-

164

FIGURE 7.1. *Charge of the Light Brigade* (David Hemmings as Captain Lewis Nolan)

uct of his time, Richardson's *Charge of the Light Brigade*, which cannot help but remind us of Tennyson's poem of the same title, challenges the moral worth of the Victorian ethos that Tennyson so fully lauded. Richardson's *Charge* charges us to question authority. Our valor and virtue are located in our moral awareness, he suggests, and our bravery is most worthily demonstrated when we do what we know and believe to be right.

Richardson was "passionate about the subject" (Richardson, 1993, 231), and he and John Osborne worked on a script based on *The Reason Why*, a work that Richardson described as a "brilliant piece of historical writing" (231). However, while the script retains much of the nippy taste of Woodham-Smith's prose, Richardson's film focuses, not on Lords Cardigan and Lucan as the book does, but on the well-trained, intelligent, and brave young Captain Lewis Nolan, who speaks out against the imbecility and ineptitude of the British military leadership.[1]

As Richardson was quite aware, the task of relating the historical background leading up to the charge of the Light Brigade at Balaclava, Crimea, in 1854 "is impossible, and especially difficult in film terms" (Richardson 1993, 239), but it was essential for what he wanted: "to do something different, to concentrate on the charge itself, on the mixture of heroism, romance, farce, and horror embodied in the actions of a much more panoramic group of characters, using as our central figure the enigmatic and dashing Captain Nolan" (231).

The real characters and events of the charge were brimful with heroism, romance, folly, and horror—courage and idiocies. As if to capture more purely these elements, Richardson tried to keep his version of the tale historically complete and accurate, down to the horse harnesses and the uniform buttons. The first cut of the film was excessive in length, and while its released version was pared to 128 minutes, the supervising editor, Kevin Brownlow, had wanted to make a second version, four and one-half hours long. He was never able to complete the project. Still, the commercial release sufficiently portrays the powerful individuals and the climate and society of Victorian England in 1854 so as to explain how and why the tragic event of the charge at Balaclava came to occur.

The film opens with an animated sequence in which the Russian bear attacks the helpless Turkish turkey, causing the sleeping English lion to awake, don a bobbie's cap, and resolutely stride forward. An animated horseman dissolves into the live-action Lord Cardigan (Trevor Howard), drilling his cavalry and getting the story underway. As soldiers drill, the young and handsome Captain Nolan (David Hemmings), back in England after serving in India, attends the wedding of army buddy William Morris (Mark Burns) and Clarissa Morris (Vanessa Redgrave). A series of scenes follows, developing the main characters while showing the sharp contrast between the lives of the upper and lower classes.

The Morris wedding reception, a bright scene filled with happy, well-fed people, is followed by the contrasting scene of a dark, dirty lower-class tenement area from which soldiers are recruited with promises of entering the respectable world of service to the queen. The contrast continues as the scene shifts to the officers' quarters. Clearly issuing from wealth and good breeding, the officers are seen lounging languidly and idly in palatial quarters until a cross-cut returns us to the world of the enlisted men, soldiers humiliated by their immediate superiors into thinking that they do not know their left feet from their right and that their worth to the cavalry is notably less than the worth of the horses who, throughout the film, are treated with greater respect and creature comforts than the men. The enlisted men reside with their wives and children in barracks that are over-crowded, dim, and shabby. These men will fight, risk their lives, and die to preserve a world order constructed of customs clearly of greatest benefit to the nobility, the officers. Richardson's sequence of contrasting scenes, at times too pointed, does insist that it should be the right, even the duty, of the common soldier to question *the reason why*.

In spirit Captain Nolan belongs neither to the world of the enlisted men nor to the world of his fellow officers. He is an outsider, made more alien from his peers by his constantly demonstrated expertise as a soldier and horseman, skills at which the other officers are, at best, merely competent. The character of Nolan is a great all-purpose composite. He demonstrates great heroism, great virtue in dealing with men and horses, and some lack of virtue in dealing with Clarissa Morris. He is made the personification of Britain's military strength, its frustration, and, finally, its inconceivable blunder. Deep though his meritorious qualities extend, Nolan is not the pure, heroic ideal as is shown early on in his betrayal of Morris, his closest friend and fellow officer, by the casual affair with Morris's newly wedded wife, Clarissa.

The traits that we see in the characters during peaceful times will explain their eventual actions in the historic charge. Lord Lucan (Harry Andrews) is as stalwart in his arrogant stupidity as Lord Cardigan is brimming with haughty ineptitude. Both are shown to be aristocratic senior officers who, in accordance with the prevailing custom, purchased their rank.

The film spends a good deal of time with Cardigan, played wonderfully by Trevor Howard, entertainingly arrogant, toplofty, and rude. In a scene lifted straight from history, Cardigan is shown strutting along a London sidewalk as lines of soldiers appear and salute him. Cardigan's feelings of exaltation are undiminished by the fact that he has arranged this "spontaneous display" by paying a shilling to each soldier for the honor. The brash Cardigan reflects the aristocratic air of superiority over the British Empire's own as he voices his bigoted resentment of soldiers and officers who served in India, despite (or because of) the fact that they actually have been engaged in battle, while he has not. Lord Lucan is not introduced until later in the film and tends to come off as merely grumpy in demeanor and barely competent militarily.

The film also makes much of Paymaster Duberly (Peter Bowles) and his wife, Fanny Duberly (Jill Bennett), who desperately want to be aristocrats though they vaguely sense the inanity and mean-spiritedness of those such as Cardigan. Fanny is used in voice-overs narrating what is really going on underneath the pretense that the aristocrats present. "Duberly says . . ." she repeatedly confides while telling us something Paymaster Duberly and most of the command may think, though certainly would never publicly say. However, having set her sights on Cardigan as a means of entry into that world, Fanny seduces him (on Cardigan's well-appointed yacht moored on the fringes of the battlefield) in a ribald, comic, and strapping sequence wonderfully reminiscent of Richardson's *Tom Jones*. Fanny, who knows how to bring out the best in Cardigan's horsemanship, leaves us bemused over what Duberly might say about *this*.

Fanny and Cardigan, much like Clarissa and Nolan, conduct themselves in strict moral probity when they are in society; however, their conduct in private is quite another matter. The scenes involving Clarissa and those involving Fanny have been harshly criticized as adding little to a film whose time constraints would have been better served in clarifying the historical gaps the movie creates. However, the Clarissa and Fanny sequences are vital to what Richardson is attempting to say: the stress on the *appearance* of proper conduct, which cuts to the heart of the Victorian ethos, would be really quite funny if it were not so very deadly—literally.

The lethalness of the importance of appearances, which reaches its deadly epic proportions at the charge itself, is rendered in miniature in the "black bottle" scene. Cardigan is shown presiding over the officers' mess as his sycophants laugh at his hazing of one of his own young officers, the unfortunate Coddington, who is forced to eat greens because he is green with inexperience. This boyish prank is devised by the brigade's commander himself—Lord Cardigan—against one of his own officers, showing Cardigan to be something of an ungentlemanly ninny. As a member of the aristocracy, however, Cardigan believes that, by birth, he is a gentleman, and, in line with the idea that his gentleman officers must look good at all times, Cardigan orders that the men drink only champagne at dinner. Ironically, in insisting on the *appearance* of strict gentlemanly comportment, Cardigan proves himself to be the epitome of coarseness. Nolan, acting as a true and consummate gentleman, orders a bottle of Moselle that a guest desires. Cardigan sees it and, convinced that the black wine bottle is porter beer—the lowly and ungentlemanly drink of the troops in India—becomes enraged. Cardigan refuses to hear Nolan's explanation, and Nolan, in turn, refuses to apologize for a social transgression that he feels he did not commit. In consequence, Cardigan orders Nolan arrested. Accusing Nolan of impropriety and absurdly arresting him because the black bottle defied a gentleman's code of conduct, Cardigan, concerned only with the appearance of propriety, acts, in reality, in a most boorish and ill-bred way—bigoted, pernicious, and vindictive.[2]

During this same dinner, the officers belittle the Russian soldiers for going to battle wearing drab gray uniforms, in contrast to the handsome short red jackets, bright gold buttons, and tight pants bought by Cardigan for his troops. The Russian uniforms are not dashing; they do not create the appearance of military glory. Concerned with the pomp of war, the dashing appearance of valor, the British officers ridicule the very feature of the Russian uniforms that makes them so much less obvious visual targets than the Light Brigade will become. For the British officers, with crowds from home transported to the battlefront to watch the spectacle as if at a parade ground, there is no point in attempting heroics if they cannot be seen doing so. The need to appear heroic, rather than to be heroic demonstrates the false sense of heroism that permeates the British military leadership.

Shortly after the incident in the officers' mess, Lord Cardigan attends a performance of *Macbeth* where the audience, having read of Nolan's arrest and angered by it, starts a chant of "Black Bottle!" In the background, we see the stage and the actors; and, if we eavesdrop on them, filtering out the film's dominating dialogue, we realize that we are watching that portion of act 4, scene 1 where the Apparition cautions Macbeth to "Beware Macduff!" as Macbeth, the king and leader of England's army, readies for battle. The prophecy clearly warns that he must beware Macduff, respect his military potency; but Macbeth is filled with a false sense of invincibility, much as Cardigan is; and Macbeth, much like the Lords Cardigan and Lucan, arrogantly believes that he is ordained to military victory. Like them, Macbeth is defeated in a battle (which he too miscalculates) on the plains.

Driven by arrogance and rivalry and stewing over the insubordination of the talented Captain Nolan, Cardigan solicits a twenty-year veteran sergeant major to spy on Nolan and report the slightest transgression back to him. The sergeant major respectfully declines, citing qualms of conscience and loyalty. Unjustly (and ironically) accused and found guilty of dereliction of duty, he is stripped of his rank and flogged in front of the soldiers, who blindly accept the judgment that they know to be iniquitous. Blind compliance, the importance of maintaining appearance above all, and the haughty ineptitude of the aristocratic leadership are the three factors, Richardson keeps reminding us, most responsible for the tragedy of the Light Brigade.

Haughty ineptitude to the point of grave imbecility characterizes Lord Raglan's (John Gielgud), behavior in a scene that parallels Cardigan's attempt to recruit a spy from his own ranks. The night before the charge, Lord Lucan captures a Russian spy who offers significant information regarding the Russian's plans for attack upon the British the next day. Amazingly, however, Raglan refuses to talk to the man or even listen to what he has to say, instead berating Lucan for even thinking that *he*, Lord Raglan, would admit a spy into his presence and dismissively scolding the Russian for being a traitor to his country.

Lord Raglan had served as Wellington's aide and had lost his sword arm at Waterloo. However, by 1854, the Raglan that we see is doddering and distracted. When first encountered in the film, he is concerned only with the huge statue of Wellington, which sits on a dolly right outside his window and in whose shadow he daily works—literally. The great symbolic hero-warrior, the Duke of Wellington who defeated the seemingly invincible Napoleon, exists as a huge, dark, rolling statue, which Lord Raglan, the current commander-in-chief does not quite know where to put or what to do with—comically emblematic of what we will later witness: Raglan's indecisive, dawdling, and ultimately lethal management of the brave and well-trained troops who are ready for battle.

Vain, pompous, and too proud or too unwitting to acknowledge that the task requires much greater military acumen than he possesses, Raglan decides to head the British expedition to Crimea himself. Mindful of the animosity of Lucan and Cardigan, officers who are about to work jointly leading brigades of men into battle, Raglan merely directs his aide, General Airey (Mark Dignam) to "do what you can to keep them apart."

Gielgud's Raglan is a marvelous cartoon of a British commander-in-chief, a live-action version of the animation used elsewhere in the film. He announces, "It's war, gentlemen!" and gives a speech about the necessity for Britain to fight the Russians in Crimea, saying at one point that he preferred to consider Turkey not as a weak "stick-man" nation but as "a young lady lashing fluttered, defenseless if she should fall to the tyrant."

The animation (by Richard Williams) incorporated into the film is done in the style of Victorian cartoons, most notably the period's *Punch* cartoons. The animation illuminates as much as it entertains, and Richardson uses it effectively "to punctuate his social criticism" (Welsh 1984, 447). In one animated sequence, the strong, masculine British lion saves a Turkish turkey turned fainting woman from the threats of the crude Russian bear, as a banner reading "Right against Wrong" unfurls. It was not the moral imperative to right a wrong that motivated England's entry into war, but rather commercial considerations. Animation is employed effectively also to explain and compress historical events as when, with wit and speed, it maps the route the British took through the Mediterranean to Constantinople and finally to Calamita Bay in Crimea. The same sequence also portrays the prevailing English attitude as British forces are shown coming from under the vast skirts of the just and powerful queen and moving through the Mediterranean in a dreamy, cloud-filled voyage to Constantinople. The sequence includes Lord Cardigan (almost as animated in cartoon form as Trevor Howard plays him) in his private yacht steaming past his superiors, Raglan and Lucan, and beyond their control. All the ships go into a dark, stormy Calamita Bay, the expedition's landing site in Crimea.

The animation took much longer to complete than either Richardson or Williams had anticipated. They had intended to use more animated sequences and were adding them right up to the film's release. The sequences in the film not only added a satirical edge but also helped explain those historical events that, while perhaps common knowledge to the average British audience, are not as well known to outsiders. An animated map of the Crimean peninsula and the terrain of the valley, as Woodham-Smith included in her book, would have been helpful to most audiences.

The British landing in Crimea is portrayed as a loosely organized, comedic undertaking where different groups of British forces, who should be working together, have little to do with one another, except to get in each other's way. The expedition includes Mrs. Duberly, other wives, and Squire De Burgh (Willoughby Goddard) who is portrayed as a personification of the worst of the pampered and idle British aristocracy. As Richardson presents him, he is impeccably dressed, grossly obese, and cruelly snobbish, only interested in war as a spectator's sport.

Once ashore, the expedition marches off into Crimea, stepping out in perfect formation, a merry parade complete with marching music. Soon, though, the music stops. There is only the faint dirgelike beat of one drum and the sound of buzzing flies. The parade ends; the overbearing heat and dust are palpable. Soldiers are scattered and dropping from horses; there is no formation; there is no water. The war has commenced.

The British first engage the Russians at Alma. Raglan is shown as inept, to the point of being comedic. When the British infantry attack on the Russians successfully drives the Russians back, General Airey rightly implores Raglan to order the cavalry to pursue the vulnerable Russians. Raglan fatuously refuses, instead wishing to keep the cavalry "in a bandbox," out of range of battle. This is both distressing to the infantrymen who remain fighting and annoying to the cavalry who want to start. One wonderfully compressed scene establishing the farcical ineffectuality of the British leadership shows General Airey, confused by Raglan's approach and seeking concrete military direction from him, inquiring, "How do you want it to go, my lord?" Raglan replies, "Of course, Airey, I should want us to win."

Richardson subtly reminds us that all battles carry horrors, even for the victors. We see British soldiers from the successful Airy skirmish lying dead and dying in the background as Mrs. Duberly complains that the battle offered her nothing to see. Her husband agrees, saying, in his affected aristocratic speech, that the battle was "dweadfully" dull because the "cavalwy" had not been used. Nolan, seeing the dead and dying, becomes frustrated at Raglan's nonchalance and his refusal to employ cavalry and insists that the cavalry could have routed the Russians and probably taken the ultimate objective of the expedition, the port city of Sebastopol. However, the leadership was so pleased to have won the battle of Alma that the English newspapers incorrectly reported that the force had actually taken Sebastopol.

The next day the battle is made legend by the Light Brigade's charge. The Russians attack the British gun positions or "redoubts," and Nolan alone foresees that the Russians plan to seize the redoubts and control the road to Sebastopol. Just as Nolan had foreseen, the Russians do overrun the British redoubts and start to cart away the British guns. Outraged and alone in his understanding that decisive military action must be taken, he mounts to the hilltop vantage point where Commander-in Chief Raglan and other on-lookers picnic and watch the heroics below. There, Nolan rightly insists that Raglan take action. He does and has Airey write down the order for the cavalry to "advance rapidly to the front." Faithful to the historical accuracy of visual details, the film's actual note looks remarkably like the real note, which still exists and was reproduced in *The Reason Why*.

Nolan delivers the order to Lucan and Cardigan in the valley below, as Raglan is shown to be drifting still further from reality, sitting in his chair explaining to Mrs. Duberly that she should look into the pretty valley where the cavalry is going to get its guns back, not into the other valley, the "nasty valley full of half the Russian army." Raglan almost seems to realize that disaster awaits, saying that riding into the nasty valley would give the cavalry a "bloody nose" which, he declares, would be "not pretty." But he is helpless to avoid it; instead he then babbles on that babies are pretty as is some table linen.

Lucan and Cardigan are in a valley and cannot see the guns being moved from the British redoubts along the Causeway Heights and in the smaller North Valley, the area they should be attacking. "Attack what!?" they cry. (Animation here would have been very helpful to explain the geography of the valley, which Lucan and Cardigan themselves did not fully understand.) So frustrated by their repeated refusal to act, by their recurrent and flagrant military complacency and ineptitude, and simply eager and impatient to get underway, Nolan snaps, yells, and points, incorrectly, to the larger North Valley. "There is your enemy!" he shouts and contemptuously gestures. Cardigan for the first time shows some military savvy and states that such an attack, that is, having cavalry charge through enemy artillery is "contrary to the practice of war." Lucan and Cardigan, who previously have never been seen agreeing on anything, momentarily look at each other as if understanding that an attack into the larger valley, which they seemingly are being ordered to make, is a terrible idea.

It was, of course. The larger North Valley was a secure Russian hold, with cannons positioned to the right, to the left, and in front of the route the British entered. What was Nolan thinking? Cardigan and Lucan indicate that they must follow orders and have no choice. The cavalry starts walking forward, Cardigan at the head. From the heights, the view of the large, well-ordered cavalry brigade moving forward is magnificent. But at the end of the valley the Russians shake their heads in disbelief and get their artillery ready. The sound of buzzing flies is heard. As the brigade goes forward, speed and excitement pick up. Nolan seems unable to contain himself and rides up out of formation and to the front. The very first shot fired by the Russians explodes, killing him. Curiously, while Richardson wished to show the horror of war, Nolan's on-screen death is not very horrific. It is subdued, quiet, anticlimatic, and much more meaningful as such. In contrast, Woodham-Smith's description has Nolan's chest torn open, sentimentally exposing his heart (1953, 245).

The brigade thunders forward, moving fast and sounding powerful. However, they are soon struck by the even stronger sound of booming Russian artillery. Men and horses are killed or knocked down and trampled by the ever-onrushing brigade. Those who continue ride straight into the Russian artillery position and engage in hand-to-hand combat with Russian horsemen and foot soldiers. As the smoke clears, the picnickers on the hilltop see stragglers returning, they see Nolan's horse come back, and they eventually realize that everything has gone terribly wrong and that the Light Brigade has been decimated.

In their worst moment, the characters' full colors are brought out. As men limp or crawl into the British position, Cardigan vents angrily about Nolan and mutters, "Has anyone seen my regiment?" He quickly declares, "Men, it was a mad-brained trick, but no fault of mine." Immediately, Raglan challenges Cardigan and says he was ordered by his superior officer, Lucan. Lucan, in turn, blames the order written by Raglan who, in turn, blames Airey who actually wrote the note containing the order. Airey yells out that he will not be blamed.

The argument continues over scenes of wounded, bloodied men shooting horses and a long shot of the valley strewn with dead men and horses. Once again, there is the sound of buzzing flies, and a shot of a dead horse goes from live action to animation.

Rather than subvert the realities of history, as the 1936 *Charge of the Light Brigade* did, Richardson's film has us stare full-face into the ineptitude, the denials, the hubris, and the folly that resulted in the Light Brigade's tragic ride into the valley of Death. Released in 1968, the movie cannot help but remind us of America's Vietnam debacle, which exposed the same human conduct and squalid power politics that Richardson's film, about a different age, exposed: gross ineptitude, hierarchical denials, blind compliance with military orders, vast hubris in the leadership, and life-destroying inanity. We are reminded of the protests that that war incited when we watch the protest scene from *The Charge of the Light Brigade*. An antiwar demonstrator, who dares to speak out against England's involvement in the Crimean War, attracts an attentive crowd. Cardigan on his charger, accompanied by select officers on horseback, rides right up into the crowd, dispersing it, and breaking up the rally. Cardigan and his chums shout to the Crimean protesters, "Go back to Russia!" in a response evocative of the "Love it or leave it" shibboleth often shouted at American protesters of the Vietnam War.

Nolan, young and idealistic and long-haired, looks like a 1968 version of an antiwar protester, not a cinematic war hero. And Lucan, Cardigan, and Raglan seem comically impossible as the highest-level commanders of the army of the world's greatest power. But, even while Richardson's *Charge of the Light Brigade* reflects the historical time in which it was produced, his film simultaneously stands as a realistic treatment of real people in a real event, people and events that would be delightfully ludicrous and amusing if they had not been real.

NOTES

1. Richardson and Osborne sought to avoid the problems that would result from "trespassing on the original digging" Woodham-Smith had done by setting up a "research department" under military historian John Mollo (the screen credit lists Mollo under "Historical Research"). However, their script borrowed so heavily from Woodham-Smith's work as to result in a lawsuit brought by actor Laurence Harvey, who at the time held the rights to the book. Legal details were worked out, including Richardson's agreement to give Harvey a small role that John Osborne had been going to play. This destroyed the friendship between Richardson and Osborne for a long time, though in the end Harvey's performance was cut from the film as released anyway. (For an account of the handling of Harvey's role, see the interview chapter, which suggests that Richardson took pleasure in cutting the role.)

2. There was an actual "black bottle" incident involving Lord Cardigan, though, as told by Woodham-Smith, it took place in 1840 and involved an "Indian" officer, Captain John Reynolds. See *The Reason Why* , 1953, 58–59.

WORKS CITED

Richardson, Tony. *The Long Distance Runner: A Memoir.* New York: Morrow, 1993.

Welsh, James M. "Tony Richardson." *The International Dictionary of Films and Filmmakers.* Vol. II. Chicago: St. James Press, 1984, 446–48.

Woodham-Smith, Cecil. *The Reason Why.* Bungay, Suffolk: Richard Clay and Company, Ltd., 1953.

CHAPTER EIGHT

King of Infinite Space:
Richardson's Hamlet (1969)

PAUL MEIER

For many theatre folk, as well as for the general public perhaps, *Hamlet* is the supreme opus of the Shakespearean canon, maybe of all dramatic literature.

For the public, the tale of the young prince learning from his father's ghost that the dead king perished at the hand of his own brother, and enraged by his mother's "o'erhasty" marriage to the usurping assassin has a special place among our tribal stories. It possesses that special quality of classics—reading it or seeing it for the first time is like *remembering* it. In the castle of Elsinore, a huge and complex drama of human action and motive is played out as vividly and resonantly as in any other play that comes to mind.

For young male actors of the heroic type, the melancholy Dane, endlessly vacillating between action and inaction, wrestling with his demons, speaking what are possibly the four greatest verse soliloquies in the language, is the role coveted beyond all others. It is the theatre game played for the very highest stakes.

For directors, similarly, taming this monster of a play, one of the bard's longest, looms as a project to make or break careers. Staging or filming it, the director engages with a parable as potent as that of Arjuna in the *Baghavad Gita*, a parable of the metaphysics of human action. The play is such an infinitely faceted jewel, with such alluring depths, that the storyteller who takes it up can be dazzled or drowned. The story is bigger than directors and can easily overpower them. Yet, almost fatally, it draws them.

Tony Richardson was drawn. In 1969, in a bold conception, he staged *Hamlet*, his only Shakespeare film, at the Roundhouse, an avant-garde London theatre space occupying a former locomotive roundhouse, and he simultaneously filmed it there, using the same actors, costumes, and almost the same settings. By day the camera watched, and, by night, the paying customers.

Yet this was no mere filmed record of a stage play for it possesses a complete synergy between camera and action, something often missing from stage plays on film. However, the adaptation for camera did not demand so total a metamorphosis as it otherwise might have, for arena-style theatre productions, or productions mounted on thrust stages, as this one was, have already built into them, by their very nature, the multiplicity of camera angles on which film thrives. In such a theatre production, sharply different from proscenium theatre where the picture frame is composed for front viewing only, the camera can "slide in" among the players, recording events already staged for viewing from any angle by an audience that almost completely surrounds it.

It was this initial, bold conception of Richardson that set up the conditions that made this film the compelling and powerful work it is. For thrust stage production, the style that Shakespeare had in mind when he wrote the play, must forego solid sets that enclose and delimit the action. For most audience members, their gaze, no matter where they sit, will always penetrate the acting space to the theoretical infinity of the space beyond. Attempts to define and delimit location in arena staging by the use of representational scenery will often fail because it tends to obstruct sight lines and, what is more important, because it makes finite the infinity of the "sacred" circle.

Theatre productions in the round, then, or in severe thrust config-urations, work best with texts that do not depend on highly defined loca-tions or with texts that have the sense of location embedded in them. Shakespeare, as we all know, wrote this kind of play, and while *Hamlet* requires a grave for Ophelia, an arras behind which Polonius must die, and one or two other scenic devices, none of the locations is so highly defined as to absolutely require representation. The theatre platform itself becomes "the space" in which the words are spoken, a space infinitely accommodating, shifting in scale and scope according to the scale and the scope of the text.

And so, because Richardson was committed to filming mostly on the same set on which the play was staged for the theatre audience (he also filmed in the building's cellars and tunnels) and because the style of the theatre production essentially precluded material boundaries to the acting space, he was almost automatically committed to the same style on film. More frequently than not, what his lens records in this remarkable film is actors lit against a very indeterminate background (a tapestry, the prosaic back wall of the theatre itself) or simply a void.

This, I suggest, is the source of the film's unique strength, for, while it is a 100 percent *film* experience rather than a hybrid, it necessarily partakes of the infinitude of the *theatrical arena*, for which the play was written. If one contrasts Olivier's *Hamlet*, say, with Richardson's, the solidity and specificity of location is one of the startling differences. Because of the specificity of place in Olivier's version, when it comes to the soliloquies, for example, the question is always begged, "Is he *thinking* this or *speaking* it?" This question arises precisely because the character is depicted on a cliff top, in a throne room, or in some other highly defined location. If the character speaks aloud, one is led to wonder who is beyond that door or around that corner who might overhear. It is in the very nature of a specifically defined location, whether constructed of wood and plaster or found in a natural outdoor setting, that such questions must arise. Olivier chose to speak much of Hamlet's soliloquy text in "voice over," perhaps recognizing this limitation of specifically defined locations. In Richardson's version, one will notice, the question of who might overhear simply never arises, because the text has been freed from the tyranny of finite space. I have never seen soliloquy work better on film than in Richardson's *Hamlet*, and I am sure it is for this reason as much as any other. To paraphrase the Dane himself, Richardson, though "bounded in a nutshell" (the cramped Roundhouse), made himself "a king of infinite space" by eschewing representational scenery.

In making this fundamental design decision, Richardson gave huge responsibility to his actors. There is almost nothing in this *Hamlet* that is not actor-generated. Of course, there are costumes and hand props, and the extensive use of torches and candles contrasting with the murky, shadowy backgrounds is very effectively scenographic, yet it is the faces and voices of the actors that provide, almost totally, the experience of this film for the audi-

FIGURE 8.1. *Hamlet* (Nicol Williamson and Judy Parfitt)

ence. There is very little music, no ocean swirling at the foot of the cliffs, no battlements, no vaulted throne rooms. At every step of the way, the *actors* carry the film, create the rhythms, the tempo, the sense of whether they are in a small or large room, and all other dynamics. They seem, too, to lead the camera at all times, never appearing to come to their "mark."

This huge reliance on the acting is another happy consequence of Richardson's initial conception—to produce simultaneously for film and stage—for theatre thrives or dies by the strengths of the players.

And Richardson not only had the phenomenal Nicol Williamson in the title role but also the equally amazing Anthony Hopkins as Claudius, Judy Parfitt as Gertrude, Michael Pennington as Laertes, Marianne Faithfull as Ophelia, Mark Dignam as Polonius, Gordon Jackson as Horatio, Roger Livesey as first player and grave-digger, and a strong supporting cast that doubled and tripled, theatre-style, in the smaller parts. It is from the interaction of these fine players, from the rhythms that they created under Richardson's direction before a live audience that the film draws its strength. Although edited by Charles Rees, his hand is almost nowhere to be seen. Many a scene consists of one complete, uncut take! Others profit from conventional intercutting between different takes shot from different points of view—the play-within-a-play most notably—but this is the exception rather than the rule. A very skilled Gerry Fisher, perhaps sometimes using a hand-held camera (for this film predates the Steadycam), unobtrusively insinuates himself among the players like one of them, making the film technology marvelously transparent. It is true that flaws in composition occasionally result, that sometimes a face is infelicitously shadowed, but often Richardson has chosen to use a technically marred take for the *performance* it records. No doubt, only purists are distracted by these minor problems for the performances are so true and strong that the camera often becomes journalistic rather than artistic, witnessing rather than creating, and errors of composition and lighting are easily forgiven.

Unlike Kenneth Branagh whose recent *Hamlet* is remarkable for keeping every single line (and runs over four hours as a result), Richardson, in common with most other directors of the play on film, cut the text extensively, and, in a relatively minor way, changed the order of the scenes, transposing some dialogue. By watching with folio in lap, one discovers that a surprising 50 percent of the text has been jettisoned, though so seamless is Richardson's literary editing that one is never jarred. Occasionally, a cut begins midline and is cobbled onto another edited half-line with a metrically balky result, yet the flow of the story is always smooth. Like many others, Richardson chose to excise completely the Norwegian subplot, a piece of surgery easy to accomplish and leaving only the faintest scar. One misses the quickened subliminal pulse generated by the mysterious and urgent preparation for war ("And why such daily cast of brazen cannon / And foreign marts for implements of war / Why such impress of shipwrights, whose sore task / Does not divide the Sunday from the week"), the sense that the secret evil of the assassination has had international repercussions for Denmark and that the crown is ultimately lost to the Norwegian, Fortinbras, a distinctly karmic consequence. But I think this a small price to pay for the swifter and more concentrated story that it buys.

With unerring film instincts, Richardson often cuts the concluding rhyming couplet of a scene, a device that greatly facilitates an actor's exit in the *theatre*, and provides satisfying prosodic scene division, but which is redundant to the *filmmaker*, with jump cuts at his or her disposal. (I am sure these lines would have been retained for the live theatre version.)

But, happily, few of Hamlet's lines are lost, for it is, of course, Nicol Williamson's now legendary performance that lies at the heart of this project. And what a blessing it is that this troubled and erratic actor's performance in this role was recorded for all subsequent performances of the role must surely take account of his. Despite appearing to be of an age with the actors playing Claudius and Gertrude, a problem perhaps less troubling to the theatre audience, Williamson's rich and varied voice, his mercurial shifts of mood, his penetrating intellectual command of the ideas, his enormous emotional range, and his astonishing charisma all combine to produce a performance of immense power and credibility. The remarkable scene with his mother (III.iv) has a breathtaking range of emotion and subtext. Whereas Olivier merely raged at his mother ("cruel" but not "kind"), Williamson reveals grief, pity, love, anger, and much more. A complex mother/son relationship can be inferred. Moreover, Judy Parfitt's Gertrude modulates Williamson's Hamlet just as much as the reverse. A strong sense emerges that these two performances evolved in tandem, unlike in many films—notorious for their short gestation—where the star's performance seems impervious to those of supporting players.

Among many other remarkable scenes by remarkable actors is the play-within-a-play (III.ii) and Anthony Hopkins' performance. In silence and stillness Hopkins conveys that Claudius is cut to the very quick by the reenactment of his poisoning of his brother, the king. His shock and horror in the seemingly endless pause before his "Give me some light! Away!" are palpable and sickening.

Memorable too, as the first player, is Roger Livesey's recitation of Aeneas' account of Priam's death which provides a potent catalyst for Hamlet's question:

> Is it not monstrous that this player here
> But in fiction, in a dream of passion;
> Could force his soul so to her own conceit
> That from her working all his visage wann'd,
> Tears in his eyes, distraction in's aspect,
> A broken voice and his whole function suiting
> With forms to his conceit? and all for nothing!
> For Hecuba!

The vital yet often marginalized role of the Player, is essential if the dramatic irony of Hamlet's own presumably broken voice and tears (confronting Gertrude, perhaps, or when confessing love for Ophelia at her grave) is to be achieved. Shakespeare, by having a player weep freely at the drop of a hat, "all for nothing," deliberately risks making "nothing" out of Hamlet's own similarly "fictional" sorrows. This aesthetic distancing is vital to what I take to be Shakespeare's overarching spiritual objectives— to render the mundane affairs of men antlike in the light of the larger story of their souls' progress. By such meticulous attention to the casting and performance of the player, and by allowing it exclusive occupancy of the lens for its duration, Richardson reveals the maturity of his vision. Olivier, in contrast, notorious for tilting productions toward his own performance, cut the player's speech entirely, Branagh larded Charlton Heston's more than competent recitation with redundant flashback enactment of its story. Richardson allowed a fine actor his moment in the sun, trusting that the performance would adequately support the play and echo eloquently later on. Again we see ensemble acting at its best, nurtured by a long run in the theatre.

At the heart of *Hamlet* is the idea of the theatre itself, so rich a metaphor for appearance and reality. Hamlet, appearing first in mourning garb, tells Gertrude:

> 'Tis not alone my inky cloak, good mother
> Nor customary suits of solemn black,
> Nor windy suspiration of forc'd breath,
> No, nor the fruitful river in the eye,

> Nor the dejected 'haviour of the visage
> Together with all forms, modes, shows of grief
> That can denote me truly; these indeed *seem*
> For they are actions that a man might *play:*
> But I have that within which passeth show;
> These but the trappings and the suits of woe.
> (Italics mine)

From the start then, the metaphors are theatrical. An actor, playing Hamlet, feigns madness. An actor, playing Ophelia, plays "real" madness. An actor, playing an actor, recites a speech from another play, and sheds "real" tears. Actors, playing Gertrude or Hamlet, in the fictive "reality" of the play, *Hamlet*, shed "real" tears. Hamlet, eschewing all surer and more logical means of verifying Claudius' guilt in the king's death, settles on the rather improbable device of presenting *The Mousetrap* (referred to in II.ii as *The Murder of Gonzago*) to the court, to determine the matter. Hamlet is so scrupulous in his demand for proof that he hesitates to act on the evidence of the ghost itself:

> The spirit I have seen
> May be the devil: and the devil hath power
> To assume a pleasing shape; yea, and perhaps
> Out of my weakness and my melancholy—
> As he is very potent with such spirits—
> Abuses me to damn me. I'll have grounds
> More relative than this: the play's the thing
> Wherein I'll catch the conscience of the king.
> (II.ii)

Yet he will trust the dubious evidence of Claudius' inevitably ambiguous reaction to the play? Shakespeare could have had Hamlet verify the ghost's veracity by any number of other stratagems. Oracle, torture, testimony of the apothecary or Claudius' confessor: any number of ways come to mind. But the theatrical metaphor suits his metaphysical purposes. Reality within reality within reality, like the hall of mirrors in Branagh's *Hamlet* is what he sought.

Any director of *Hamlet* must take account of this overarching metaphor and be judged by the resonances he allows it to evoke. Richardson, to my mind, succeeded especially well in this matter. The scenographic indeterminateness is the first way in which he introduces this important slipperiness and elusiveness, as I have already argued. He achieves it in several other significant ways.

The ghost: Richardson's choice in representing the ghost is to herald its appearance by a sound effect (a shimmering, metallic, gonglike sound), by a blinding light on the faces of those who see the ghost, and by having its lines "voice over." These add up to a stunningly effective choice. It neatly stops the audience from speculating about the technology used to create the ghost effect, an unfortunate weakness of many productions where the ghost is personated visibly by an actor, or where tricks of lighting or other special effects are employed. Ironically, Richardson's ghost, conjured in the audience's imagination by such gentle means, is as "real," if one can use such a term of a ghost, as any other I can imagine. (Gielgud's portrayal of the ghost in Branagh's *radio* production of *Hamlet* succeeds equally well.) The fact that Williamson himself provides the ghost's voice, compounds the brilliance of Richardson's concept. It could be thought of as both "doubling" by an actor, and as suggesting that only Hamlet can hear the ghost, and inside his own head at that. On both counts a satisfying ambiguity is produced.

Richardson, by this one device, proves himself an artist of extraordinarily mature sensibilities. And his choice did not inflate the budget by as much as a penny. Again, in allowing imagination to fill the deliberate vacuum, the metaphor of theatre as a place of slippery and elusive meaning is powerfully invoked. Richardson, by this point in his career, with *Look Back in Anger, The Entertainer, The Loneliness of the Long Distance Runner, A Taste of Honey,* and *Tom Jones* all on his resume, had enough clout in the industry to have taken his crew down the road to Shepperton or Elstree, to have commanded a budget twenty or thirty times greater, and to have ordered up big sets and special effects. However, he knew he did not need it. The play demanded a theatrical spaciousness in which its philosophical profundities could echo.

One more example of how Richardson invoked the metaphor of the theatre to pose large philosophical questions is the extensive use of double-casting, almost never seen on film but very common in the theatre. In mainstream filmmaking, the ontology of character identity is bound to that of the actor. We cast people who "look like" the character, who have the "right look," who are the same age, nationality, gender, and so on. And we cast them in only one role at a time. The theater, by contrast, while not eschewing type casting entirely, is more willing to evoke certain dissonances by virtue of casting stratagems. When dissonances of this kind are used correctly and in the right kind of play, they can be a powerful way of hinting at the slipperiness of meaning, identity, and character. When one meets, in act 4, an actor one met in act 2 in a different role, that slipperiness can be very strong indeed. It seems to say to us, "You see! *All* of these characters are fragile, unstable, transmutable things! Their outside appearance is not the real 'them!'"

So in asking Roger Livesey who played the first player to do the grave digger as well, with no attempt to mask the fact that the same actor was appearing again (indeed, that voice could only belong to Roger Livesey!), Richardson was parting company with mainstream film convention. He does not do this for a mere whim, and surely not to save a salary, but because to do so is to uncover yet another layer in the theatre metaphor.

The only weak performance in this otherwise very strongly acted film is Marianne Faithfull's Ophelia. Williamson could not find the chemistry with his girlfriend that he could with his mother!

Why are we moved so little by Ophelia in this film? Her plight is surely the most pitiable of all, for she has no karmic ties to the House of Denmark. She is innocent. Hamlet throws her over in presumable disgust with all women after his mother's unconscionable marriage to her first husband's assassin. Hamlet gives himself the luxury of playing at madness, yet Ophelia is driven to despair and a "doubtful" death by the loss of Hamlet's love. Despite the highly sympathetic nature of the role, Faithfull fails to move us in either the loss or the insanity. She speaks the "O what a noble mind is here o'erthrown" speech very poorly, and she is not helped in what she must accomplish in the role by what I take to be Richardson's hint at an incestuous relationship with Laertes, her brother. Ophelia, in act 1, scene 3, reclines luxuriously at full length, while Laertes, his face just a few inches above hers, rather jealously it seemed to me, cautions her against accepting Hamlet's advances. She does not take this warning at all seriously and mockingly cautions him against hypocrisy, as if she knows, only too well, that Laertes is not himself chaste. There are three lingering mouth kisses between brother and sister, the final one guiltily broken off at Polonius's entrance.

Although this contributes to the general rottenness of the state of Denmark (or perhaps it is just a free-love thing that has more to do with the sixties), Faithfull is not equal to incorporating this incest idea into Ophelia's psyche. The suggestion of incest by Richardson's staging and direction merely undercuts the rather conventional "wronged innocent" that is the sum of his actress's performance.

As a sidebar, I have always wondered why Ophelia is so often played as pretty in her madness, and such is the case in this film. Does it have something to do with the pastoral overtones suggested by the flowers? Madness, in my experience, is a shocking and ugly thing. To have shown, alternatively, Ophelia as dirty, self-lacerated, and blazing, would have been a satisfactorily shocking indictment of Hamlet's dilettantish scrupulousness. To posit a *pretty* Ophelia is to miss that Gertrude's lyrical and possibly euphemistic description of the girl's suicide may have been to spare Laertes' feelings, or, alternatively, to prevent him from avenging it. In any event, it is to miss the serious unpleasantness that the play proposes. I feel Richardson, in his casting, his conception, and his direction, failed to realize adequately this strand of the story.

Yet in revisiting all the major *Hamlet* films in order to set Richardson's in context for myself, I found his, far and away, the most moving, the most coherent, the most intelligent and trusting of the text and the one that most thoroughly achieves the grandeur of tragic vision and metaphysical resonance inherent in the play. Yet, for all this, at £350,000 or so, it must have been easily the cheapest to make!

Today, thirty years later, when special effects and overproduced action overshadow the work of actors and writers in film, eclipsing the drama's primary mission—to provoke consideration of the human condition—Richardson's *Hamlet* is a shining example of a mature poetic sensibility, as well as one of lean and muscular filmmaking.

CHAPTER NINE

Narrative Voice and "Chorus on the Stage" in Tom Jones (1963)

JUDITH BAILEY SLAGLE AND ROBERT HOLTZCLAW

Following some general critical notice and acclaim in the late 1950s and early 1960s with a series of films exploring the challenges of working-class life in present-day England (*Look Back in Anger*—1958, *A Taste of Honey*—1961, *The Loneliness of the Long-Distance Runner*—1962), Tony Richardson sought a change of pace for his next film project. In 1958, Richardson and frequent collaborator John Osborne had established their own film company, Woodfall Film Productions Ltd., and a series of relative critical and financial successes had afforded Woodfall the clout to negotiate with established studios for financial and distribution help in projects of interest to both Richardson and Osborne. For his follow-up to *Runner*, Richardson decided that he wanted "to get away from the rainy, industrial cities of the North. [I] wanted something full of color and fun and it suddenly hit me that *Tom Jones*, which I'd loved since childhood, was it" (Wakeman 1988, 881). In the late summer of 1962, United Artists agreed to finance the film at a budget of just over $1 million, and John Osborne agreed to write the screenplay adaptation of the Henry Fielding novel, continuing his collaborative series with Richardson.[1]

The finished product was, quite simply, a smashing success. *Tom Jones* was a critical and financial hit in both the United States and England, grossing between $30 million and $40 million and winning four Oscars (for best film and best director), as well as awards from the British Film Academy as best film and best British film. Among the accolades, both critical and box-office, were, "one of the most successful cinematic adaptations of a novel ever made, and . . . one of the most imaginative of comic films, a classic in its own right" (Battestin 1971, 164); "much appreciated by audiences—who turned up in record numbers the world over" (Shipman 1993, 260); "Richardson's *Tom Jones* . . . emerges not merely as an entertaining adaptation but as a witty exploration of cinematic styles" (Insdorf and Goodman 1981, 37); "a watershed movie [with] immense influence on . . . the film industry in Britain [and the way that] American power operated on British talent" (qtd. in Wakeman 1988, 881); "a lusty, rollicking comic masterpiece. . . . It is a maxim of film criticism that a good film cannot be made from a good book, but *Tom Jones* is a glorious exception" (Johnson 1980, 1760).

It is this last comment that, in part, drives our forthcoming discussion of Richardson's *Tom Jones*. Examples of classic novels being made into classic, award-winning films are indeed rare, and the particular scope and complexity of Fielding's novel in particular make the adaptation all the more noteworthy. We focus most specifically on the role of the *narrator* in *Tom Jones*, as a key element in the novel's depth and structure and as a central feature of the film's success, albeit in transformed ways. To explore this use of narrative voice in the novel and the film, we will move through four steps of discussion and analysis: the role of narrator in *Tom Jones*, the novel; a comparison between Fielding's narrator and Richardson's narrator; the role of the narrator in *Tom Jones*, the film; and other narrator-equivalent devices in Richardson's film. Through this exploration, the significance of the narrative voice in *Tom Jones*—novel and film—can come more fully into view.

THE NOVEL—FIELDING'S NARRATOR

After a lapse of seven years from the appearance of *Joseph Andrews*, his first novel, in 1742, writer Henry Fielding, who had been working in the meantime as a lawyer and magistrate, provided the sophisticated London reading public with a comic epic novel using many of the same plot, structural, and narrative techniques used in *Joseph Andrews*. *Tom Jones* (1749) was virtually an overnight sensation. Fielding initially received hundreds of pounds for the manuscript, and the printer could not produce copies of the novel fast enough. While *Joseph Andrews* had been rather quickly crafted as a parodic response to Samuel Richardson's *Pamela*, *Tom Jones* had the advantage of a more studied construction, however, borrowing some of the best elements of *Joseph Andrews*. Plot similarities include mysteries of parentage, journeys, and episodic mini-climaxes (inherited from earlier picaresque novels such as *Don Quixote*) that demonstrate Fielding's playwrighting skills as a constructor of scenes. Structural similarities between *Joseph Andrews* and *Tom Jones* include separate books within each novel with introductory author/narrator comments, but *Tom Jones's* structure is somewhat more complex than is *Joseph Andrews's*, as *Tom Jones's* first six books deal with young Tom's initiation into the world, the middle six books with his life on the road and separation from loved ones, and the last six with his return to London and return to grace.

While this overall structure of initiation, separation, and compensation is similar to the construction of *Joseph Andrews*, the introductions to many of the chapters of *Tom Jones* are more consistently focused—many containing treatises on the novel as a genre—than the chapter introductions in *Joseph Andrews*. With *Tom Jones*, Fielding begins to educate the public about the craft of writing a novel rather than simply attacking one that he deems bad, and through this process he calls attention to his narrator's self-awareness. As Robert Alter explains, Fielding transmits

> all action through the medium of a knowing, beneficent narrator whose presence creates for the reader, as Wayne Booth has put it, "a kind of comic analogue of the true believer's reliance on a benign providence in real life." . . . *Tom Jones* is obviously the product of a book-writing narrator—we are constantly made aware of how the narrator imposes patterns on the stuff of reality. (1968, 18, 101)

In chapter 2 of book 1, the narrator declares, "Reader, I think proper, before we proceed any farther together, to acquaint thee that I intend to digress through this whole history as often as I see occasion; of which I am myself a better judge than any pitiful critic whatever" (Fielding 31). And in book 2 he further explains that he is

> in reality, the founder of a new province of writing, so I am at liberty to make what laws I please therein. And these laws my readers,

whom I consider as my subjects, are bound to believe in and to obey; with which that they may readily and cheerfully comply, I do hereby assure them that I shall principally regard their ease and advantage in all such institutions; for I do not, like a *jure divino* tyrant, imagine that they are my slaves or my commodity. (65–66)

However, this pseudo-objective narrator is very *often* a tyrant, always keeping readers aware of the fact that they are reading a carefully constructed novel with a clear plan and periodically subjecting these readers to lectures on virtue, prudence, and other qualities he considers valuable and underappreciated: "Let this, my young readers, be your constant maxim: that no man can be good enough to enable him to neglect the rules of prudence, nor will Virtue herself look beautiful unless she be bedecked with the outward ornaments of decency and decorum" (118). Soon after this little moral lesson, the narrator pleads, "I ask pardon for this short appearance, by way of chorus, on the stage" (118), but, of course, such an apology by no means indicates that he will not return. His lectures on prudence and his singling out of Bridget Allworthy as one whose "prudence was as much on the guard as if she had had all the snares to apprehend, which were ever laid on her whole sex" (30) help set up one area of the novel's central focus—the irony of, and discordance between, appearance and reality—for the "prudent" Bridget is a superb actress. Martin Battestin explains that, as in *Joseph Andrews*, Fielding's story in *Tom Jones* is one of human nature in English society, "but a story that filters the harsh realities of lust and injustice through the distancing medium of the narrator's reassuring Augustan prose" (1987, 112).

The narrator's sermonizing joins with his comments on the art and craft of writing a novel as his two most prominent features in Fielding's novel. While the use of this "reassuring" omniscient narrator is a feature that unites *Tom Jones* with *Joseph Andrews*, Tony Richardson did not include the narrator when he followed up his film version of *Tom Jones* with a film of *Joseph Andrews* (1977). No directorial technique separates the two films more decidedly, as narrator and narrative technique provide the same type of artifice, though less intrusive and with a slightly different focus, in Richardson's *Tom Jones* as in Fielding's novel. The narrator's centrality to the meaning—and to the enjoyment—of *Tom Jones* is such that it is difficult to imagine either Fielding's novel or Richardson's film without him.

THE NARRATOR IN THE NOVEL
AND THE FILM: A COMPARISON

Given this centrality of the narrator to Fielding's novel, and Richardson's decision to use a narrator in his film as well, a next logical step is to analyze the two narrators in terms of changes (additions, alterations, deletions) in the transfer from novel to film. Omission and streamlining are necessities in almost any adaptation, particularly of a novel the length of *Tom Jones*, yet a discussion of *what* is chosen for inclusion and exclusion can be instructive in an understanding of both versions, separately and in tandem. As Geoffrey Wagner explains in *The Novel and the Cinema*, "Sometimes a change in character or scene may actually fortify the value of its original on the printed page," and this alteration by the filmmaker may become an enhancement, or a commentary, rather than an infidelity (1975, 224).

Many critics have commented on the presence of the narrator in Richardson's *Tom Jones* as one of the film's chief virtues, expressing a general appreciation that the director (and his screenwriter) chose to carry the device forward. Martin Battestin maintains that it is Richardson's (Osborne's) ability to duplicate much of the original text, especially Fielding's "deliberately self-conscious, artificial narrative techniques," in the medium of film that makes *Tom Jones* such a superior production to that of *Joseph Andrews* (1987, 111). Battestin also explores the importance of the narrator in both versions of *Tom Jones*: "Osborne's commentator is a clever adaptation of Fielding's celebrated omniscient narrator, whose presence is constantly felt in *Tom Jones*. . . . It has been remarked that the most important "character" in Fielding's novel is the author-narrator himself. . . . Osborne's commentator functions correspondingly" (1971, 170). Similarly, in his film textbook *Understanding Movies*, Louis Giannetti cites *Tom Jones* as "an example of a faithful adaptation," pointing out that "John Osborne's screenplay preserves much of the novel's plot structure, its major events, and most of the important characters. Even the witty omniscient narrator is retained" (1996, 388). Thus the two narrators (novel and film) are often grouped together in praise, but a closer comparison of them reveals more about their function and importance in their respective works.

While differences between the two narrators are numerous (and some will be discussed below), the spirit of Fielding's original text does not suffer nor transform dramatically in Richardson's film version. Fielding uses his narrator, in places, to expound on the process of writing a novel, thus making his readers see that, in part, he has written a novel about writing novels; Richardson expounds, in a different way, on the process of making a film (discussed later in this chapter), allowing his viewers to see that, in part, he has made a movie about making movies. The narrator used by each artist serves several functions beyond these self-reflexive ones, including plot explication or transition, characterization of Tom himself, and the delivery of proverbs deemed useful or educational for the audience.

Richardson's film moves quickly through books 1 and 2 of Fielding's novel, galloping through Mr. Allworthy's discovery of baby Tom between the bedsheets, his subsequent accusation that Jenny Jones is the infant Tom's mother, and his decision to raise Tom at Allworthy Manor. In a sense, the film's rapid arrival at Tom's life as a young man is an echo of the novel's narrator, who states at the beginning of book 3 that he will "pass over several large periods of time in which nothing happened" to arrive at more interesting, more attention worthy, subjects (1979, 97). The film, then, actually begins its focus on Tom with the material from the novel's books 3 and 4, introducing Tom's two main love/lust interests, the heroic Sophia Western and the lusty Molly Seagrim. After some earlier, primarily expository comments (to be discussed later in this chapter), the film's narrator arrives most prominently with material from what would be book 5 of Fielding's novel, the illness of Mr. Allworthy. Many of his comments in the film, though certainly in the spirit of Fielding, are not taken directly from the novel, while others are quite accurate copies. One example of the latter occurs when Tom, rejoicing at Mr. Allworthy's recovery from illness, encounters Molly in the "thickest part of the grove": "Jones probably thought one woman better than none, and Molly as probably imagined two men to be better than one" (216). This last adventure with Molly, along with Squire Western's discovery that Sophia is in love with Tom, results in the hero's exile from the Allworthy estate and from Sophia, in book 6; for, as the film's narrator perceptively explains, the "forces of sobriety [were] gathering against Tom."

Book 7, Fielding's discourse on life as theater, finds Tom on the road to Bristol and Sophia planning to run away from home in order to avoid marrying Mr. Blifil. Richardson uses the narrator at this point to condense and speak his way through a large volume of the novel's text, moving viewers to the next important action scenes of both the novel and the film. He does this by omitting the novel's philosophical story of the Man of Mazard Hill, advancing the audience to the lively scene where Tom rescues Mrs. Waters (Jenny Jones, although viewers are not aware of her true identity at this time) from assault (book 9 of the novel). Her clothes have been partly torn away in this scene, and the film narrator explains that Tom was reluctant to look back at her in her state of disarray, lest the fires of temptation consume him. Fielding, somewhat more explicit in the novel, writes of "her clothes being torn from all the upper part of her body, her breasts, which were well formed and extremely white, attracted the eyes of the deliverer" (415). The film, of course, can *show* viewers as much of Mrs. Waters' allure as is considered necessary for the scene, but the novel's more detailed language makes for an interesting alteration some 214 years later.

When Tom offers Mrs. Waters his coat to help hide her nakedness, Fielding's narrator explains that "Jones offered her his coat but, I know not for what reason, she absolutely refused the most earnest solicitations to accept it" (so much for omniscience!); Tom himself then declares, "I will entirely remove it [her embarrassment] by walking before you all the way; for I would not have my eyes offend you and I could not answer for my power of resisting the attractive charms of so much beauty" (417). Thus Fielding and Richardson both set the audience up for the coming seduction scene, in which, clearly, neither participant is innocent. After all, the exonerating film narrator insists, "heroes, whatever high ideals they have, are mortal, not divine." He, like the novel's narrator, attempts to be honest about Tom's weaknesses of the flesh (and other flaws) while still building a case for his essential humanity—in spite, or because, of his essential humanness. What Fielding does in this section of the novel and elsewhere, as Robert Alter explains, "is to make the self-conscious activity of the narrator, who stands, as it were, between us and the stage of action, an integral part of the novelistic event" (194). Much of Richardson's success in the film arises from his ability to accomplish a comparable feat on his own, somewhat modified, terms.

Richardson next uses the narrator after Sophia, Mrs. Fitzpatrick, Squire Western, and the rest of the motley group "coincidentally" converge on the inn at Upton (book 10). In the film, Tom finds an article of Sophia's attire after she has dropped it, thus realizing she is near. As the film narrator so eloquently expresses it: "It is hard when a woman leaves a man nothing but memories and a muff." In the novel, however, Tom's discovery of the muff is less happenstance; Fielding has Sophia resolutely leave the muff, along with a note, in Tom's room for his discovery, allowing her a more aggressive role in the courtship.

As each unsuspecting character leaves the inn to fall prey to the evils of the city, the film narrator advances the plot by skipping over portions of the novel, moving to Tom's search for Sophia at the London home of the debauched Lady Bellaston and the Vauxhall Gardens masquerade (book 13). In the film, the narrator explains that with his "usual good breeding" the narrator will not follow Tom and Lady Bellaston to the bedroom. This moment echoes one of the narrator's earliest comments in the movie: Richardson's first scene featuring a semi-adult Tom is one involving some sexual activity between Tom and Molly. Here, in one of the film narrator's first lines to the audience, he says, "It shall be our custom to leave such scenes. In this way, we shall try to make up for our incorrigible hero." So, early in the movie, the narrator indicates some "selective editing" will be used to help shape our perception of Tom, and now, back to the present and the scene between Tom and Lady Bellaston, the narrator once again pulls away, this time acknowledging his *own* virtues ("good breeding") rather than Tom's vices. The effect and the motivation—to spare us from the details of Tom's misdeeds—are the same.

Fielding trims these lovemaking scenes between Tom and Lady Bellaston in the novel as well, using the narrator both to defend Tom and to plant innuendo:

> He knew the tacit consideration upon which all her favours were conferred, and as his necessity obliged him to accept them, so his honour, he concluded, forced him to pay the price . . . and to devote himself to her from that great principle of justice by which the laws of some countries oblige a debtor who is no [sic] otherwise capable of discharging his debt to become the slave of his creditor. (615–16)

While Tom submits to Lady Bellaston in order to gain knowledge of Sophia's status and whereabouts, this desired noble end does not forgive his decadent means, even for Fielding.

At this point in Richardson's film, the narrator returns to read for the audience a letter that Sophia has managed to get to Tom after his sham marriage proposal to Lady Bellaston. In the letter, Sophia advises Tom that he must not come to her house again, as she fears their love will be discovered, and she advises Tom to be patient. "'Tis said that hope is a bad supper that makes a good breakfast," the film's proverb-spouting narrator assures, while the novel's less optimistic narrator confirms that "this letter administered the same kind of consolation to poor Jones which

Job formerly received from his friends" (637). And, like Job, Tom's troubles increase in both novel and film: Squire Western, Blifil (the status-and-wealth-seeking Western's chosen mate for Sophia), and Mr. Allworthy all converge on London, and Tom is forced into a sword fight, orchestrated by Sophia's angry cousin, Harriet Fitzpatrick, with Harriet's estranged husband, Mr. Fitzpatrick (book 16).

As the film moves to the jailed Tom awaiting the hangman for his alleged fatal stabbing of Fitzpatrick during the duel, the narrator explains that Blifil has dispatched a lawyer to convince Mrs. Waters that she should help seal Tom's doom even as Partridge searches for someone to prove Tom's innocence. Richardson must now propel his film audience through the remaining 150 or so pages of Fielding's novel in the remaining few minutes of what is already a comparatively long film. Thus, the film narrator's role becomes increasingly important as he steps even more to the forefront as our guide both to what is happening and how we should react to what takes place. In the novel (book 18) the philosopher Mr. Square produces a letter to prove Tom's innocence, while in the film there is word of a letter that will reveal Tom's true parentage. Absent from the novel is the film's "nick-of-time" rescue scene in which Squire Western saves Tom from the gallows at literally the last moment (the noose is already around his neck!). During this dramatic rescue, the film's narrator asks us to contemplate yet another maxim: "To die for a cause is a common evil; to die for nonsense is the devil," and then, as Tom is saved, the narrator reminds us of his degree of control over the situation, finishing the epigram with, "and it would be the devil's own nonsense to leave Tom without a rescuer." This moment recalls a scene earlier in the film when Tom, off on the road to London, is challenged to fight with a rowdy soldier after the soldier has insulted Sophia's virtue. In this earlier scene, when it appears that Tom has been killed by the offending soldier, the film's narrator informs us that "a hero cannot be lost until his tale is told," and suddenly Tom is up and alive again. This degree of narrative control—present, of course, in any work of fiction—is seldom so explicitly stated. So Tom Jones manages to survive the first dangerous situation because he *is* the hero and there is more story to tell, and later, he survives the hanging because it would be the "devil's own nonsense" to kill him off after having come so far. He has truly been wrapped in the author/director/narrator's protective arms, a narrative conceit most novels and films are unwilling to acknowledge so directly.

While the film narrator admits to this bit of fakery and manipulation as Tom is rescued at the hanging, Fielding manages to prolong the suspense a bit in book 17 of the novel:

> [P]oor Jones . . . so destitute is he now of friends and so persecuted by enemies that we almost despair of bringing him to any good, and if our reader delights in seeing executions, I think he ought not to lose any time in taking a first row at Tyburn.
> This I faithfully promise . . . we will lend him none of the supernatural assistance with which we are entrusted upon condition that we use it only on very important occasions. (753–54)

Richardson creates a similar level of "will he be saved?" suspense in the film by having Tom's neck noosed and ready for hanging before his last-second rescue, but Fielding, by having his narrator explicitly state, before the fact, that he will *not* resort to divine narrative intervention to help Tom out of this predicament, gives his narrator an even more dramatic role. He will, he says, allow Tom to *die* before he will manipulate events and "forfeit our integrity or shock the faith of our reader" (754).

Of course, Fielding does find a way to extricate Tom without offending his narrator's high sense of integrity. Tom's education in the novel is now complete, as he accepts all the blame for his actions and for his lack of good judgment and prudence: "I am myself the cause of all my misery," he concludes in the final book (791). This conversion and great lesson learning is less obvious in Richardson's film, as the film wraps up quickly after Tom's miracle rescue from the gallows, and the film's last words—spoken by the narrator—focus on Tom's happiness and survival, ending with "for I have lived today." Fielding chooses to be more pragmatic in the novel than does Richardson in the film, for when Squire Western finally learns that Tom is innocent of attempted murder *and* will be heir to the Allworthy estate, he is now eager for the match with his daughter, Sophia. This is, after all, a novel about economics, not heroism. "No sooner, then, was Western informed of Mr. Allworthy's intention to make Jones his heir than he joined heartily with the uncle in every commendation of his nephew, and became as eager for her marriage with Jones as he had before been to couple her to Blifil" (828). All ends well in both novel and film, but, interestingly, Fielding's version is often more "modern" than Richardson's in its representation of patriarchal and economic power structures and in its comparatively dark comments on forced marriage, attempted rape, political intrigue, and other concerns. Additionally, much of Fielding's narrator's witty arguments and observations about literary critics, about every aspect of writing, about life as theatre, about genius, learning, and experience, and about various "moral" subjects are jettisoned in the necessarily condensed and more story-driven film version. As Robert Alter has observed, Fielding's "narrator makes us continually aware of his rhetoric," like Nabokov in *Lolita* or Joyce in *Ulysses* (199). Richardson's use of the narrator in his film version is comparable but somewhat transformed. To say one version is "better" than the other is to raise more questions than are answered; to say each is an artistic triumph within its medium, given its aims, is to award both the praise their creators deserve.

THE FILM—RICHARDSON'S NARRATOR

Just as there are many readers of *Tom Jones* who never saw Richardson's film version (certainly in the first two hundred years of its publication!), there are also many viewers of the film who have never read Fielding's novel. The first part of this chapter looked at the narrator's role in the novel as a way of leading into the second section's comparison of Fielding's and Richardson's narrators; now we explore the narrator's role in the film as it stands alone, not in comparison to the novel but as a separate event—the way that millions of viewers who have never read the novel must have experienced the film. As one reviewer noted, "Although it cannot show every scene from the novel, [Richardson's film] remains remarkably faithful to the spirit of the work; yet a viewer who has never heard of the novel can also completely enjoy and appreciate the film" (Johnson 1980, 1760).

Films with narrators are not rare, but as a device the narrator is still uncommon enough to be noticed, and remarked upon, when it occurs. Many times a film's narrator is a character from the film itself, often providing voice-over reactions to, and reflections on, the events unfolding onscreen. In *Tom Jones*, however, the narrator is nondiegetic—not arising from within the space or world of the story—and his byplay with the audience functions on more different levels than does a standard diegetic (character from within the film) narrator or even a traditional omniscient narrator.

The voice of the film's narrator is that of Irish character actor Michael MacLiammoir. He was in his midsixties at the time of the filming; although he had a long and distinguished acting career, he did not appear in many films (his most notable, perhaps, was Orson Welles' *Othello* in 1952). It is not likely that his voice was familiar to many moviegoers, and, since he never appears as a visible character in the film itself, he accomplishes Richardson's apparent goal of functioning as a "voice" with no identity outside its role in the film: a commentator who knows and controls all and can provide guidance, or confusion, or lessons, when needed.

On a most basic level, Richardson's narrator helps to advance the plot and provide transitions between scenes, functioning in the ways a traditional narrator often does, in both films and novels. Thus, he will provide comments such as "Our hero was now on the road to London" or "An old acquaintance arrives," sometimes imparting useful information to clarify events or indicate a new direction in the narrative, while at other times providing seemingly unnecessary, but perhaps reassuring, evidence that he is still with us and is still observing (and controlling) the events on the screen.

Moving somewhat beyond this most traditional narrative function, the film's unseen voice also offers occasional poems and proverbs that are meant to provide commentary—sometimes ironic, sometimes humorous—on events and characters within the film. These interjections start to develop a personality for the narrator, investing him with a depth of purpose that goes beyond merely reporting and linking, and into interpreting and suggesting. Early in the film, the narrator offers a poem about how "ladies" should not be jealous of other ladies' romantic successes; the poem is delivered as some apparently jealous ladies are throwing various items at Molly, the object of Tom's desires. The narrator's musings are not always delivered as poetry, but they are often in the guise of general observations while being clearly linked to the material on screen: "There comes a time when men in a constant state of readiness for war will slip their leashes, and fight like dogs," he offers, providing partial explanation for the ease with which Tom and the soldier who insults Sophia's honor end up fighting.

The narrator's affection for Tom, and his hope that viewers will feel the same way, is apparent from early in the film, when even Tom's philanderings are presented as the understandable activities of "our incorrigible hero," and later, when Tom frolics with Molly as part of his celebration of Mr. Allworthy's recovery from grave illness, the narrator attempts partially to excuse Tom's behavior by reminding us that "wine will dull the senses." Tom's misdeeds are not glossed over by the film or the narrator, but they are often presented and explained as the human failings of an essentially good and decent man. Viewers would most likely grow fond of Tom even without the narrator's help, but he does surface periodically to remind us to keep Tom's misdeeds in perspective.

To help provide even more emphasis on his narrator's comments, Richardson also inserts a musical cue to signal an impending comment. At several intervals of the film (particularly in the middle third), the narrator disappears for comparatively long stretches of time. A careful viewing (and listening) reveals that Richardson employs a repeated harpsichord interlude on the soundtrack—brief but identical in each use—to signal that the narrator is about to speak: while relatively subtle, it functions as a clear indicator to viewers that our guide has yet another important comment to make. Such a device seems ultimately unnecessary, as no real preparation is needed for the audience to hear and process the narrator's ideas, but the musical motif works to increase our awareness of the narrator's presence ("there's that music again") and to draw more attention to his role as commentator, outside of the often hectic world of the story itself.

Viewers of *Tom Jones* who have never been readers of *Tom Jones* will most certainly notice, and at times appreciate, Richardson's narrator. While he does not appear as extensively, or function on all of the same levels, as Fielding's narrator (as discussed in the previous section), he emerges as a character in his own right, within the film but outside it at the same time and able to use that distance to guide the narrative and shape viewer reactions.

NARRATOR-EQUIVALENT DEVICES IN THE FILM

While the preceding section dealt with Richardson's use of the narrator in some of the same ways as Fielding's narrator, there remains one important area of Fielding's novel that Richardson's narrator never truly approaches: as discussed previously, the novel's narrator spends quite a bit of time commenting on the process of writing (and reading, and reviewing) a novel itself. Wisely, Richardson abandons this element of the narrator's written comments in his film; the words would lose their self-reflexive quality in this different medium, and too many of Fielding's discourses, while appropriate in the space of his long novel, would demolish the pace of Richardson's film. However, this does not mean that the idea of an artist commenting, within his work, on the process of creating that work is lost in the transfer to film. Instead of using the narrator himself to speak about and draw attention to the art of filmmaking, though, Richardson employs other devices that function as equivalents to this element of the novel's narration. "Fielding enriches his narrative with what he calls 'poetical embellishments'—similes, metaphors, hyperboles, parodies, mock-heroic passages, and an abundance of quotations from . . . [other] writers. Richardson translates these verbal instruments into filmic processes, which serve to chronicle not only the story but also the development of cinema as an art form" (Insdorf and Goodman 1981, 37). These devices arise quite often and, in every case, serve to remind viewers of the properties of cinema, of the options available to a director and the conventions we take for granted until they are violated on the screen. In this way, Richardson's narrative-driven *Tom Jones* works as well, on a parallel plane, as a demonstration of, and comment on, the art of filmmaking itself.

Among the devices Richardson uses to accomplish this goal are manipulations of camera speed and editing techniques. The film begins as a silent movie, in this respect echoing *Tom Jones*, the novel, as an early example of its particular genre. After this opening sequence, Richardson, at various times, employs freeze frame, stop-motion, and even fast-motion camerawork, all functioning to draw attention to the filmmaking process itself (traces of the French New Wave) and to remind us of the narrator/storyteller's control over the pace and direction of the presentation. In these ways, his playfulness with the properties of cinema functions as a clear parallel to Fielding's narrator.

Fast-motion sequences include the Keystone Kops-ish chase scene when all the characters converge at the Upton Inn, an element that highlights the absurdity of the coincidence and the manic pace of this section of the narrative. Stop-motion work is used during the leisurely montage sequence, which serves to illustrate Tom and Sophia's developing love for one another. This comparatively long, dialogue-less segment of the film borders on self-mockery at times, with soft music, shots of flowers and gondolas, loving close-ups, and so on; but the humor achieved, in part, through stop-motion camera manipulation helps to undercut the excessive sentimentality and helps to retain Fielding's tone from the novel, somewhere between a straight, sentimental presentation and a total, mocking dismissal of the nascent romance. Among Richardson's notable uses of freeze frames is the scene-ender when Tom and Lady Bellaston kiss, referred to earlier. As the narrator informs viewers that his "good breeding" prevents him from allowing us to see what happens *after* the kiss, the action stops in a frozen pose, emphasizing the director's ability literally to "freeze" and control what material is revealed on screen. There are other examples of all of these camera devices, as well as numerous editing tricks (creative wipes, iris shots, etc.), but they need not all be catalogued here. Suffice it to say that these stylistic choices are a key component in Richardson's successful appropriation of Fielding's use of the narrator to comment on the very art form in which the creator is working.

Richardson also draws attention to the art of filmmaking itself through his violation of the "fourth wall" principle in *Tom Jones*. On several occasions, characters in the film address the camera/audience directly, sometimes with just a knowing glance, and sometimes with a comment or question. Characters look directly into the camera (Sophia in the aforementioned "love montage" for example) or give it a fleeting acknowledgment (Tom yells "Help!" to the camera as he runs by during a chase at the Upton Inn), or control what the camera is allowed to see from *their* side of the lens (Tom covers the camera when it lingers too long on the barely clothed Mrs. Waters). There are also longer, even more obvious violations of the traditional boundary between actor/character and audience. After his fight with the soldier who insults Sophia's virtue, Tom is awakened the next morning by a maid/attendant and told to leave. As he dresses, he notices that £500 he had with him the night before are now missing, and he becomes quite agitated, yelling at the maid and finally turning to the camera and saying, "Did you see her take the £500?" These and other interjections serve as frequent reminders that this is all artifice; we are watching a film, created at the filmmaker's pleasure and capable of veering in any direction, violating any convention, that the director desires. It is easy to forget about the artifice of a camera until a character within a film decides to remind us. In this way, such manipulations serve as equivalents to the narrator in the novel; both are mechanisms for delivering the story and both comment, in their own distinct ways, on the very art form through which they are presented.

One final example serves both to highlight Richardson's use of other devices to approximate Fielding's narrator *and* to draw attention to the narration of the film itself, bringing us full circle in this exploration of "narrative voice." Near the end of the film, as Richardson rushes to explain and tie up Fielding's plot, the truth of Tom's parentage is revealed. Richardson presents the scene in which Mrs. Waters tells the truth to Mr. Allworthy in a manner that, in essence, teases the audience. The doors are closed before Mrs. Waters begins her explanation, and the film audience remains outside in the hall, unable to hear what is going on; instead, we are left to wait and watch a succession of freeze-framed images of Partridge and Mrs. Miller as *they* attempt to eavesdrop through the closed door. Richardson, here, reminds us of his control of the proceedings and of his (or any director's) ability to reveal information to the audience whenever he sees fit. We may be let in on a secret before characters are informed, or, as in this case, we may be deliberately kept outside as information is revealed, forced to eavesdrop on eavesdroppers, to no avail. Soon after this little frustration, however, Richardson has a bit more fun and plays with narrative convention once again. In the next scene, Mrs. Waters turns directly to the camera/audience and explains, for our benefit, exactly what Mr. Allworthy has just learned. Her speech completed, she then runs back to join the other characters in the action that is going on behind her. The film's omniscient narrator could just as easily have delivered this information, of course, but Richardson chooses to use diegetic narration in this instance, having a character literally leave the story for a moment to talk to us and then turn around and jump back into the fray. This bends all conventions of separation and "fourth-wall" construction to be sure, but that is precisely the director's intention as he continues to play with, and draw attention to, the options and conventions of his chosen means of storytelling. In all these ways, he is truer to the spirit of Fielding's narrator than if he had simply allowed the film's narrator to speak some of the novel's words concerning writing and prose construction.

In short, Richardson takes Fielding's sprawling novel and condenses it but remains true to both its general story and its overall tone. Changes in plot and characterization have been noted, but the ultimate impression is one of an eighteenth-century masterwork translated into a classic of cinema, faithful to the original while adventurous in its use of properties of its own medium. One key element in understanding and appreciating both works lies in considering the roles played by the narrators. It is rare, indeed, for a classic novel to emerge as a classic film, but Richardson manages to keep many of Fielding's strengths while putting his own cinematic stamp on the material.

NOTE

1. Osborne's role in the creation of Richardson's *Tom Jones* is a major and important one. Throughout this chapter, when we refer to Richardson's film and to various script matters within it, we are ever mindful of Osborne's contribution as screenwriter.

WORKS CITED

Alter, Robert. *Fielding and the Nature of the Novel.* Cambridge, MA: Harvard University Press, 1968.

Battestin, Martin C. "Fielding on Film." *Studies in the Eighteenth Century, Papers presented at the Sixth David Nichol Smith Memorial Seminar.* Ed. Colin Duckworth and Homer Le Grand. Special issue of *Eighteenth-Century Life* 11.1 (1987): 110–13.

———. "Osborne's *Tom Jones:* Adapting a Classic." *Film and Literature: Contrasts in Media.* Ed. Fred H. Marcus. Scranton, PA: Chandler, 1971, 164–77.

Fielding, Henry. *The History of Tom Jones, A Foundling.* New York: New American Library, 1979.

Giannetti, Louis. *Understanding Movies.* 7th ed. Englewood Cliffs, NJ: Prentice Hall, 1996.

Insdorf, Annette, and Sharon Goodman. "A Whisper and a Wink." *The English Novel and the Movies.* Ed. Michael Klein and Gillian Parker. New York: Frederick Ungar, 1981, 36–43.

Johnson, Timothy W. "Tom Jones." *Magill's Survey of Cinema.* Series 1, volume 4. Englewood Cliffs, NJ: Salem, 1980, 1760–63.

Shipman, David. *Cinema: The First Hundred Years.* New York: St. Martin's Press, 1993.

Wagner, Geoffrey. *The Novel and the Cinema.* Rutherford, Madison, etc.: Fairleigh Dickinson University Press, 1975.

Wakeman, John, ed. "Tony Richardson." *World Film Directors: 1945–1985.* New York: H. W. Wilson, 1988, 878–83.

CHAPTER TEN

Henry Fielding Revisited: Joseph Andrews *(1977)*

JAMES M. WELSH

For some, *Tom Jones* (1749) will be considered Henry Fielding's comic masterpiece and Tony Richardson's most spirited and innovative film. Richardson's later film of Fielding's earlier novel, *Joseph Andrews* (1742), was considered by many as merely an attempt on Richardson's part to duplicate his earlier Hollywood triumph. In both instances, Richardson faced a similar challenge, that of compressing an oversized narrative to the time limitations of a feature film, and in both Richardson found similar solutions, substituting antics for action, subordinating the comic to the burlesque ("the exhibition of what is monsterous and unnatural," to quote Fielding describing his "comic epic in prose") and transforming satire into farce. However, one might just as easily argue that the comic methods Richardson first developed for *Tom Jones* were further sophisticated in *Joseph Andrews,* that his second visitation of the eighteenth century is the more successful in its control of Fielding's material, and that *Joseph Andrews* is in fact the better adaptation, or so it seems to me.

The first problem involves the issue of verbal versus cinematic narration. The voice of the Fielding narrator guides the reader through the text and mediates the reader's understanding of what has taken place. The presence of the omniscient Fielding narrator would be difficult if not impossible to capture on film. This sort of expansive, digressive, and, at times, didactic narrator would be an anachronism for twentieth-century readers, let alone a mass audience of nonreaders that might constitute the film audience. And yet a Fielding novel would not and could not be the same if Fielding's narrative voice were removed. All that would remain of *Joseph Andrews* or *Tom Jones* would be the picaresque story, populated by rogues, villains, thieves, hypocrites, fops, fools, and a very few good-hearted (or good-natured) characters.

These novels would therefore seem to be unfilmable, and yet Tony Richardson managed to catapult his career to the Academy Award level with his treatment of *Tom Jones*. Both of Richardson's Fielding "adaptations" were in fact transformations or translations. To translate is to change, and just as good translators take liberties with the text, so did Richardson take liberties in transforming Fielding's novels into another medium in such a way that the films were brilliantly "faithful" to the spirit—if not exactly the letter—of the text. Expectations will have to be scaled down, in other words, if discriminating readers are to be satisfied.

Any attempt to evaluate the success of a cinematic adaptation will necessarily involve a close study of the *process* of transformation. Any lengthy novel adapted to the screen will have to be compressed, and, as a consequence, narrative moments, subplots, and whole groupings of characters may have to be excised. In *Joseph Andrews*, for example, there are six clergymen against whom the learning and decency of Parson Adams may be measured. In Richardson's film, there are only two clergymen, and the character of Parson Adams is diminished as a consequence. Moreover, the Fielding narrator is at pains to explain the theory of satire operative in the novel. Nothing of this survives in the film, which attempts to transform Fielding's satire merely into farcical action that may, in the best of sequences, demonstrate Fielding's satirical ideals.

Certainly, the film is inventive and unquestionably amusing in the way it represents *some* of the adventures of Joseph Andrews and Mr. Abraham Adams, but it cannot be considered a substitute for the novel. As early as 1936, Gilbert Seldes wrote in the *Saturday Review of Literature* that "a good movie cannot be faithful to the original book or play," that, in other words, adaptations must be corrupt, that viewers will "remember the plot, as it is expressed in action," not in words (1936, 4). In this regard, Richardson's *Joseph Andrews* is a corruption of the novel, but could it be otherwise? Much more is at issue than pure "fidelity" here, and one could still argue that the story has been effectively transformed into

FIGURE 10.1. *Joseph Andrews* (Ann-Margret and Peter Firth)

another medium. Richardson's *Joseph Andrews*, like *Tom Jones* before it, is transformed into a high-spirited romp through the eighteenth century. The disjointed comic pace and the farcical action in adapting comic novels came to constitute part of Richardson's signature style. Richardson's comic mask is distinctive, in other words.

The film begins with exposition while the credits are running with shots of a very young Joseph serving as a pageboy to Sir Thomas Booby (Peter Bull) and his wife (Ann-Margaret), with the singing of Jim Dale's Pedlar voiced over the image: "He was such a gentle boy, such a pure and gentle boy, that no one could his company deny." After the opening credits, there is a shot of Joseph grown up (Peter Firth), taking part in a bucolic (and sexually symbolic) May Day celebration that features his beloved Fanny Goodwill (Natalie Ogle) as Queen of the May. When Joseph takes off his shirt to climb a greased pole, Lady Booby watches him attentively and lustfully from afar.

In the next sequence, Parson Abraham Adams (Michael Hordern), the moral ballast of Fielding's novel, is introduced when he approaches the Booby estate, where lunch is being served on the lawn. This good man is defined by his clumsiness. He trips and falls on the table and the food and manages to kick old Booby's gouty foot. The film exploits the farcical side of Parson Adams and defines his muscular Christianity and moral courage almost entirely through his actions, as when, much later in the film, he saves Fanny from being ravished; he does not expound on moral philosophy in the film nearly as much as he does in the novel, and his serious dimension as a scholar is generally ignored in the screenplay by Allan Scott and Chris Bryant and the screenstory by Tony Richardson.

Richardson's approach is to simplify the characters as well as simplifying the sprawling picaresque narrative written "in imitation of the manner of Cervantes, author of *Don Quixote*," as the title page of the first edition of 1742 declares. Henry Fielding (1707–1754) entitled the novel *The History of the Adventures of Joseph Andrews, and of his Friend, Mr. Abraham Adams*. Though Richardson's film compresses and simplifies Fielding's narrative, it manages to dramatize the main "adventures" so that the shape of the narrative, with its many surprising discoveries at the end, is absolutely clear. In this respect, the novel is well adapted. What is most notably absent from the film is the commanding presence of Fielding's loquacious omniscient narrator, who is at pains to define his comic and satiric purposes in this "comic romance," this "comic epic in prose; differing from comedy, as the serious epic [differs] from tragedy" (1961, 7).

The "Author's Preface" clearly explains Fielding's satiric method, which intends to hold up affectation ("the only source of the true Ridiculous") for ridicule, pointing out that affectation proceeds from one of two causes—vanity or hypocrisy.

Fielding holds particular contempt for hypocrites. Affectation that proceeds from hypocrisy is "nearly allied to deceit; yet when it comes from vanity only, it partakes of the nature of ostentation" (1961, 10). A vain person lacks the degree of virtue he may pretend to have, but the avaricious person, the hypocrite, "is the very reverse of what he would seem to be." None of this meditation upon the art and nature of satire is conveyed in the film, but Richardson shows its consequences and surely understands how the ridiculous arises from the discovery of affectation and yields "pleasure and surprise." As Fielding writes, "To discover anyone to be the exact reverse of what he affects, is more surprising, and consequently more ridiculous, than to find him a little deficient in the quality he deserves the reputation of" (1961, 11).

Fielding's Parson Adams is a paradigm of moral courage, a Christian hero, a good-natured (as compared to a merely good-humored) man, but he is not perfect. In chapter 8 of book 4, for example, after Adams has lectured Joseph and Fanny about moderation and restraint and the virtue of patience, he is led to believe that his youngest son has been drowned. When thus put to the test, he does not respond to his grief with anything like moderation, and when he then discovers the boy's life was saved by his friend the Pedlar, "The parson's joy was now as extravagant as his grief had been before" (1961, 266). Not then recognizing his own hypocritical behavior, Adams resumes lecturing Joseph: "No, Joseph, do not give too much way to thy passions, if thou dost expect happiness," only to be reminded by Joseph that "It was easier to give advice than to take it." Adams can only respond, reasonably enough, that "the loss of a child is one of those great trials where our grief may be allowed to become immoderate" (267).

In the novel, this episode is informed by the author's earlier mediation on the nature of hypocrisy. All Tony Richardson can do is to show Parson Adams responding in panic and grief to the news that his son has drowned. Richardson apparently assumes his viewers will understand the situation and hope that the smarter ones will have read the novel, but to show the episode out of the context of the Fielding narrator is merely to make Adams appear to be more foolish and ridiculous than he is. Before the mistaken drowning incident, Richardson does suggest the Parson's

212

FIGURE 10.2. *Joseph Andrews* (Peter Firth, reclining; Ann-Margret, hovering)

hypocrisy by having Mrs. Adams (Helen Fraser) remark, "He's about as moderate as a buck rabbit!"—which is at best a crude substitution. Informed viewers—those who have read and reflected upon the novel (surely a tiny minority)—will of course be able to recognize the episode and understand it in context. However, viewers who have not read the novel will only catch part of the meaning, but they will understand in general what is going on. Richardson uses a sort of cinematic shorthand that readers of Fielding will quickly comprehend. In other words, the subtext is telegraphed effectively through the action.

By dispensing with the charming but long-winded Fielding narrator, Richardson is able to shorten and shape the novel to suit his purposes. Richardson also has to ignore the novel's implications as parody and the fact that Fielding was responding to what he regarded as the moral absurdity of Samuel Richardson's novel *Pamela; or Virtue Rewarded* (1740). No doubt, few viewers will understand the significance of Joseph's being the brother of Pamela Andrews, a character Fielding borrowed from the earlier novel, and will not fully grasp the humor of her vanity and affectation as played by Karen Dotrice in the film. But students of literature will know where the character comes from and understand Fielding's distaste for her hypocritical and manipulative "virtue." Virtue, Fielding asserted, should be its own reward.

The expansive novel involves four "histories"—that of Joseph Andrews, of course, but also those of Leonora and Horatio, Leonard and Paul, and Mr. Wilson—and not all of these can be adapted to a feature film of reasonable length. Richardson includes the history of Mr. Wilson (Ronald Pickup) because it is vital to the unraveling of the plot. In the film, Wilson's story is abbreviated as a comic romp of a naive young man who goes to the city and is corrupted by it, becoming involved with an actress named Belle (Ann-Margret, again, later to become Lady Booby, a manipulative tart, in other words), losing his fortune, and being left with an illegitimate child. Wilson's story is filmed in the style of a silent movie and told with remarkable economy. The other histories are dispensible since they traditionally have been regarded as digresssions. However, they are thematically linked to the main plot since they all concern love and marriage, fickle love as contrasted to true love, but twentieth-century viewers are not likly to miss them.

Other thematic strands are also jettisoned from the film adaptation, such as the discourse on faith versus good works in book 1, revealed through comparisons between Adams and his less worthy counterparts,

FIGURE 10.3. *Joseph Andrews* (Ann-Margret and Beryl Reid)

Barnabus and Trulliber, and the distinctions Fielding scrupulously makes between good nature and good humor. The narrative strands of the motion picture are thin and superficial when compared to the novel, but that is an inevitable consequence of its transformation to cinema. In this instance, literal fidelity simply is not possible, and one has reason to doubt that the adaptation would be more successful if extended to the length of a television mini-series and given the BBC "Masterpiece Theatre" treatment. Richardson has provided a quick sketch that certainly is true to the spirit of the novel, more so than even *Tom Jones*, which made Richardson a Hollywood fixture. David Watkin's cinematography provides a gorgeous visual reconstruction of Fielding's eighteenth-century England—a very pictorial countryside and a very congested cityscape, as witnessed by Joseph's entrance with the Booby coach into the city of Bath, where Sir Thomas not only takes but is taken by the waters.

Another major accomplishment of this film besides the cinematography and the art direction (by Michael Annals) is the casting, which includes many of Britain's most gifted character actors. There are cameo performances by John Gielgud (as the Doctor who comes calling at the Tow-Wouse Inn), for example, Hugh Griffith (as Squire Western), and Dame Peggy Ashcroft (as Lady Tattle, briefly seen). Peter Firth and Natalie Ogle perfectly represent the loving innocence of Joseph and Fanny. Firth had emerged from the West End success of his portrayal of Alan Strang in Peter Shaffer's *Equus* and had alreday demonstrated a talent for capturing the confusion of a young man bewildered by the adult world. Visually, moreover, he was perfect for the part. But Molly Haskell had reservations about the way he played Joseph Andrews: "[I]n a role that is more show than substance but which nevertheless holds our attention, Firth is cover-boy dull," she wrote. "There is none of the tension between ambition and voluptuous passivity that marked the young Michael York, or the cocky vitality of Albert Finney—both of whom made that most literary of protagonists, the bumbling naïf, come roguishly alive" (1978, 71).

However, Beryl Reid is brilliant as Mrs. Slipslop; even though the character may be less loquacious than she is in the novel, she is no less foolish, and her vanity is as stunning as her lust for "Joey" is threatening. Slipslop is defined by her affectation and her language abuse, "a mighty affecter of hard words," as Fielding describes her. "I always enjoy loquation with a man of learning," she tells Parson Adams in the film, but Richardson reduces her Slipslopisms to a bare minimum. Fielding turns her diction into a running joke, but Richardson has to get on with the story.

Thus, Richardson's caricature is more rapidly drawn than Fielding's, with fewer, broader strokes and with far less ink and shading. But Slipslop is a vain and empty, corpulent, foolish creature, and Richardson effectively reduces her to a quick sketch, all bust and bustle, likewise, the vulgar Mrs. Tow-Wouse, bloodied from slaughtering chickens, whose character can be summarized by her single remark, "Common charity, a fart!"

Parson Adams is another matter, however, and this richly drawn, amusingly pedantic, good and generous but socially awkward, bumbling clergyman cannot be reduced by caricature into a merely farcical, ecclesiastical buffoon. Fielding describes Adams as "a character of perfect simplicity; and as the goodness of his heart will recommend him to the good-natured, so I hope it will excuse me to the gentlemen of his cloth" (1961, 12). The foibles of Adams are reflected by Fielding's comic mirror, but always with affection and compassionate, deferential respect. Adams is one of the most remarkable comic creations in English literature, nearly the equal of Sir John Falstaff, and certainly the equal of Sir Toby Belch. To represent his character adequately on screen would be a challenge for the most gifted of filmmakers. Richardson's rendering finally falls short of the mark, but the spirit of Adams permeates the film. Without resorting to constant voice-over narration, which would have weakened the film's pace, one doubts that any film director could achieve him any better.

There is reason to ponder what, exactly, is being adapted in this Fielding film. Obviously, Richardson attempts to adapt an intractable novel to another medium. A recognized literary classic is adapted to suit the unsubtle and even vulgar tastes of a popular mass audience. Eighteenth-century morals are adapted to a twentieth-century context. Joseph and Fanny are transformed into flower children. After one particularly brutal attempted rape by the effeminate Beau Didapper's burley manservant (Del Henny), Joseph strikes a blow for decency and leads Fanny out of the forest, her bodice ripped, her breasts bared submissively, despite her modest attempts to cover them (in contrast to the breasts bared defiantly by the lecherous older female predators). The temptation is too much even for Joseph, and the two enjoy each other's bodies in a field of flowers gloriously photographed by David Watkin. This gives a sense of frantic urgency to later implications of incest. Fanny and Joseph are seen as children of the 1960s as well as of the 1740s, but the film makes light of the sacrament of matrimony and disturbs the novel's moral center.

Fielding's satire and irony are reduced and "adapted" to slapstick and farce. Adams is made over into a bumbling, bewigged clown from his first appearance, stripped of his dignity and his many admirable qualities. One sees less of his courage, compassion, and generosity, and one hears less of his moral philosophy as Joseph becomes clearly the central figure, replacing Fielding's naive Christian hero, who is turned into a sort of sidekick and fool. The problem is that the novel belongs as much to Adams as it does to Joesph.

The novel's major "digressions" are partly ignored or reduced and adapted to ballad form by Jim Dale's musical pedlar, who sings the tale of his "raggle-taggle gypsy girl" (though Jenny Runacre only superficially resembles a true Gypsy). In the film, the pedlar becomes as major a character as Mr. Wilson, whose "history" is abridged and transformed into a silent movie shot through a comically distorted lens.

Perhaps significantly and symbolically, Chris Bryant, who had a hand in writing the screenplay, also plays the "wicked Squire's steward" (of book 3) who attempts to assist in Fanny's debauchery, just as he has also assisted in the rape of the novel. The "adventures" of book 3 are much changed, suffice it to say, and not necessarily for the better—a black mass, with Fanny's body being served up by perverse "nuns," a miraculous escape involving mock heroics and farcical action, faithful more to the spirit than the substance of the text. Richardson gives in too easily to the temptations of spectacular debauchery.

The reunion of Joseph and Pamela at the end, the revelations of Gammar Andrews, Wilson's discovery of the strawberry birthmark, a night of confusion and farcical adventure are all played out in keeping with the reader's expectations. At the end of the novel, all the good characters are rewarded. Mr. Booby grants Fanny a fortune of £2,000. The problem of incest is resolved. Fanny and Joseph are married. The pedlar is "made an exciseman" by Mr. Booby, and Parson Adams is granted an annuity of £130. Fielding leaves no loose ends. Richardson's film follows these details but ends differently from the novel, after Fanny and Joseph are married, as Joseph is about to disrobe for his nuptial night and is caught in the act by a freeze frame.

It is a truism to say that the book was better, but usually film adaptations of classic novels fall short of the mark. The loquaciousness of Fielding's narrator and the massive scope of this "comic epic in prose" cannot finally be successfully adapted to the screen. It can only be transformed into something else, made agreeable and entertaining in this instance by the adaptor. Richardson produces a parallel visual text that is less sophisticated, necessarily less epic, less ambitious, and unfortunately (but to a degree necessarily) stunted. Many characters are simply discarded (there are six clergymen in the novel, for example), others transplanted (Pauline Jameson's Lady Tittle and Peggy Ashcroft's Lady Tattle remark on Lady Booby's undue attention to her footman in Bath, for example, not in London). Toward the end, the film indulges in spectacles of rampant debauchery. But could it have been otherwise?

Reviews tended to dismiss Richardson and the film because it seemed to them that Richardson was cynically trying to duplicate or top himself and revive his slumping career, but one wonders how many of them were familiar with Fielding's huge novel. Stanley Kauffmann, who surely was familiar with the novel, wrote in the *New Republic* that "Richardson keeps running scared, as if he were afraid of boring the audience with a historical picture if there's not a lot of tempo and tits" (1978, 27). For Kauffmann, the film was more "hectic" than comic. Lawrence F. Laban praised Richardson, however, for having translated "the satire and narrative voice in ways that are accessible to modern audiences, rather than slavishly imitating the novel" (1981, 28). Molly Haskell wrote that "this second adaptation of a Henry Fielding novel to be directed by Tony Richardson is in many respects superior to the earlier film." Richardson captures the English countryside "with the richly appreciative love of an insider," while at the same time capturing "a more acerbically raunchy view of eighteenth-century England" (1978, 71).

Vincent Canby of the *New York Times* proved to be Richardson's strongest critical advocate, however. Canby praised *Joseph Andrews* as "the year's most cheerful movie to date, and probably the most neglected movie of the decade" (1978, D21). Had others shared his enthusiasm, Richardson's later Hollywood career might have taken a different and more productive course.

WORKS CITED

Canby, Vincent. "Films to Break—or Make—A Vacationer's Summer Doldrums." *New York Times* (11 June 1978): D21.

Fielding, Henry. *Joseph Andrews and Shamela.* Ed. Martin C. Battestin. Boston: Houghton Mifflin Co., 1961.

Haskell, Molly. "MOMO Meets Momus." *New York* (24 April 1978): 71.

Kauffmann, Stanley. "British Tailorings." *The New Republic* (13 May 1978): 27.

Laban, Lawrence F. "Visualizing Fielding's Point of View." *The English Novel and the Movies*. Ed. Michael Klein and Gillian Parker. New York: Frederick Ungar, 1981.

Seldes, Gilbert. "The Vandals of Hollywood: Why a Good Movie Cannot Be Faithful to the Original Book or Play." *The Saturday Review of Literature* (17 October 1936): 3–14.

CHAPTER ELEVEN

Reflections on Class: Tom Jones *(1963) and* Joseph Andrews *(1977)*

KENNETH S. NOLLEY

A gentleman? If he's a gentleman, he's innocent; I've never hanged a gentleman in my life.

> —Squire Western in *Joseph Andrews*

They can't hang an innocent man! They have done often enough before.

> —Mrs. Waters and Tyburn Turnkey in *Tom Jones*

It is widely held that Tony Richardson's early work was centrally concerned with class issues—issues that were lost in the enlarged budgets of his success. *Tom Jones* and *Joseph Andrews*, then, are generally viewed as lighter, commercial works, with little or no connection to the earlier, "serious" films. Thompson and Bordwell, for example, refer to Richardson's early work as coming from the short-lived "Kitchen Sink" period of British filmmaking. "*This Sporting Life* failed, and the unexpected success

221

of another, very different, Woodfall film swerved filmmakers in new directions. Turning away from harsh realism, Richardson adapted a classic British comic novel in *Tom Jones* (1963). . . . Backed by United Artists, the big-budget color film borrowed heavily from the French New Wave. It became a huge hit and won several Academy Awards" (1993, 555).

Mast and Kawin tell the story of Richardson's career in much the same way. "Later Richardson films—*Tom Jones* (1963), *The Loved One* (1965), *The Charge of the Light Brigade* (1968), *Joseph Andrews* (1977)— leave the grime of working-class England and the bitterness of social-outcast laborers far behind. (Success seems to take its toll on anger and agony.) The angry naturalistic sincerity of the four early films is replaced by higher budgets, bigger casts, and colorful settings, thousands of miles or hundreds of years distant from industrial Britain" (1992, 393).

There is something to this contention, but it rests on a too-simple analysis of the early films as well as the two films adapted from Fielding's novels, treating *Tom Jones* as a light-weight bit of commercial pandering, quite apart from the serious social preoccupations of the earlier films, and assuming that *Joseph Andrews* is merely a failed attempt to capitalize upon the critical and financial success of *Tom Jones*.

Certainly Richardson did not recall the films that way in his autobiography. Of *Tom Jones*, he said, "I felt the movie to be incomplete and botched in much of its execution. I am not knocking that kind of success—everyone should have it—but whenever someone gushes to me about *Tom Jones*, I always cringe a little inside" (1993, 169).

One might argue that Richardson's reaction is merely a defensive ploy for his having sold out, but his assessment of *Joseph Andrews* is likewise at odds with the usual view. Richardson argues that in spite of the publicists, he was trying to do something quite different in his second Fielding adaption than in the earlier film, and that it failed commercially because his intentions were not in synch with the taste of the late 1970s. "The public today seems to have antennae of extraordinary sensitivity to what it wants to see, and *Joseph Andrews* was simply not to the taste of the time. I believe it to be a much better-made film than *Tom Jones*, but coming after it, it was inevitably judged in comparison" (1993, 297).

I am inclined to believe that the shift of emphasis in *Tom Jones* and *Joseph Andrews* is the product of a complex relationship to issues of class (only one of which is expressed as simple desire to cash in); accordingly, I want to explore the treatment of class in these two adaptions, and I hope to show that the early films were never so completely immersed in issues of class as they often have been represented to be, and that although *Tom Jones* betrays some interests of the early films, it retains certain other connections to those early works; further, I hope to show how Richardson's fondness for *Joseph Andrews* may well be due in part to the fact that it restores some of the missing elements of earlier vision and that in spite of the overwhelming tendency of critics to write off *Joseph Andrews* as a failure, there may be some good reasons why Richardson preferred the later film.

TOM JONES

Richardson said that *Tom Jones* represented for him a change of pace from his previous work (1993, 158), but it certainly must have seemed to be somewhat familiar ground to him as well. The story centers on an outsider—on a character who, like Jo in *A Taste of Honey* and Colin in *The Loneliness of the Long Distance Runner*, is excluded by the circumstances of his birth from the world of power and privilege. Jo, in fact, like Tom, is illegitimate. And the film treatment of the story emphasizes the prejudices of a society that classifies people on the basis of their parental origins. Blifil's first comment in the film, for example, exemplifies such unwavering prejudice: "I am afraid, my dear tutors, that neither of you can touch his bastard's heart."

Further, the film is replete with references to the state of class relations in eighteenth-century England; as Raymond Durgnat says, "Molly Seagrim's cottage isn't a pretty thatched affair suitable for an Antique Shoppe tea-cosy" (1970, 109). And beyond the rather grim life of Squire Allworthy's gamekeeper and his family, we are shown cottager's animals trampled by horses in the hunt, Squire Western's sexual predation on his female employees; Partridge's desperation, which leads him to attempt robbery and to beg a job as servant from the indigent Tom; the appalling squalor of life and death in the London streets; the worse squalor of life in Tyburn gaol; and the way public executions served to encourage lower-class conformity while simultaneously providing public entertainment.

There are plenty of things in *Tom Jones*, then, for all its rollicking good humor, to tie it to the bleak vision of the films that immediately precede it. Yet the film is undoubtedly less than sharply focused on this misery engendered by an unequal society. The silent film treatment of the opening segment suggests immediately that the main preoccupation of the film will be with personal rather than social justice. Squire Allworthy

FIGURE 11.1. *Tom Jones* (Albert Finney on donkey)

appears initially to be sympathetic precisely because he deals generously with the baby in his bed, and the subsequent narrative dilemmas generally hang upon whether one ought to mete out harsh judgment or to deal forgivingly with people in the world.

The argument in favor of generous judgment, even at the expense of social justice, is expressed particularly in the forgiveness that must finally be meted out to Tom for his wenching; in the end, that forgiveness extends from his dalliances with Molly through what might just as well have been Oedipal incest with Jenny (Jones) Waters, though the film is so resolutely pitched in favor of forgiveness that even this taboo hardly merits a second thought.

It is particularly remarkable that the Allworthy of the film, who was bemoaning precisely these tragic consequences of unbridled passion before Mrs. Waters appeared with the revelation of Tom's true parentage, seems to forget or relinquish this particular judgment and ends up begging *Tom's* forgiveness, rather than the reverse, arguing that he has used Tom cruelly. This latter assertion seems slightly incredible, given the focus of the film, which does not raise any serious question about the justice of property ownership and the laws of inheritance.

This tendency in the film to deflect serious judgment, particularly away from its hero, has also led scholars of the novel to fault the film as lacking the high moral seriousness of its source. Martin Battestin's early comment is typical: "What is missing from the film is . . . that 'moral seriousness' which underlies all of Fielding's humor and his satire and which makes of *Tom Jones* not merely a frivolous, if delightful romp through English society, but a complex symbolic expression of its author's Christian vision of life" (1967, 33).

However, Fielding's own preoccupation with personal ethics is undoubtedly rooted largely in the class debates of his day. The atmosphere that gave rise to Fielding's novels, particularly the enthusiastic reception of Samuel Richardson's *Pamela*, was highly charged with class concerns of the sort that Leslie Fiedler sums up in a passage worth quoting in its entirety:

> Superficially, the literary war of the sexes reflects a psychological fact of bourgeois self-consciousness, institutionalized in bourgeois life; symbolically, it stands for a more complex sociological phenomenon: for class war in eighteenth-century England. Part of the appeal of the seduction novel rested surely on its presentation of the

conflict of aristocracy and bourgeoisie within the confines of the boudoir. Typically the Lovelace character is a nobleman, the girl he attempts to seduce of humbler stock. Sometimes, like Clarissa, she is rich and bourgeois, occasionally she is poor; and the seducer is sometimes given anti-democratic speeches, in which he scorns the notion of a marriage that will bring him neither profit or distinction. Against such cold class-consciousness and self-seeking are balanced the arguments of sentimentality: that it is the quality of the soul which counts, that the truest nobility is piety, etc., etc. In this sense, the novel is the long-delayed answer of the lower classes to the courtly *pastourelle*, the love debate of shepherdesses and noblemen, which ends typically with a tumbling in the grass. It is a protest, democratic and sentimental at once, against the courtly love codes and the sexual tyranny which they disguised. It rejects alike the conviction that love must be adulterous and the off-hand assumption that the lord of the manor has a right to take whatever girl of inferior rank is pleasing to him. On the one hand, the bourgeois novel insists that the premarital period is the proper time for love and legitimate marriage is its only proper consummation; on the other, it asserts the sexual rights of its daughters as persons, capable of consent or refusal. But its protest against seduction is metaphorical as well as literal; through Richardson a whole class cries: We will be raped and bamboozled no more! (1960, 54)

If this was, in essence, the drift of Samuel Richardson's work, Fielding stood to some degree on the other side of the political fence from his rival among early novelists. A child of the rural aristocracy, he set out first to answer *Pamela* with *Shamela*, a venture that led next to *Joseph Andrews* and later to *Tom Jones*. In *Shamela*, Fielding recast Richardson's naive lower-class girl as a shrewd sexual politician rather than an innocent victim; by *Joseph Andrews*, he had adopted a narrative formula a bit more like Richardson's in that he focused on the adventures of a naive lower-class figure amongst a group of randy social betters, except that Fielding inverted the gender of his hero so that the principal lower-class figure at sexual hazard in his book was male—a pattern he retained in *Tom Jones*.

One important effect of this inversion was to make the seductions in his novels more comic than potentially tragic and thus to mute substantially the metaphorical protest of which Fiedler spoke. And perhaps what is more important, Fielding employed a stock comic device in both

Tom Jones and *Joseph Andrews*—the confusion of identity—which caused the apparent class difference that drove the plot to evaporate in the end. Thus, the prejudice shown against Tom throughout the novel, reprehensible as it is shown to be, is finally demonstrated to be misplaced and mistaken because he was, in fact, an unrecognized child of privilege all the time. And the story (both Fielding's and Richardson/Osborne's) finally *can* exonerate quality of soul and generosity of spirit over social ambition and a too narrow insistence on social identity, precisely because the marriage of Tom and Sophie will not compromise the system of primogeniture and entail, but will rather consolidate the wealth and power of two important families into one.

This is precisely why Raymond Williams has argued that the morality of Fielding's novel is so deceptively conservative:

> It is the morality of a relatively consolidated, a more maturely calculating society. From such a position, the cold greed of a Blifil, the open coarseness of a Squire Western, can be noted and criticized; but calculation, and cost, are given a wider scheme of reference. Love, honour, physical pleasure, loyalty: these, too, have to be brought into the reckoning with incomes and acres. The humanity is of a resigned and settled kind: firm and open when faced by the meaner calculators, but still itself concerned to find the balance— the true market price—of happiness. (1973, 63)

And Williams's point is that Fielding's very preoccupation with personal morality is a statement of class interest, in this case the class interest of the rural squirarchy becoming increasingly aware of the power of the marketplace in rural affairs—affairs increasingly governed by concerns with profit and loss, with investment and return, with the adoption of the new iron plow and selective breeding.

Perhaps it is particularly the purchase of the novel's happy ending at such a low price to the privileged that has also led many critics to value Richardson's first adaption of *Tom Jones* lower than the early films. And yet, if there was any social radicalism in those earlier films, it was modest and undoctrinaire at best. There is little sense in *A Taste of Honey*, for example, of the social mechanisms that keep Jo and her mother in their place. John Hill has pointed out that there is almost no treatment in these early films of collective identity or of the formative conditions of labor; the films operate as if one can and should understand working-class people entirely apart from the workplace and in terms of their personal (and therefore largely individualized) lives (1986, 138–39).

There is some social analysis in *The Loneliness of the Long Distance Runner* (perhaps the most socially serious of Richardson's films), particularly in that Colin does seem to understand: (a) the Faustian bargain that industry exacts from labor, and (b) the way that economic consumption becomes an inescapable trap. Even in *Loneliness*, however, Richardson provides no sense that circumstances can change nor any vision of collective action; Colin's refusal to finish the race, his withholding of his labor at this critical moment, is an individual act of rebellion, which can achieve at best a quite pyrrhic victory and offers little more promise of redemptive change than his father's refusal to go into a hospital. Eugene Quirk has argued that Richardson's film compromised the much stronger and more potent social analysis in the source, Alan Sillitoe's story (1981, 170).

Perhaps the most interesting parallel in the early films to the ending of *Tom Jones* is in *The Entertainer*, another John Osborne script. Archie Rice is, of course, another self-destructively independent hero like Colin, but the character who stands out and partially redeems the bleakness of the ending is Joan Plowright's Jean, Archie's daughter, who returns home in the film to do what she can for the family as it crumbles, secure finally in the knowledge that her well-bread fiance, Graham, is waiting for her with the comfort of his privileged life and the excitement of his open sports car. Jean's (and our) impotence before Archie's failure is painful, but it is made more survivable by the options she still retains, just as the brutalities of the eighteenth-century class system, as briefly painful as they are in Richardson's *Tom Jones*, are softened by Tom's escape from poverty and the gallows into Allworthy's inheritance and the waiting arms of his heiress love.

To read Richardson's account of his own life is to realize that he had no necessary desire himself to stay close to his relatively modest origins as the son of a chemist from Shipley in Yorkshire. His description of university life at Oxford is revealing in this regard:

> Just as it's impossible to write anything bad enough about English public schools, it's impossible to say anything good enough about Oxford. Keep the dreaming spires, sink the punts in the Isis—for the first time in one's life just to be young was very heaven. You went past the heavy wooden gates, met the porter at the lodge, were assigned some paneled dark rooms for two up an old staircase—a

sitting room with two bedrooms attended by some ancient "scout" who waited on you, made the beds, attended to your wishes. (1993, 66)

For all that one might say about Richardson's dislike of the British establishment, his anger was never so alienating as that of some of his characters, such as Colin. And Richardson's class interest is an interest rooted in the world of small shopkeepers, not factory workers or the rural peasantry. His resentment of the privilege maintained by a hereditary aristocracy is real enough and is expressed in his satiric treatment of the public school crowd in *Loneliness* just as it is in the fox hunt sequence in *Tom Jones*. In both, he tends to emphasize the violation of the individual, however, rather than the exploitation of a class of people. This focus is rooted in his twentieth-century bourgeois origins, just as Fielding's tolerant Christian humanism was rooted in the eighteenth-century country houses of the West country.

JOSEPH ANDREWS

Richardson's decision to film Fielding's first novel certainly brought him back to some of the themes and preoccupations of *Tom Jones*, but it is important not to assume that the differences in tone and focus between the two films are entirely the result of the triumph of commercial concerns over aesthetic or moral judgment.

In certain ways, *Joseph Andrews* provided the same sort of structural preoccupations as *Tom Jones*. The story centers on a young couple whose naive love is quite apart from calculation or economic concern and on the ways in which that love is put at hazard by the cupidity of a calculating, mainly aristocratic, world. Again, the hero appears to be a child of the dispossessed but is revealed in the end to be heir to the privilege of the rural squirarchy represented here by Wilson, Joseph's true father. Again, there is the threat of incest, though Joseph avoids it through the constancy of his love for Fanny rather than through the blind luck of revealed parentage that saves Tom Jones.

It is interesting that the threat of incest in *Joseph Andrews* is driven by the randiness of Lady Booby rather than the weakness of the hero, and indeed the threats that the world of privilege poses to Joseph and Fanny are considerably more vicious than the threats posed in *Tom Jones*, particularly in the film: Lady Booby actually does throw Joseph out on the street for refusing her sexual favors and becomes, in the process, a figure of greater menace than her alter ego, Lady Bellaston, in *Tom Jones*; more to the point, Fanny is under repeated sexual threat, whether it be by the man on the road early in the film, by "rough justice" dispensed by the drunken and half-mad Squire Western, by the sexual-religious obsessions of the wicked squire, or by the advances of Beau Didapper.

Like the earlier film, *Joseph Andrews* contains multiple scenes evoking the coarseness of eighteenth-century life, the harshness of class relations, the casual acceptance of brutality in everyday experience. The prison sequences, in particular, recall the harsh portrayal of Tyburn, and the street scenes in Bath, rife with prostitution and horse manure, are comparable to the Hogarthian images of London streets in *Tom Jones*.

In the end, the hitherto unrecognized and illegitimate child of privilege marries the daughter of a miller, and that social union is presented as redemptive in both the film and the book. In a sense, this central aspect of the narrative that Fielding devised and Tony Richardson accepted is much closer to Samuel Richardson's plot in *Pamela* than either *Shamela* or *Tom Jones*; we are led to approve a marriage that crosses class lines, but that does so quite apart from calculation and the quest for social advantage. In fact, because both Joseph and Fanny see themselves as being from the serving classes throughout, the plot is not even open to the implication of calculation and impure motive that Fielding found in *Pamela*.

The source of this purity of motive is, of course, individuals reared in the working classes. Alternatively, there are no members of the gentry in *Joseph Andrews* who represent the level of kindness and sensitivity that Allworthy does in *Tom Jones*. As a group in Richardson's later film, the aristocracy are even more self-absorbed, more obsessed with satisfying their appetites, more given to exploitative excess, particularly in sex, than their counterparts in *Tom Jones*.

In fact, Joseph and Fanny represent a kind of ideal that seems impossible in the earlier modern films as well. In *A Taste of Honey*, Jo seeks a romantic attachment with Jimmy, but in spite of the fact that he assures her that he will return (much as Joseph does Fanny), Jo and we know that she will never see him again. Colin wishes, too, that he could be at the beach at Skegness with Audrey forever, but he knows that such an idyll is impossible. However, Joseph and Fanny's unswerving loyalty to each other is prefigured by the constancy of the elder Andrews's relationship in the film, a parallel that suggests that such love is not unique. The lives of Jo's and Colin's parents suggest, however, what romance means among the working classes in those films—fantasies and lies designed to ward off loneliness for the men and indigence for the women.

Richardson's film begins with the spring festival, which involves Joseph's pulling the leek from between the legs of the female fertility figure at the top of the pole and presenting it to Fanny—an expression of desire suppressed and displaced. The final shot of the film is a freeze frame with the two lovers about to consummate their marriage on their wedding night. This, and only this, is what they (and we) have come to want through the film, as opposed to the union of two estates and the promise of a next generation heir "tomorrow nine-month."

What frustrates and retards this moment more than anything else in the plot, of course, is the license and duplicity of the upper classes, just as the circumstances of poverty and the socially constructed misapprehension that material consumption can bring happiness serve to frustrate and prevent fulfilling relationships in the modern films from Richardson's earlier period. So, unlike *Tom Jones*, *Joseph Andrews* as a film does not finally sell out or compromise its vision of lower-class integrity in favor of social advantage and material success. At the same time, all the film manages to offer by way of narrative resolution is this vision of a lovingly fulfilled sexual relationship.

Thus, like Richardson's version of *Tom Jones* and like the Fielding novels upon which both films are based, the film version of *Joseph Andrews* does exonerate quality of spirit over social ambition. Jane Haspel argues that it emphasizes the morality of choice (1991, 125); again, the film ends focusing on individual and moral issues rather than political and economic issues. And yet, because the sexual choices of the privileged classes in the film have been so consistently and brutally exploitative, so dismissive of consequences for others, the morality of personal choice here has some significant political and social consequences.

Thus, Richardson's Joseph, who is so stubbornly resistant to the appeals of wealth and the power it can purchase, becomes in this regard most like Colin in *The Loneliness of the Long Distance Runner*, arguably the most independent and purely proletarian of the heroes in the earlier films.

THE COUNTRY AND THE CITY, TODAY AND YESTERDAY

There is an interesting difference between the way in which the early films set in the twentieth century construct the city/country split and the way in which the Fielding adaptions (and their sources) do so. In both *A Taste of Honey*, for example, and *The Loneliness of the Long Distance Runner*, the plot tends to move from the world of the city to the country and back to the world of the city once again. Jo's life in her film is thoroughly urban, although she and Geoffrey make a day trip into the countryside. Colin's life is just as thoroughly tied to Nottingham, though he and his friends have their idyllic escape to the beach at Skegness for a weekend.

In both films, the city is portrayed as a lonely place, a world of isolation and alienation; the country, on the other hand, is portrayed as a space where one can imagine and briefly experience connection with other individuals, but where one cannot remain. Thus Jo meets Jimmy, the black sailor she loves briefly, in an empty landscape of oil tanks and filthy canal banks. Colin and his friend Mike steal a car from a street full of parked vehicles but devoid of people, a deserted landscape presided over by the cooling towers of a nuclear power plant in the background. And the streets through which Colin and Mike wander before and after they rob the bakery are almost completely deserted.

John Hill contends that through these images, the city in the films is "emptied of socio-historic content" (1986, 136). Certainly, it is true that these images offer little that can encourage an analysis of the economic organization of the city; again, the effect is to turn attention toward the personal and away from the collective and structural and to construct the behavior of the poor as driven by their own self-destructive impulses at least as much as by the lightly examined nature of their situation.

In Fielding's novels (and consequently Richardson's adaptions), the country is fraught with tensions, even if those tensions are finally made, for the most part, to seem manageable. There are tensions between classes, just as there are tensions between competitors for the same resources. But the city is constructed as seething with activity, and that activity is even more consistently driven by self-interest and ambition than is activity in the country. In both city and country, the plight of the poor is clearly constructed as the product of the cupidity and greed of the wealthy. And the movement of the plot is precisely the reverse of the early films—from country to city and back again.

The early films with their twentieth-century settings suggest a resolutely urban and commercial culture in which a concern with money and material success dominates all aspects of life, particularly the life of the poor; the country is conceived of as a kind of unrealizable fantasy space where one can imagine a world that might be driven more by tenderness than profit, even if one cannot make that world accessible. The Fielding films borrow an earlier vision of the city, one where the city can be conceived of as territory to be rejected because the world of the country is still an inhabitable possibility and the seething world of urban commercialism still seems at least partially escapable.

For Fielding, of course, the advancing concern with financial advantage over personal integrity appeared to emanate more from the city than the country, perhaps because he, like most members of his class, associated the problems of the age with the rising entrepreneurial spirit of trade, a spirit they resisted but finally had to accommodate. Accordingly, he began his career with a comic indictment of ambition masquerading as morality for a servant girl on the make in *Shamela*; years later, his work moved increasingly to resolve the tension between generosity and competition, and he constructed a comic story in which moral repentance fronts for and justifies the social advancement of his hero in *Tom Jones*. This development proved finally to be relatively lenient in its judgment of the ambition of the rural aristocracy.

In Richardson's career, of course, *Tom Jones* precedes *Joseph Andrews*. The relatively superficial social protest of the earlier film (which slyly transmutes into a reassertion of the status quo in the marriage of Tom and Sophie) is followed years later by a portrait of a much more consistently independent hero in Joseph and a less economically compromised resolution in the union of Joseph and Fanny.

Richardson appropriates the historical perspective of the eighteenth century to transform the mythic space of the country into an inhabitable site of resistance to the unrestrained competition of modern society, albeit one devoid of any concrete exploration of the structuring principles and formal operations of that emerging entrepreneurial world. Insofar as the earlier Richardson films had always seemed to define the threat to his characters in individual terms, perhaps that kind of threat seemed increasingly manageable as his career prospered and Woodfall built a relatively solid base of commercial success. In any case, *Joseph Andrews* in particular seems to have provided a vision of resistance purer and more necessary than the one in *Tom Jones* and more hopeful and resilient than he had managed earlier in his more celebrated era of social seriousness.

Is it fair to say, then, that Richardson's adaptations of Fielding do call attention to the facts of class division and exploitation, just as they reveal the misery of the poor to be more the result of the irresponsibility of wealth than do the earlier films in which the ruling classes are at best visible on the fringes of the plot. However, through their retreat into the past, they offer few tools for meaningful and effectual analysis of the problems of contemporary society, though in that sense they are quite closely linked to the contemporary films of Richardson's earlier career, which did not offer much of that sort of analysis either.

John Hill argues that the British films of the realist period prior to the release of *Tom Jones* "appear to occupy an ambivalent space. While they undoubtedly assisted in 'opening up' the British cinema with their innovative contents and more socially inquiring attitudes, they were, in the end, something less than radical" (1986, 174). Much the same must be said of *Tom Jones* and *Joseph Andrews*, which preserve the critical attitudes of their predecessors, even though that criticism never extends much beyond the limits of safe social consensus.

WORKS CITED

Battestin, Martin C. "Osborne's *Tom Jones*: Adapting a Classic." *Man and the Movies.* Ed. W. R. Robinson. Baton Rouge: Louisiana State University Press, 1967.

Behrens, Laurence. "The Argument of *Tom Jones.*" *Literature/Film Quarterly* 8.1 (1980): 22–34.

Durgnat, Raymond. *A Mirror for England: British Movies from Austerity to Affluence.* London: Faber and Faber, 1970.

Fiedler, Leslie. *Love and Death in the American Novel.* Rev. ed. New York: Dell Publishing Company, 1960.

Haspel, Jane Seay. "Sex and Moral Purpose in *Joseph Andrews.*" *Literature/Film Quarterly* 19.2 (1991): 122–26.

Hill, John. *Sex, Class and Realism: British Cinema 1956–1963.* London: The British Film Institute, 1986.

Mast, Gerald, and Bruce F. Kawin. *A Short History of the Movies.* Fifth edition. New York: Macmillan Publishing Company, 1992.

Quirk, Eugene F. "Social Class and Audience: Sillitoe's Story and Screenplay." *Literature/Film Quarterly* 9.3 (1981): 161–71.

Richardson, Tony. *The Long Distance Runner: A Memoir.* New York: Morrow, 1993.

Thompson, Kristin, and David Bordwell. *Film History: An Introduction.* New York: McGraw-Hill, Inc., 1993.

Williams, Raymond. *The Country and the City.* New York: Oxford University Press, 1973.

CHAPTER TWELVE

Revisiting and Re-Visioning: A Delicate Balance *(1973) and* The Hotel New Hampshire *(1984)*

EDWARD T. JONES

While several of Tony Richardson's most esteemed films of the past have undergone some devaluation in the intervening years, a case can be made for revisiting and re-evaluating some previously disparaged examples that merit renewed appreciation. Two representative titles of this latter group include *A Delicate Balance* (1973) and *The Hotel New Hampshire* (1984), both of which were poorly received by critics and the public at the time of their initial releases. They seem, in some ways, fresher today than they did originally and deserve recognition as worthy adaptations by a director renowned for his film versions of stage plays and prose fiction.

A Delicate Balance was the third release from the eight-feature subscription series of movie adaptations of contemporary stage plays, produced by the Ely Landau Organization for the American Film Theatre, exhibited commercially for a two-day run in U.S. movie theatres in 1973 and 1974. Richardson's film version of Edward Albee's 1966 Pulitzer Prize-winning drawing-room drama followed in the series two enormously successful predecessors, John Frankenheimer's adaptation of Eugene O'Neill's *The Iceman Cometh* and Peter Hall's film version of his acclaimed stage production of Harold Pinter's *The Homecoming*. The Pinter/Hall antecedent may have been particularly damaging for Richardson's *Delicate Balance*. In any comparison, the Albee adaptation was usually judged somehow deficient. By this time in the early seventies, *A Delicate Balance* itself was being viewed rather negatively as a play. It was widely held that the Pulitzer Prize awarded to it was reparation for the neglect of the earlier *Who's Afraid of Virginia Woolf* by the judges. Albee subsequently went into an eclipse that lasted a number of years before his resurrection as a national treasure in the nineties with recent successes such as *Three Tall Women*. Likewise *A Delicate Balance* enjoyed a successful revival on the New York stage in 1996 with the Lincoln Center Theatre's production of Albee's play directed by Gerald Gutierrez to much critical endorsement.

On the surface, notwithstanding the presence of David Watkin as Richardson's director of photography for both films, based on the style of production and the tone of the material, few movies would seem more opposite than *A Delicate Balance* and the film version of John Irving's best-selling 1981 novel, *The Hotel New Hampshire*. Albee's restrained, understated comedy of manners, ascetic, even classical, and Irving's farrago of the family romance share little stylistically but considerably more thematically as this essay attempts to show. Taken together as films, they demonstrate the range and daring of Tony Richardson in adaptations.

Into the carefully modulated and controlled upper-middle-class domestic space of Tobias and Agnes in *A Delicate Balance* comes Julia, their thirty-six-year-old daughter whose fourth marriage is breaking up, and then their best friends, Henry and Edna who seek refuge from some existential anxiety—what they term the "terror" that has driven them out of their own home. Besides these outside intrusions is Agnes and Tobias's resident challenge to their delicate marital balance in the person of Claire, Agnes' sister who drinks excessively and embarrassingly in part to alleviate her desire for Tobias. Moreover, in typical Albee fashion, there are references to a dead child, a little boy, Julia's sibling, whose demise has resulted in the end of conjugal relations between husband and wife. Anthony S. Abbott succinctly sums up the conflicts in Albee's play in the following:

> People can no longer change. Julia cannot stay married. Claire cannot stop drinking. Tobias cannot love Harry in the way that a best friend ought, Edna and Harry cannot stave off the terror, and Agnes

239

FIGURE 12.1. *A Delicate Balance* (Katherine Hepburn and Joseph Cotton)

is limited to the role of maintaining order in her household, through aesthetics, through grace and manners, through decency. As she says, "There is a balance to be maintained, after all, though the rest of you teeter, unconcerned, or uncaring, assuming you're on level ground." (1989, 179)

Richardson's film version of the play has the good fortune of Katharine Hepburn's Agnes and Paul Scofield's Tobias. The latter character chooses comfort over confrontation as he explains in his discourse about a cat that suddenly seemed to stop liking him and was subsequently put to death. Scofield's matter-of-fact reading of this scene chillingly makes it the emotional turning point of the play, thus establishing the basis of Tobias's failure with his wife, his daughter, and his best friends. Richardson showcases another equally distinctive vocal performer with Katharine Hepburn's Agnes in yet one more stellar Yankee portrayal by her. As numerous critics and commentators of Albee have acknowledged over the years, women are usually the blazing sources of energy in his plays, and Richardson underscores this fact in his film, especially with Hepburn and Kate Reid's Claire. In the case of Claire, the director and Kate Reid keep the character from the caricature she often becomes in productions of the play. The two actresses in the film version offer complementary portrayals that make Tobias' moral hesitancy almost inevitable surrounded by such women whom he compares at one point— with the addition of daughter Julia, played as a petulant, immature young woman by Lee Remick—to the witches in *Macbeth*.

The American Film Theatre presentations manage to capture a compromise between stage and screen; the directors traditionally do not "open up" their play texts as film adaptations often do. However, Richardson does offer modest alternatives to the handsome living-room set with a conservatory sequence, a very brief shot of a bedroom, and the dining room on occasion.

Early in the film version Richardson and his director of photography, David Watkin, place Agnes and Tobias in two shots at the edge of the frame with space, often dark but sometimes filled with a piece of sculpture, separating them. Later, a similar *mise en scene* is used in the conservatory sequence for Agnes and Julia as well as Julia and her father, with a plant dividing the speakers in the middle of the frame. Perhaps this arrangement suggests a pivot that provides a visual correlative for its own delicate balance. Lights from lamps and white shades on lamps are often

FIGURE 12.2. *The Hotel New Hampshire* (Beau Bridges, Jodie Foster, Rob Lowe, and Wallace Shawn)

used for dramatic effect with the most notable example being the substantial slash of a white lampshade that divides the frame with Claire who concludes the first act, saying "I was wondering when it would begin . . . when it would start" (Albee 1967, 58).

Joseph Cotten as Harry and Betsy Blair as Edna wear black, which contributes to their sinister quality even as they display their neediness and vulnerability to their longtime friends. Actors are often placed in depth with addresses given to the back of foregrounded characters in a set-up found frequently in film noir and similarly expressive in Albee's context.

One somewhat distracting visual element in this film version, at least from the perspective of the late nineties, is the confluence and clash of the women's prints in their attire against the heavily patterned wallpaper in the dining-room scenes. Otherwise David Brockhurst's art direction seems attractive and appropriate. Lighting to denote passages of day and night works especially well in Richardson's film, suggesting as Jay Cocks noted in his review of *A Delicate Balance*, "the dark distances between night and morning" (1974, 39). Light thrown on Agnes at the end of the film, as she stands by the brightening window, hints at her moral illumination: "They say we sleep to let the demons out—to let the mind go raving mad, our dreams and nightmares all our logic gone away, the dark side of our reason. And when the daylight comes again . . . comes order with it. . . . Come now; we can begin the day" (175). With that Albee has the curtain fall, while Richardson preserves the integrity of the domestic space for the credits.

A further assessment of *A Delicate Balance* will be deferred until a sense of Richardson's *The Hotel New Hampshire* has been obtained.

John Irving's fiction usually pivots between Eros and Thanatos, as indeed Edward Albee's *A Delicate Balance* seems equally poised. In *The Hotel New Hampshire*, the pleasure principle in its own way transcends the death instinct, despite a substantial body count along the way. Irving is a romancer and a satirist or mock-romancer who incorporates romance patterns into the modern novel. He weds representationalism and abstract design to give a kind of double vision whereby characters, objects, and events are seen at once as themselves—particulars, individuals—and as suggestions of or embodiments for universals, essences, and archetypes.

Like Irving's novel, Richardson conceives *The Hotel New Hampshire* as a fairy-tale love story. From the opening sequence of the titles where the Berry family is shown sitting on a bed listening to their favorite story of their mother's and father's romance to the closing apotheosis of family unity and survival in dream—symbolic of art—which defeats the mortality presented in the narrative itself, fear, awe, and love animate the film of *The Hotel New Hampshire.* Richardson's choice of music by Jacques Offenbach strikes exactly the right note as score for the axiom supplied by Irving's King of Mice that life is serious, but art is fun. The distinguishing feature both of Irving's novel and Richardson's film version is magical transformation of life becoming art, presented with comic-elegiac tenderness, even innocence, in the midst often of brutal language and cruel action.

Of course, Freud, Sigmund rather than the bear-trainer Freud of Irving's novel and Wallace Shawn's portrayal in Richardson's film, destroyed innocence of the mind, and Irving's characters are as much children of Kierkegaard as of Freud, meditating on dread, on the sickness-unto-death, on fear and trembling. Yet that meditation often is qualified by laughter; the characters' faith in dream, art, love, and renewal becomes priceless because it is absurd.

Richardson retains Irving's structural design of the novel, focusing on the hotels that Win Berry and his family occupy. More remarkably, the director/screenwriter keeps the novel's central metaphors in the much more literal texture of the film. As might be expected, the difference in the two media relative to metaphor presents problems in transference; however, the cross-graining of "real" experience that film provides so fully produces an equivalency of Irving's own prose technique. The hotels stand for the family itself, and Father Berry's dream of his hotel as a New Eden can be both celebrated and undercut in novel and film. Certainly, if metaphors are taken too ingenuously, they come back to haunt as inexplicable ghosts, and Richardson's film version does not completely avoid this condition, especially in its repetition of key phrases and metaphors, which prove more oppressive visually and aurally on film than they do in the literary text. Symbol sometimes becomes only signal; metaphor merely image. The film viewer, nevertheless, appreciates that Sorrow floats both literally as the deceased, stuffed family dog and metaphorically as well. Likewise, the recurring advice of the novel "to keep passing open windows" resonates in Richardson's film version. The Berry sister, Lilly, who succeeded in writing a best-selling novel about trying to grow, finds she is not large enough to continue writing critically acclaimed and commercially successful fiction and repudiates the axiom by plunging out the fourteenth floor of the Stanhope in Irving's novel. In the film, the scene

244

FIGURE 12.3. *The Hotel New Hampshire* (Wilford Brimley, Beau Bridges, and bear)

has been changed to the Ritz-Carleton and Lilly's suicide takes place in an environment recalling an earlier hostelry from something like *Last Year at Marienbad*. The film intertextuality seems quite in keeping with Irving's allusive method in the novel.

Richardson preserves at least some of Irving's literary allusions. The poetry of Donald Justice, which figures prominently in the latter part of the novel, is eliminated, but reference to the ending of Fitzgerald's *Great Gatsby* is skillfully integrated into the film. Initially, the Fitzgerald passages are read to the Berry children during their stay in Vienna by the virginal terrorist, Miss Miscarriage, well played by Amanda Plummer, with German accent. One of the causes of Lilly's suicide presumably was her inability to produce prose as compelling as Fitzgerald's, and Irving's own conclusion to *The Hotel New Hampshire* demonstrates his ambition toward the same model. The evocative apotheosis Richardson supplies for his film version is consistent with his literary source. Richardson, like John Irving, takes as the essence of romance its affinity with the world of the imagination. Characters are linked to attitudes, world views, dreams, and ideas. Interaction with others and with life hardens, alters, or reverses these attitudes. The final confrontation is with death, real or symbolic.

Richardson's large cast is extremely well chosen with Beau Bridges as Father; Lisa Banes as Mother, Wallace Shawn, mentioned earlier as Freud, the bear trainer; Natassja Kinski as Susie the bear; Jennifer Dundas as the diminutive Lilly; Wilford Brimley as Iowa Bob, the grandfather; Paul McCrane as Frank, the elder homosexual brother of the Berry siblings; and numerous others such as Matthew Modine, for example, in the dual roles of Chipper Dove, the rapist, and the pornographer/anarchist in Vienna. The principal emotional events of the novel and the film are the gang rape of the adolescent Franny (Jodie Foster) and the consummation followed by subsequent transcendence of the incestuous relationship between Franny and her brother John (Rob Lowe), the novel's narrator. Critics generally praised Jodie Foster's tough-talking portrayal in the film, but Rob Lowe's John was less warmly received, perhaps unfairly.

Lowe's assignment is more difficult than Foster's, since he must play the realist in a family of dreamers and would-be artists. Irving includes descriptions of a movie made from Lilly's book within his novel made, of course, from the same material of his own narrative, which Richardson has adapted; the character of John was turned into "a lifeless combination of sweetness and stupidity" (Irving 1981, 372). This fate Richardson and Rob Lowe try to avoid in the film. Some might argue that Richardson should have taken to heart more of the cautionary model of how not to film this material from the novel itself. The visual concentration on the process of John's weight-lifting in the film conveys a measure of the novel's underpinning for this character who prepares physically to shoulder the caretaking of his eccentric father and often oppressed siblings, connecting John with his deceased grandfather, Iowa Bob.

One of the most provocative parallels in the novel Richardson struggles to work out cinematically with some measure of success. That is the anarchists' bomb meant to destroy the Vienna State Opera and the incestuous time bomb between John and Franny Berry. In voice-over narration, John informs the viewers that all he can do is think about Franny as he and his father are seen walking past the opera house in Vienna. After the anarchists' plot has been foiled and the terrorists murdered in what Richardson's script refers to as "the good old American way," Susie walks with John in Manhattan and observes, "You and Franny have a bomb between you. One day it will blow you both away unless you do something about it." Shortly thereafter, Franny calls John and tells him, "It's now or never." Richardson indulges in a speeded-up sequence, sparingly used here in contrast to his earlier *Tom Jones*, as John sprints across town to Franny's hotel room. Once there Richardson shows how that incestuous passion is defused or exploded by a marathon session of love-making between brother and sister. The bedroom sequence is cut with inserts to the alarm clock face passing the hours and intercut by appearances of Lilly at the locked door, seeking entrance. Franny's claim to her younger sister that she is writing a novel has its own symbolic fitness in the context of the whole.

At the end of the novel, Susie, the former disguised bear, initially the human substitute for the deceased ursine State-O-Maine, at last able to face herself as a human being, turns the last Hotel New Hampshire into a rape crisis center. Richardson does not make this hotel metamorphosis clear in the film, except perhaps indirectly as he shows the hotel as a refuge into which members of the Berry family withdraw for protection against the cruelty of the world.

In the novel, the now blind Win Berry, his affliction the price he paid for saving the Vienna State Opera, unknowingly provides therapy for rape victims whom he assumes are paying hotel guests. He sets forth his philosophy of what a great hotel should do for its patrons, and Richardson retains a portion of his declaration here quoted from the novel: "If you come to a great hotel in *parts*, in broken pieces . . . when you leave the great hotel, you'll leave it *whole* again. We simply put you back together again, but this is almost mystically accomplished—this is the sympathy space I'm talking about—because you can't *force* anyone back together again; they have to grow their own way. We provide space" (1981, 393). More recently in American literature, Joan Didion has presented the hotel scene in a less sanguine guise, notwithstanding characters who seem as inclined to hotel life as Win Berry himself.

Masculinity in John Irving is often the locus of tragedy, violence, and sometimes farce, but it frequently has a nurturing, redemptive dimension as well. For every Chipper Dove who rapes, there is a Junior Jones who reclaims the victim's self-possession or a John Berry who marries Susie the Bear, herself a former rape victim, and convinces her that she is indeed a beautiful woman. Some years ago, after Irving's novel became a best-seller, Joseph Epstein cast doubt on the author's typical protagonists: "These John Irving heroes, these sweet bruisers, are also permanently puerile, young men whose chief experience occurred in adolescence—it's downhill after your middle-teens, says a character in *The Hotel New Hampshire*—and who have been able to arrange things so that, whatever their chronological age, they never quite have to leave adolescence" (1982, 63). Rob Lowe's portrayal of John Berry is consistent with the strength and limitation of Irving's own characterization. Indeed, upon reviewing Richardson's film and rereading Irving's novel, one may find that the succinctness of the film and the imaginative sequences of the director/screenwriter actually give the pleasurable and qualitative edge to the movie version, however heretical that may sound.

Irving nods toward F. Scott Fitzgerald in the following passage almost at the end of the novel to reaffirm the romance tradition in which he is working:

> So we dream on. Thus we invent our lives. We give ourselves a sainted mother, we make our father a hero; and someone's older brother, and someone's older sister—they become our heroes, too. We invent what we love, and what we fear. There is always a brave, lost brother—and a little lost sister, too. We dream on and on: the best hotel, the perfect family, the resort life. And our dreams escape us almost as vividly as we can imagine them. (1981, 400)

Comparably, in Richardson's final sequence, Lilly grows beautifully as the presiding angel over the last Hotel New Hampshire; the dead are restored to exuberant life—as it was when the parents first worked at Arbuthnot-by-the Sea before World War II and fell in love. This retrospective idyll is choreographed as a waltz with the beautiful family and their friends enjoying the fullness of life. Faithful to Irving but perhaps truer to himself as a filmmaker, Richardson offers his benediction along with the apotheosis.

Both Albee's play and Irving's novel deal with particular gender vulnerabilities and the difficulties each sex experiences in understanding the burdens assumed by the other gender. Albee's Agnes says she is a drill sergeant, taking upon herself the physical and mental agon for preserving balance as John Berry does in *The Hotel New Hampshire*. Moreover, she manages the household as one might a hotel: "She runs the house, for what that's worth: makes sure there's food, and not just anything, and decent linen" (1981, 136). She does insist that "men decide the moral issues" (138) such as whether Harry and Edna should stay in the haven they have appropriated as best friends. Claire reminds Julia who protests interlopers in her old room, "You're laying claim to the cave! Well, I don't know how they'll take to that. We're not a communal nation, dear; giving, but not sharing, outgoing, but not friendly" (100). This remark might transfer to the dark underside of the Hotel New Hampshire. By the same token, as Vincent Canby observed in his review of the recent revival of Albee's play, "Just beneath the placid, well-ordered surface of this household, there are histories of frigid marriage, infidelities, lost children (dead and unborn) and lifelong friendships based solely on convenience" (1996, C-11). That quotation suggests something of forward illumination for Richardson's version of *The Hotel New Hampshire*.

To be sure, Albee's "terror" and favorite Irving catch-phrases like "sorrow floats" and the "undertoad" from *The World According to Garp* share a similar signification. Both *A Delicate Balance* and *The Hotel New Hampshire* are about sanctuary and the need to act with love. In his film versions of both works, Tony Richardson preserves a realistic representation but with hints of allegoric stylization. These latter attributes seem more interesting and provocative now than at the time of the films' original release. The respective literary sources for Richardson's films may have begged some of the questions they raise, which likewise affected subsequent film treatments of them. That is to say only that Richardson's versions of both works are perhaps as faithful to the weaknesses of his sources as he is to their strengths. It is not possible to have the virtues of a writer (or a filmmaker) without certain opposites, if not necessarily his vices.

In these two studies of the American family and the tensions of different generations within it, Richardson's *A Delicate Balance* and *The Hotel New Hampshire* employ an almost contrapuntal technique by which themes occur in close succession and overlap, presented with grave but also festive wit. Looking at the two films together yields unexpected thematic parallels. While these films may be among his lesser achievements, they yet bear witness to Richardson's skill, intelligence, and imaginative compassion often shown especially in his work with actors. For example, he does equal justice to the aging Katharine Hepburn and to the youthful Jodie Foster and their male counterparts, Paul Scofield and Rob Lowe. Richardson remains a broad, bold, simultaneously revelatory and celebratory filmmaker—an "original" adaptor, to end with an oxymoron or, perhaps better, a balancer who willingly risks absurdity to affirm life and art. Thus, Albee and Irving serve as congenial collaborators for this director.

WORKS CITED

Abbott, Anthony S. *The Vital Lie: Reality and Illusion in Modern Drama.* Tuscaloosa and London: University of Alabama Press, 1989.

Albee, Edward. *A Delicate Balance.* 1966. New York: Pocket, 1967.

Canby, Vincent. Review of *A Delicate Balance. New York Times* (22 April 1996): C11.

Cocks, Jay. Review of *A Delicate Balance. Time* (14 January 1974): 39.

Epstein, Joseph. "Why John Irving Is So Popular." *Commentary* (June 1982): 59–63.

Irving, John. *The Hotel New Hampshire.* New York: Dutton, 1981.

CHAPTER THIRTEEN

American Contexts: A Delicate Balance *(1973)* *to* Blue Sky *(1990–94)*

JAMES M. WELSH AND BRUCE HUTCHINSON

Richardson's Hollywood career probably peaked too early with *Tom Jones* in 1963. Other successes were to follow, but nothing to match the commercial and industry impact of Richardson's first Fielding adaptation. Scattered critics judged *The Hotel New Hampshire* (1984) a successful adaptation of John Irving's novel that marked, in the opinion of *Variety,* "a career highpoint for Richardson" (qtd. in Radovich 1995, 151). Moreover, *The Charge of the Light Brigade* (1968) was a *succès d'estime,* though not universally admired. Stanley Kauffmann, never one to admire Richardson's work, praised *The Charge of the Light Brigade* as "easily the best spectacle since *Lawrence of Arabia* and more ambitious than Lean's picture since it wants to dramatize not one man's life but a civilization" (1968, 32), just as Vincent Canby was to praise *Joseph Andrews* ten years later. But Canby stood nearly alone in his admiration of *Joseph Andrews,* and in fact Richardson had few critical successes after *Tom Jones.*

Despite the casting of Mick Jagger in the lead, *Ned Kelly* flopped in 1970, and Richardson's next film, an adaptation of Edward Albee's *A Delicate Balance* (1973) was not at all well received, despite a stellar cast that

252

FIGURE 13.1. *Ned Kelly* (Mick Jagger as Ned Kelly)

included Katharine Hepburn, Paul Scofield, Lee Remick, Kate Reid, Joseph Cotton, and Betsy Blair. In 1966 the play had won Albee the Pulitzer Prize and was a success on Broadway in a production that featured Jessica Tandy and Hume Cronyn. Moreover, Albee himself wrote the screenplay and kept it quite close to the original award-winning play about an upper-middle-class family in Connecticut and the "delicate balance" of love and hate they have achieved.

At the head of the family is Agnes (Katharine Hepburn), the matriarch who is clearly in charge. Her husband, Tobias (Paul Scofield), seems content to let Agnes make the decisions and keeps busy largely by mixing drinks for the others. Claire (Kate Reid), Agnes's alcoholic sister, finds herself constantly under attack by her sister and mildly defended by Tobias. The family's "delicate balance" is then threatened when two old friends, Harry and Edna (Joseph Cotton and Betsy Blair), come for what is evidently a permanent visit. Gripped by an unknown or unspeakable fear, they refuse to return home. Shortly afterward, Agnes and Tobias's daughter, Julia (Lee Remick), returns home after the failure of her fourth marriage. Her return escalates the vitrolic discourse after Julia discovers that Harry and Edna now occupy her room.

The critical reception of *A Delicate Balance* serves as a case in point to demonstrate the direction Richardson's career had taken. By 1973 the critical tide had turned against Albee, however, and Ely Landau was criticized for selecting the play for his American Film Theatre project. "Today Albee seems diminished by time as does his rhetorical florid, hollowly bitchy world," Paul Zimmerman wrote in *Newsweek* (1973, 113). Molly Haskell responded in similar terms: "Interspersed with lines that rarely achieve the dubious status of a 'one-liner' are speeches, generally given by Agnes, the house intellectual, in which a string of subordinate and parenthetical phrases are meant to suggest the image of a mind in search of itself but sound more like a grocery-list metaphysics" (1973, 93). The *Time* critic found the text "pompous, windy, arch; it is a series of tableaux shaped out of crushed ice" (Anon. 1973, 39).

Such comments would indicate that Albee's play did not age gracefully at all. The dialogue comes across as whiny and petty and therefore makes the characters seem rather small and uninteresting. Even Richardson felt that the play and script were lacking: "I found the play itself, the more we worked on it, unsatisfying in its emotional underpinnings. Edward's mandarin dialogue is fascinating, and modulated with impeccable rhythms—satisfying for performers to handle—but the moral dilemmas at the core seem small in comparison with the intricacy of the trappings" (1993, 282).

Richardson's statement is especially interesting in the light of events before the film's production. When Richardson was first approached by the American Film Theatre, he had been offered either John Osborne's *Luther* or Eugene Ionesco's *Rhinoceros*. Both of these he turned down. When he was later offered the chance to direct *A Delicate Balance*, he found the offer more tempting. He had directed the first English double bill of Albee's works with *An American Dream* and *The Death of Bessie Smith*. Moreover, though he had encountered problems with playwrights writing screenplays, he had been impressed by Albee's script for a film about Rudolph Nureyev. Through these encounters he had developed a respect for Albee, which led to his acceptance of the project. Yet, in the end, it was Albee's script that proved problemmatic for both Richardson and the critics.

Despite the script problems, Albee was not the only person to receive critical blame for the film's failure. Richardson himself and Landau's choice of him were also criticized. The primary problem was Richardson's decision to shoot the film as a recorded play rather than as a cinematic event. Critics accused the film of being stagy, ponderous, and lacking in vitality. Though Richardson directed for both stage and screen, his decision to shoot the film as a recorded play conflicted with his usual penchant for location shooting. The result was a clash of style and technique. As a staged film, *A Delicate Balance* should have been shot in a studio to allow for maximum flexibility of blocking and equipment set-up. However, Richardson's desire to use locations to create a stronger sense of reality created a situation in which quarters were cramped and cast and crew were often restricted and uncomfortable (Radovich 1995, 137). The result is a staged film with little movement or vitality.

Despite these problems, the film was praised for its cast. Hepburn's turn as Agnes was the most often cited, with *Variety* judging her performance "superb." Kate Reid was also singled out for praise. Reviewing the film for the *Monthly Film Bulletin*, Sylvia Millar wrote: "Kate Reid invests the intellectual clarity of the character with a witch-like sense of mischief and humour" (1976, 50). The high praise given to Kate Reid as Clair was somewhat ironic, since she was not Richardson's first choice for the role. Kim Stanley, reputedly an alcoholic herself, was originally cast as the alcoholic sister. In fact, Richardson himself wrote that his attempts to rehabilitate Stanley by casting her as Clair became a mission to him. However, it became clear during the rehearsals that Stanley would not work out in the role (Richardson 1993, 280–81).

The film's other main strength was David Watkin's cinematography. His harsh, blunt style of lighting was appreciated by most critics who felt it served to enhance the play's attempt to reveal the harsh, naked truth about these people. "Watkin uses a kind of embellished natural light," the *Time* critic wrote. "His uncluttered compositions can shock the eye with a shaft of light from a table lamp or lull it with a suggestion of the dark distances between night and morning. His craftsmanlike photography, at least, makes the film worth watching" (Anon. 1973, 39).

In short, then, *A Delicate Balance* proved to be an interesting failure. When an adapted screenplay is criticized, it is usually the translation to film rather than the original source that comes under fire. However, *A Delicate Balance* was seen as an outdated, petty play by the time it made its way to film, and most critics seem to have felt there was little point in adapting the play at all. Richardson seemed trapped between directing *A Delicate Balance* as a play on film or as a cinematic event in its own right. The result was a filmed play that was even more stagnant than most attempts at filming a recorded play.

Nearly ten years later, in 1982, Richardson found a project that required location shooting in Texas along the Mexican border, mainly in El Paso and Laredo. *The Border* gave him an opportunity to work with Jack Nicholson, whom Richardson had known since 1964, supported by Harvey Keitel, Warren Oates, and Valerie Perrine. Saddled with a nitwit materialistic wife, Marcy (Valerie Perrine), Charlie Smith (Nicholson) is talked into moving from California to El Paso so Marcy can buy her dream house and be close to her friend Savannah (Shannon Wilcox), whose husband Cat (Harvey Keitel) gets Charlie a job as a border guard. He is befriended by Cat and Big Red (Warren Oates), head of the local border patrol, but soon finds himself involved with a corrupt operation. As his marriage continues to disintegrate, Charlie gets involved with Maria (Elpidia Carrillo, a Latina in her first American role), a beautiful, noble, innocent Mexican widow whose child is stolen from her. She is as dignified as the American women, Marcy and her friend Savannah, are ridiculous. But none of the women in this movie really have much substance or dimension. Like most of the men as well, they are cardboard, allegorical figures, and as such they cannot be very engaging.

The only exception is the Nicholson character, whose wife gets him head over heels in debt, but Cat, the husband of his wife's friend Savan-

FIGURE 13.2. *The Border* (Jack Nicholson and Harvey Keitel)

FIGURE 13.3. *The Border* (Jack Nicholson and Adalberto Cortez)

nah, offers Charlie a solution. Most of the border guards, it seems, are on the take. By turning crooked, Charlie might be able to pay his bills, but he finds himself dealing with bad hombres on both sides of the Mexican-American border, and he "draws the line" at murder. None of these corrupt characters has much respect for human life. When they steal the Mexican woman's baby for a ($25,000) blackmarket adoption, Nicholson shifts his allegiance and decides to help her, whatever the cost or consequences may be. In brief, *The Border* was an unusual and off-beat picture for Richardson to have made.

The film's production history is a little unclear. The story was conceived by producer Edgar Bronfman, Jr., after reading a series of articles in the *Los Angeles Times* in 1977. The story concept was then turned over to writers Deric Washburn (who had earned an Academy Award nomination for his work on *The Deer Hunter* [1978]), Walon Green, and David Freeman. As Richardson remembers the production, he and Deric Washburn disagreed about how the story should be developed: "He wanted the mythic and monumental; I believed in the precise and the realistic—the human scale" (1993, 259–60). And at that point David Freeman was brought onto the project, and, later on, Walon Green to help with the rewrites.

The *Variety* review suggested that the film as released might not have reflected the director's intentions, though in his memoirs Richardson takes a contrary position: "Once I'd edited the movie, I was still dissatisfied with it. After a lot of thought, I proposed a new ending," and, after re-shooting, Richardson claimed, "I liked and still like the new ending better" (1993, 263). As *Variety* reported, however, it was not the director's but the studio's decision: "Universal decided to go back and shoot a much more up-beat ending where Nicholson emerges as a hero" (Anon. 1982, 16). By and large, the characters were too often weak and foolish, and the screenplay was scrambled, with the ending reshot to meet Universal expectations.

The strength of this picture depended upon the way Nicholson registered frustration and outrage and his rendering of a potentially decent man caught up in a moral dilemma produced by an astonishingly corrupt world. Richardson found Jack Nicholson "wonderfully flexible on each take" but was a bit disappointed because he had expected "more challenge, more dialectic, more disagreement" in his collaboration with the actor. "I have always felt making a movie to be the kind of collaborative process where everyone had to give everything critically and constructively, and often I felt Jack could have contributed more to the whole" (1993, 262–63).

Variety found Richardson's direction "murky and disjointed" and, finally, "uninspired." But not all of the reviews were unfavorable. Reviewing the film for *Rolling Stone*, Michael Sragow described it as "an engaging, invigorating social protest against the crime and injustice perpetrated by the U.S. Border patrol" and found its "depiction of the corruption rife in the border patrol [to be] devastating and damning." Sragow claimed that this "Goya-like mural of bloodshed and corruption" was Richardson's "most powerful piece of filmmaking yet," adding that never before had "this British filmmaker worked so comfortably in an American milieu" (1982, 45).

The Hotel New Hampshire, adapted from John Irving's novel, also opened to mixed reviews two years later, in 1984. On the negative side, Rita Kempley, reviewing the film for the *Washington Post Weekend*, wrote that Richardson, "who wrote the scatological screenplay, works at a frantic pace, trying to stuff all of Irving into this psychodramatic allegory, this long dark comedy of horror, readily accepted by Irving's zany zombies" (1984, 3). Her colleague Gary Arnold attacked Richardson's "facile condensation" of Irving's novel and its "literary assault techniques," shameless in the way it shifts emphasis from "the lewd to the sanctimonious on a moment's notice." Arnold criticized Richardson for falling back on the "one-highlight-after-another" approach of *Tom Jones*, "with little flickers of speeded-up slapstick" (1984, C8).

However, Lou Cedrone of the *Baltimore Evening Sun* was far more positive, claiming that *The Hotel New Hampshire* "was never as enjoyable as [Irving's] previous book, *The World According to Garp*. As a film, however, *Garp* was not so good as the book. As a film, *The Hotel New Hampshire* is better than the book" (1984, B1). Cedrone believed that the film managed "a very workable mixture of elements that are seemingly incompatible." Richardson originally considered doing the novel as two films, Cedrone explained, but later changed his mind: "It was a very sound decision. Done as two movies, *The Hotel New Hampshire* might show its seams. As one, it moves along at a very fast and funny pace" (B4), as indeed it does. This film deserved better than it got from many critics.

No doubt, Richardson had become Americanized during the years he spent in Hollywood, but his most successful work in an "American milieu" (*The Hotel New Hampshire*, after all, is international in scope) came at the very end of his filmmaking career. The film *Blue Sky* resem-

FIGURE 13.4. *Blue Sky* (Tommy Lee Jones and Jessica Lange)

bled *The Border* in the troubled relationship it presented between a decent and well-intentioned husband, Hank Marshall (Tommy Lee Jones), and his dissatisfied wife, Carly (Jessica Lange), but there the resemblance ends. Carly is not a silly materialist like Marcy Smith, but a dreamer who longs for a life better than what her husband has provided in the military.

"Blue Sky" is a code for a government project to study the effects of radiation, particularly from open-air nuclear tests, which the military wants to continue, as well as underground testing, which also releases radiation. "Blue Sky" suggests the invisibility of nuclear radiation, which cannot be seen, felt, or tasted but has life-threatening long-range consequences. At issue here are the terrible decisions made by the United States government and the military to develop programs of nuclear testing without regard for ordinary citizens who might be contaminated as a consequence. The film was certainly timely, since when it was released in 1994, a congressional investigation into such matters was underway. Records classified "Top Secret" that were stored at Los Alamos were still protected under the veil of national security, but allegations had been made that the military had made use of human guinea pigs to calculate the effects of radiation. That is exactly the issue Richardson's film addresses.

The screenplay by Rama Laurie Stagner, Arlene Sarner, and Jerry Leichtling branches out in two directions, then, the personal and the political. It was loosely based upon the childhood memories of screenwriter Rama Stagner about the personal and marital problems her parents experienced in 1962, when her father was stationed in Anniston, Alabama. In the screenplay, Hank Marshall is a military scientist, a nuclear engineer who comes to believe that the radiation released by nuclear testing is dangerous. He believes that nuclear tests should be conducted underground, but none of his military superiors will take his warnings seriously. Blue Sky is the program that measures nuclear contamination resulting from nuclear testing. As a scientist, Hank seeks the truth, but the military is only interested in short-term results. Because he is a man of integrity who is willing to question authority, Hank's military career is not very secure.

Hank is further saddled by the outrageous behavior of his neurotic wife, Carly, who constantly embarrasses him with her flirtatious behavior. While they were stationed in Hawaii, Carly would sunbathe topless, exhibiting herself to the military helicopters flying overhead; she is not only an exhibitionist but also an adulteress and possibly a nyphomaniac. She believes she could have been a movie star; in Hawaii she emulates

FIGURE 13.5. *Blue Sky* (Tommy Lee Jones, Jessica Lange, and Powers Boothe)

Brigitte Bardot, and in Alabama she dresses like Marilyn Monroe. She appears to live in a world of self-deluded fantasy, suggesting that she may be mentally unbalanced.

However, Hank loves Carly and is astonishingly tolerant of her flamboyant and sometimes hostile behavior. Her daughters are distressed by her unpredictable temper tantrums. When Hank is called away from home to measure radiation at a nuclear testing site in Nevada, Carly plays the tease and is ultimately seduced by base commander Vince Johnson (Powers Boothe), but they are not discreet and are discovered together by Carly's older daughter and her seducer's son. The daughter forces her mother to call Hank and confess her indiscretion to him.

Upon his return, Hank confronts the commander, not about his adultery, but about his stonewalling stance on nuclear policy. Hank loses his temper, strikes the commander, and ends up in the stockade. The commander then persuades Carly to sign papers that will put her husband in the base hospital, where he is drugged senseless. She believes that by signing the papers, she will get him released from the stockade, and she does not understand the political motives until she sees what the military doctors have done to Hank.

Carly finds her husband's Blue Sky dossier at home and learns that at the site of one test, two cowboys were "cooked" when they inadvertently rode their horses too close to the testing ground. Moreover, they were not warned that they had been exposed to radiation. Carly's natural instinct is to dramatize events, so she drives to Nevada to locate the cowhands and explain what has happened to them and to ask them to testify, but they refuse. Even though their faces are blistering from radiation poisoning, they believe in their government and are uncooperative.

When Carly learns that another test is scheduled, she steals a horse and rides onto the testing ground herself just before the device is to be detonated. The press, waiting in the bunkers for the explosion, then seek her out, sensing a story. In this way, Carly gets the attention of the military and manages to negotiate her husband's release and discharge. The film ends with Hank and Carly free to seek a better life outside the military.

The film was very well received. Todd McCarthy of *Variety* praised the film as "a solid melodrama from the 1950s," in which "a small number of characters define themselves in terms of their interaction within well-proscribed physical and social limits" (1994, 41). In *Newsweek* David Ansen wrote that *Blue Sky* felt "like a Hollywood film from another era" because of "its belief that character can drive a movie," adding "that there is nothing more fascinating than the complexities of the human heart" (1994, 64). Ansen seemed to agree with McCarthy who wrote that the picture "feels like a throwback, but in a refreshing way."

This film is also a "throwback" in another way because of its political message. Nuclear fear was a common component of motion pictures during the cold war, so it is a little surprising to see a film with a nuclear message after the collapse of communism and the fall of the so-called Iron Curtain during the late 1980s, yet this film is a potent reminder that we are all living with the consequences of nuclear politics. People tend to forget that the nuclear dilemma remains with us, though a latent nightmare so far during the 1990s.

Blue Sky was an appropriate capstone to Richardson's career. Hank Marshall is a living emblem of the motto that emerged very early in Richardson's work: resist authority. Moreover, the film proved to be Oscar-worthy when Jessica Lange was nominated for an Academy Award for Best Actress, and went on to win not only the Academy Award but a Golden Globe as well. According to Aljean Harmetz, Orion's game plan for *Blue Sky* was to get Oscar nominations for both Lange and Tommy Lee Jones, difficult since the film had been shelved since it was completed in 1990, when Orion "toppled into bankruptcy while the director, Tony Richardson, was editing the film" (1995, II, 18). Jones was running in a stronger field, however, so only half of the strategy worked. But there would have been no strategy, and no awards, had it not been for the skill of Tony Richardson, working at the top of his form. The film was a worthy exit performance and a forceful reminder to the "new" Hollywood of what a well-executed film could achieve.

WORKS CITED

Anon. "*A Delicate Balance.*" *Variety* (31 October 1973): 625.

Anon. "Tableaux of Ice." *Time* (14 January 1974): 39.

Ansen, David. "A Director's Swan Song." *Newsweek* (26 September 1994): 64.

Arnold, Gary. "Vacant 'Hotel.'" *The Washington Post* (17 March 1984): C8.

Berg. "*The Border.*" *Variety* (27 January 1982): 16.

Cedrone, Lou. "Wacky Comedies Debut Today." *The Baltimore Evening Sun* (9 March 1984): B1, B4.

Harmetz, Aljean. "Bear Hunting in Oscar Season: Five Strategies." *New York Times* (29 January 1995): II, 11, 18–19.

Haskell, Molly. "The Long Night of the Suburban Soul." *Village Voice* (13 December 1973): 93.

Kauffmann, Stanley. "England Expects." *The New Republic* (22 October 1968): 32, 47.

Kempley, Rita. "'Hotel New Hampshire': Ugh." *The Washington Post Weekend* (9 March 1984): 3.

McCarthy, Todd. "*Blue Sky.*" *Variety* (12–18 September 1994): 41.

Millar, Sylvia. "*A Delicate Balance.*" *Monthly Film Bulletin* 43.506 (1976): 50–51.

Radovich, Don. *Tony Richardson: A Bio-Bibliography.* Westport, CT: Greenwood Press, 1995.

Richardson, Tony. *The Long Distance Runner: A Memoir.* New York: Morrow, 1993.

Sragow, Michael. "Jack Nicholson Catches Fire in 'The Border.'" *Rolling Stone* (18 March 1982): 45.

Zimmerman, Paul. "Theatre in the Camera." *Newsweek* (3 December 1973): 113.

A TONY RICHARDSON
FILMOGRAPHY

1956 *Momma Don't Allow.* Co-directed with Karel Reisz. Photography by Walter Lassally. Edited by John Fletcher. BFI documentary. 22 mins.

1959 *Look Back in Anger.* Produced by Harry Saltzman for Woodfall. Screenplay by Nigel Kneale and John Osborne. Cinematography by Oswald Morris. Edited by Richard Best. Cast: Richard Burton (Jimmy Porter), Claire Bloom (Helena Charles), Mary Ure (Alison Porter), Edith Evans (Mrs. Tanner), Gary Redmond (Cliff Lewis), Glen Byam Shaw (Colonel Redfern), Phillis Nielson-Terry (Mrs. Redfern), Donald Pleasence (Hurst), Jane Eccles (Miss Drury), S. P. Kapoor (Kapoor), George Devine (Doctor), Walter Hudd (Actor), Jordan Lawrence (Producer), Bernice Swanson (Sally). 101 mins.

1960 *The Entertainer.* Produced by Harry Saltzman for Woodfall. Screenplay by John Osborne and Nigel Kneale. Cinematography by Oswald Morris. Edited by Alan Osbiston. Cast: Laurence Olivier (Archie Rice), Joan Plowright (Jean), Brenda de Banzie (Phoebe), Roger Livesey (Billy Rice), Alan Bates (Frank Rice), Albert Finney (Mick Rice), Daniel Massey (Graham), Shirley Ann Field (Tina), Thora Hird (Mrs. Lapford), Miriam Karlin (Soubrette), Geoffrey Toone (Hubbard), James Culliford (Cobber Carson), Gilbert David (Brother Bill), Tony Longridge (Mr. Lapford), McDonald Hobley (TV Star), Charles Gray (Columnist), Anthony Oliver (Interviewer), Max Bacon (Charlie Klein), George Doonan (Eddie Trimmer), Jo Linden (Gloria). 96 mins.

1960 *A Subject of Scandal and Concern.* A BBC Television production. Screenplay by John Osborne. Cast: John Freeman (Narrator), Richard Burton (George Holyoake), Rachel Roberts (Mrs. Holyoake), George Devine (Mr. Justice Erskine), Nicholas Meredith (Mr. Alexander), Nigel Davenport (Mr. Bartram).

1961 *Sanctuary.* Produced by Richard D. Zanuck for 20th Century-Fox. Screenplay by James Poe, based on *Sanctuary* and *Requiem for a Nun,* by William Faulkner. Cinematography by Ellsworth Fredricks. Edited by Robert Simpson. Cast: Lee Remick (Temple Drake), Yves Montand (Candy Man), Bradford Dillman (Gowan Stevens), Harry Townes (Ira Bobbitt), Odetta (Nancy Mannigoe), Reta Shaw (Miss Reba), Strother Martin (Dog Boy), Howard St. John (Governor Drake), Jean Carson (Norma), William Mims (Lee), Marge Redmond (Flossie), Jean Bartel (Swede), Hope DuBois (Mamie), Enid James (Jackie), Dana Lorenson (Connie), Pamela Raymond (Cora), Linden Chiles (Randy), Robert Gothie (Gus), Wyatt Cooper (Tommy), Kim Hector (Bucky Stevens), Voltaire Perkins (Judge), Wilton Felder (Musician). 90 mins.

1961 *A Taste of Honey.* Produced by Tony Richardson for British Lion/Woodfall. Screenplay by Shelagh Delaney and Tony Richardson. Cinematography by Walter Lassally. Edited by Anthony Gibbs. Cast: Dora Bryan (Helen), Rita Tushingham (Jo), Robert Stephens (Peter), Murray Melvin (Geoffrey), Paul Danquah (Jimmy), David Boliver (Bert), Moira Kaye (Doris), Herbert Smith (Shoe Shop Proprietor), Valerie Scarden (Customer), Rosalee Scase (Nurse), Veronica Howard (Gladys), Eunice Black (School Mistress), Margo Cunningham (Landlady), Jack Yarker (Ship's Mate), John Harrison (Cave Attendant), A. Goodman (Rag and Bone Man), Janet Rugg and Sonia Stephens (Girls on Pier). 100 mins.

1962 *The Loneliness of the Long Distance Runner.* Produced by Tony Richardson for British Lion/Woodfall. Screenplay by Alan Sillitoe. Cinematography by Walter Lassally. Cast: Tom Courtenay (Colin Smith), Michael Redgrave (Governor), Avis Bunnage (Mrs. Smith), James Bolam (Mike), Julia Foster (Gladys), Topsy Jane (Audrey), Alec McCowen (Brown), Joe Robinson (Roach), Dervis Ward (Detective), James Cairncross (Mr. Jones), John Bull

(Ronalds), William Ash (Gunthorpe), Raymond Dyer (Gordon), Peter Kriss (Scott), Philip Martin (Stacey), Anthony Sager (Mr. Fenton), Peter Madden (Mr. Smith), John Thaw (Bosworth), Christopher Williams (Public School Boy), Anita Oliver (Alice), Brian Hammond (Johnny), John Brookling (Mr. Green), Michael Brown (Public School Boy), Christopher Parker (Bill), Frank Findlay (Booking Office Clerk), Peter Duguid (Doctor), Arthur Mullard (Chief Officer), Maurice Perry (First Prison Officer), Derek Fuke (Shop Assistant), Evelyn Lund (Shop Assistant), Reginald Smith (Commissionaire), Robert Percival (Tory Politician), Maeve Lesley (Shop Assistant), Canna Kendall (Shop Assistant), Ray Austin (Craig), Douglas Robinson (Second Prison Officer), John Porter Davison (Borstal Boy). 104 mins.

1963 *Tom Jones.* Produced by Tony Richardson for Woodfall. Screenplay by John Osborne, based on the novel by Henry Fielding. Cinematography by Walter Lassally. Edited by Anthony Gibbs. Cast: Albert Finney (Tom Jones), Susannah York (Sophie Western), Hugh Griffith (Squire Western), Edith Evans (Miss Western), Joan Greenwood (Lady Bellaston), Diane Cilento (Molly Seagrim), George Devine (Squire Allworthy), Joyce Redman (Mrs. Waters and Jenny Jones), Rachel Kempson (Bridget Allworthy), Wilfred Lawson (Black George), David Warner (Blifil), Micheàl MacLiammòir (Narrator), James Cairncross (Parson Supple), Patsy Rowlands (Honor), Angela Baddeley (Mrs. Wilkins), Jack MacGowan (The Barber said to be Tom's father), John Moffatt (Square), Peter Bull (Thwackum), Freda Jackson (Mrs. Seagrim), Redmond Philips (Lawyer Dowling), Mark Dignam (Lieutenant on the road to London), Julian Glover (Northernton), Avis Bunnage (Landlady at the George Inn), Rosalind Knight (Mrs. Fitzpatrick), Lynn Redgrave (Susan, Upton Inn), George A. Cooper (Mr. Fitzpatrick), Jack Stewart (MacLachlan), Rosalind Atkinson (Mrs. Miller), David Tomlinson (Lord Fellaman). 128 mins.

1964 *The Loved One.* Produced by John Calley and Haskell Wexler for MGM. Screenplay by Terry Southern and Christopher Isherwood, based on the novel by Evelyn Waugh. Cinematography by Haskell Wexler. Edited by Anthony Gibbs. Cast: Robert Morse (Dennis Barlow), Jonathan Winters (Wilber Glenworthy and Harry Glenworthy), Anjanette Comer (Aimee Thanatogenos), Rod Steiger

(Mr. Joyboy), Dana Andrews (General Brinkman), Milton Berle (Mr. Kenton), James Coburn (Immigration Officer), John Gielgud (Sir Francis Hinsley), Tab Hunter (Guide), Margaret Leighton (Mrs. Kenton), Liberace (Mr. Starker), Roddy McDowall (D. J., Jr.), Robert Morley (Sir Ambrose Abercrombie), Lionel Stander (Guru Brahmin), Ayllene Gibbons (Joyboy's Mother), Martin Ransohoff (Lorenzo Medici), Paul H. Williams (Gunther Fry). 116 mins.

1966 *Mademoiselle.* Produced by Oscar Lewenstein for Woodfall-Procinex. Screenplay by Jean Genet (English translation by Bernard Frechtman). Cinematography by David Watkin. Edited by Anthony Gibbs. Cast: Jeanne Moreau (Mademoiselle), Ettore Manni (Manou), Keith Skinner (Bruno), Jane Berretta (Annette), Umberto Orsini (Antonio), Mony Reh (Vievotte), Georges Douking (Priest), Rosine Luguet (Lisa), Gabriel Gobin (Police Sergeant), Pierre Collet (Marcel), Jean Gras (Roger), Georges Aubert (Rene), Antoine Marin (Armand), Gerard Darrieu (Boulet). 103 mins.

1967 *The Sailor from Gibraltar.* Produced by Oscar Lewenstein and Neil Hartley for Woodfall. Screenplay by Tony Richardson, Christopher Isherwood, and Don Magner, based on the novel *Le Marin de Gibraltar,* by Marguerite Duras. Cinematography by Raoul Coutard. Edited by Anthony Gibbs. Cast: Jeanne Moreau (Anna), Ian Bannen (Alan), Vanessa Redgrave (Sheila), Zia Mohyeddin (Noori), Hugh Griffith (Legrande), Orson Welles (Louis of Mozambique), Gabriella Pallotta (Girl at the Dance), John Hurt (John), Theo Roubanis (Theo), Brad Moore (Brad), Wolfgang Hillinger (Wolf), Eleanor Brown (Carla), Umberto Orsini (Postcard Vendor), Erminio Spalla (Eolo), Fausto Tozzi (Captain), Massimo Sarchielli (Massimo). 91 mins.

1967 *Red and Blue.* Produced by Oscar Lewenstein and Lindsay Anderson for Woodfall. Screenplay by Tony Richardson and Julian More. Cinematography by Billy Williams. Edited by Kevin Brownlow. Cast: Vanessa Redgrave (Jacky), John Bird (Man on Train), Gary Raymond (Songwriter), Michael York (Acrobat), Amaryllis Garnet (Songwriter's Girl), Douglas Fairbanks, Jr. (Millionaire). 35 mins.

1968 *The Charge of the Light Brigade.* Produced by Neil Hartley for United Artists. Screenplay by Charles Wood. Cinematography by David Watkin. Edited by Kevin Brownlow and Hugh Raggett. Cast: Trevor Howard (Lord Cardigan), Vanessa Redgrave (Clarissa), John Gielgud (Lord Raglan), Harry Andrews (Lord Lucan), Jill Bennett (Mrs. Duberly), David Hemmings (Captain Nolan), Peter Bowles (Paymaster Duberly), Mark Burns (Captain Morris), Howard Marion-Crawford (Sir George Brown), Mark Dignam (Airey), Alan Dobie (Mogg), Willoughby Goddard (Squire), T. P. McKenna (William Howard Russell), Corin Redgrave (Featherstonehaugh), Norman Rossington (Corbett), Ben Aris (Maxse), Leo Britt (Scarlett), Helen Cherry (Lady Scarlett), Peter Wooodthorpe (Valet), Rachel Kempson (Mrs. Codrington), Donald Wolfit ("Macbeth"), Valerie Newman (Mrs. Mitchell), Andrew Faulds (Quaker Preacher), Ambrose Coghill (Douglas), George Douking (St. Arnaud), Ben Howard (Pridmore), Roger Mutton (Rupert Codrington). 141 mins.

1969 *Hamlet.* Produced by Neil Hartley for Woodfall/Filmways. Screenplay adapted from Shakespeare by Tony Richardson. Cinematography by Gerry Fisher. Edited by Charles Rees. Cast: Nicol Williamson (Hamlet), Gordon Jackson (Horatio), Anthony Hopkins (Claudius), Judy Parfitt (Gertrude), Mark Dignam (Polonius), Marianne Faithfull (Ophelia), Michael Pennington (Laertes), Ben Aris (Rosencrantz), Clive Graham (Guildenstern), Peter Gale (Osric), John Carney (Player King), Richard Everett (Player Queen), Roger Livesey (Lucianus and Gravedigger), Robin Chadwick (Francisco), Ian Collier (Priest), Michael Elphick (Captain), Mark Griffith (Messenger), Anjelica Huston (Lady in Waiting), Bill Jarvis (Courtier), Roger Lloyd-Pack (Reynaldo), John Railton (Sailor), John Trenaman (Bernardo), Jennifer Tudor (Lady in Waiting). 119 mins.

1969 *Laughter in the Dark.* Produced by Neil Hartley for Gershwin-Kastner/Marceau/ Woodfall. Screenplay by Edward Bond, based on the novel by Vladimir Nabokov. Cinematography by Dick Bush. Edited by Charles Rees. Cast: Nicol Williamson (Sir Edward More), Anna Karina (Margot), Jean-Claude Drouot (Hervé Tourace), Peter Bowles (Paul), Sian Phillips (Lady Elizabeth More), Sebastian Breaks (Brian), Kate O'Toole (Amelia

More), Sheila Burrell (Miss Porley), Edward Gardner (Chauffeur), Helen Booth (Maid), Willoughby Goddard (Colonel). 104 mins.

1970 *Ned Kelly.* Produced by Neil Hartley for Woodfall. Screenplay by Tony Richardson and Ian Jones. Cinematography by Gerry Fisher. Edited by Charles Rees. Cast: Mick Jagger (Ned Kelly), Allen Bickford (Dan Kelly), Geoff Gilmour (Steve Hart), Mark McManus (Joe Byrne), Serge Lazareff (Wild Wright), Peter Sumner (Tom Lloyd), Ken Shorter (Aaron Sherritt), James Elliott (Pat O'Donnell), Clarissa Kaye (Mrs. Kelly), Diana Craig (Maggie Kelly), Susan Lloyd (Kate Kelly), Alexi Long (Grace Kelly), Bruce Barry (George King), Frank Thring (Judge Barry). 103 mins.

1973 *A Delicate Balance.* Produced by Ely Landau for American Film Theatre. Screenplay by Edward Albee. Cinematography by David Watkin. Edited by John Victor Smith. Cast: Katharine Hepburn (Agnes), Paul Scofield (Tobias), Lee Remick (Julia), Kate Reid (Claire), Joseph Cotton (Harry), Betsy Blair (Edna). 132 mins.

1974 *Dead Cert.* Produced by Neil Hartley for Woodfall. Screenplay by Tony Richardson and John Oakley, based on the novel by Dick Francis. Cinematography by Freddy Cooper. Edited by John Glen. Cast: Scott Antony (Alan), Judi Dench (Laura), Michael Williams (Sandy), Mark Dignam (Tudor), Nina Thomas (Penny), Julian Glover (Lodge), Joseph Blatchley (Joe Nantwich), John Bindon (Walter), Dervis Ward (Albert), Ian Hogg (Bill Davidson), Annie Ross (Mrs. Mervyn), Bill Fraser (Cresswell), Sean Lynch (Sid). 99 mins.

1977 *Joseph Andrews.* Produced by Neil Hartley for Woodfall. Screenplay by Allan Scott and Chris Bryant, based on a story by Tony Richardson and the novel by Henry Fielding. Cinematography by David Watkin. Edited by Thom Noble. Cast: Peter Firth (Joseph Andrews), Ann-Margret (Lady Booby), Michael Hordern (Parson Adams), Beryl Reid (Mrs. Slipslop), Natalie Ogle (Fanny), Jim Dale (Pedlar), Peter Bull (Sir Thomas Booby), Karen Dotrice (Pamela), John Gielgud (Doctor), Hugh Griffith (Squire Western), Peggy Ashcroft (Lady Tattle), Timothy West (Mr. Tow-Wouse), Wendy Craig (Mrs. Tow-Wouse), James Villiers (Mr. Booby), Ronald Pickup (Mr. Wilson), Murray Melvin (Beau Didapper), Kenneth Cranham (Wicked Squire), Norman Rossington (Gaffer

Andrews), Patsy Rowlands (Gammer Andrews), Penelope Wilton (Mrs. Wilson), Pauline Jameson (Lady Tittle), Vanessa Millard (Betty), John Gielgud (The Doctor), Alfie Lynch (Postilion), Dan Meaden (Coach Driver), Gerald Cross (Lawyer to Coach), Jenny Runacre (The Gypsy) Jonathan Cecil (Fop One), Vernon Dobtcheff (Fop Two), Patrick Durkin (Trotter), Steven Berkoff (Greasy Fellow), Gawn Grainger (Scout), Chris Bryant (Wicked Squire's Steward), Helen Fraser (Mrs. Adams), Willoughby Goddard (Fourposter Innkeeper), Richard Goolden (Squire Western's Clerk), Del Henny (Didapper's Valet), Nigel Humphreys (Birdcatcher), Tim Piggott Smith (Cornet), Stefan Gates (Young Joseph), Shannon Skinner (Young Pamela), George Raistrick (Booby Steward), Declan Mulholland (Resurrectionist), Sandra Dorne (Whore in Traffic Jam), Ken Mason (Dancing Master), Brian Glover (Goaler), Timothy Bateson (Master of Hounds), Janet Webb (Fat Nun), Maggie Wright (First Nun), Michael Balfour and Robert Ashby (Ruffians). 104 mins.

1978   *A Death in Canaan.* Produced by Robert W. Christiansen and Rick Rosenberg for Warner Brothers TV. Screenplay by Thomas Thompson and Spencer Eastman, based on the book by Joan Bartrhel. Cinematography by James Crabe. Edited by Bud Smith. Cast: Stefanie Powers (Joan Barthel), Paul Clemens (Peter Reilly), Tom Atkins and Kenneth McMillan (Police Officers), Jacqueline Brooks (Defence Attorney), Brian Dennehy and Conchita Farrell (Neighbors), William Bronder (Judge). 150 mins.

1982   *The Border.* Produced by Edgar Bronfman, Jr., for Universal/ RKO/Efer. Screenplay by Deric Washburn, Walon Green, and David Freeman. Cinematography by Ric Waite and Vilmos Zsigmond. Edited by Robert K. Lambert. Cast: Jack Nicholson (Charlie), Harvey Keitel (Cat), Valerie Perrine (Marcy), Warren Oates (Red), Elpidia Carrillo (Maria), Shannon Wilcox (Savannah), Manuel Viescas (Juan), Jeff Morris (J. J.), Mike Gomez (Manuel), Dirk Blocker (Beef), Lonny Chapman (Andy), Stacey Pickren (Hooker), Floyd Levine (Lou), James Jeter (Frank), Alan Fudge (Hawker), William Russ (Jimbo), Gary Grubbs (Honk), Gary Sexton (Slim), Billy Silva (George), William McLaughlin (Donny), David Beecroft (Kevin), Esther Sylvey (Secretary). 107 mins.

1984 *The Hotel New Hampshire.* Produced by Neil Hartley and James Beach for Orion. Screenplay by Tony Richardson, based on the novel by John Irving. Cinematography by David Watkin. Edited by Robert K. Lambert. Cast: Rob Lowe (John), Jodie Foster (Franny), Paul McCrane (Frank), Beau Bridges (Father), Lisa Banes (Mother), Jennie Dundas (Lily), Wallace Shawn (Freud), Wilford Brimley (Iowa Bob), Nastassja Kinski (Susie the Bear), Seth Green (Egg), Wally Aspell (Hotel Manager), Joely Richardson (Waitress), Jobst Oriwal (German Man), Linda Clark (German Woman), Matthew Modine (Chip Dove and Ernst), Elie Oren (King of Mice), Amanda Plummer (Miss Miscarriage), Roger Blay (Arbeiter), Timothy Webber (Wrench), Jean-Louis Roux (Old Billig), Sharon Noble (Babette), Lorena Gale (Dark Inge), Michele Scarabelli (Chip Dove's Girlfriend) Gayle Garfinkle (Doris Wales and Screaming Annie), Robert Thomas (Harold Swallow), Cali Timmins (Bitty Tuck), Dorsey Wright (Junior Jones). 110 mins.

1986 *Penalty Phase.* Produced by Tamara Asseyev Productions. Screenplay by Gale Patrick Hickman. Photography by Steve Yaconelli. Edited by David Simmons. Cast: Peter Strauss (Judge Kenneth Hoffman), Jonelle Allen (Susan Jansen), Karen Austin (Julie), Melissa Gilbert (Leah Furman).

1988 *Shadow on the Sun.* Tamara Asseyev and Stefanie Powers for Tamara Asseyev Productions/New World. Screenplay by Allan Scott. Photography by Steve Yaconelli. Edited by Robert K. Lambert. Cast: Stephanie Powers (Beryl Markham), James Fox (Mansfield Markham), Timothy West (Charles Clutterbuck), Claire Bloom (Lady Delamere), Nicola Paget (Amanda Orchardson), Trevor Eve (Denys Finch Hatton). 240 mins.

1990 *The Phantom of the Opera.* Produced by Ross Milloy for Saban/Scherick Productions. Screenplay by Arthur Kopit, based on the novel by Gaston Leroux. Photography by Steve Yaconelli. Edited by Robert K. Lambert. Cast: Charles Dance (Erik, the Phantom), Burt Lancaster (Carriere), Ian Richardson (Cholet), Andrea Ferreol (Carlotta), Teri Popo (Christine), Adam Storke (Count Philippe). 240 mins.

1990 *Hills Like White Elephants.* Produced by David Brown and William S. Gilmore for David Brown/HBO Showcase as part of the trilogy *Women and Men: Stories of Seduction.* Screenplay by Joan Didion and John Gregory Dunne, based on the story by Ernest Hemingway. Photography by Steve Yaconelli. Edited by Robert K. Lambert. Cast: Melanie Griffiths (The Girl) and James Wood (The Man). Total running time for the whole trilogy, which also includes *The Man in the Brooks Brothers Suit,* directed by Frederic Raphael, and *Dusk before Fireworks,* directed by Ken Russell: 90 mins.

1994   *Blue Sky.* Produced by Rohert H. Solo for Orion. Screenplay by Rama Laurie Stagner, Arlene Sarner, and Jerry Leichtling. Photography by Steve Yaconelli. Edited by Robert K. Lambert. Cast: Jessica Lange (Carly Marshall), Tommy Lee Jones (Hank Marshall), Powers Boothe (Vince Johnson), Chris O'Donnell (Glenn Johnson), Amy Locane (Alex Marshall), Anna Klemp (Becky Marshall), Carrie Snodgrass (Vera Johnson), Mitchell Ryan (Ray Stevens), Dale Dye (Colonel Mike Anwalt), Tim Scott (Ned Owens), Annie Ross (Lydia), John J. Fedak (Adjutant), Michael McClendon (Lt. Colonel Jennings), Merlin Marston (Lt. Colonel George Land), Dion Anderson (General Derrick), Gary Bullock (Doctor Vankay), Angela Paton (Dottie Owens), Ray Sergeant (Administrative First Sergeant). 101 mins.

SELECTED
BIBLIOGRAPHY

Albee, Edward. *A Delicate Balance.* New York: Pocket Books, 1967.

Alpert, Hollis. "Britain's Angry Young Director." *Saturday Review* (24 December 1960): 48–49.

Ansen, David. "A Director's Swan Song." *Newsweek* (26 September 1994): 64.

Armes, Roy. *A Critical History of the British Cinema.* New York: Oxford, 1978.

Baker, Peter. "Peter Baker Sees Courtenay Lose and Richardson Win the Race." *Films and Filming* 8 (November 1962): 32.

Barron, James. "Tony Richardson, the Director of 'Tom Jones,' Is Dead at 63." *New York Times* (16 November 1991):27.

Bartlett, C. J. *History of Postwar Britain, 1945–1974.* London: Longman, 1977.

Battestin, Martin C. "Fielding on Film." *Eighteenth Century Life* 11 (May 1987): 10–13.

———. "Osborne's *Tom Jones:* Adapting a Classic." *Virginia Quarterly Review* 42 (1966): 387–93.

Behrens, Laurence. "The Argument of *Tom Jones.*" *Literature/Film Quarterly* 8.1 (1980): 22–34.

Berg. "*The Border.*" *Variety* (27 January 1982): 16.

Betts, Ernest. *The Film Business: A History of British Cinema, 1896–1972.* London: Pitman Publishing, 1973.

Billington, Michael, and Derek Malcolm. "Exiled Maker of the Court." *Guardian* (16 November 1991): 25.

Bremmer, Charles. "Film World Mourns Its 'Angry Young Man.'" *The* [London] *Times* (16 November 1991):20.

Canby, Vincent. "Films to Break—or Make—A Vacationer's Summer Doldrums." *New York Times* (11 June 1978): D21.

Caughie, John, with Kevin Rockett. *The Companion to British and Irish Cinema.* London: BFI/Cassell, 1966.

Cocks, Jay. Review of *A Delicate Balance. Time* (14 January 1974): 39.

Courteney, Tom [*sic*]. "The Loneliness of the Long Distance Runner." *Films and Filming* 8 (September 1962): 10–13.

Curtis, Anthony. "Tony Richardson." *Financial Times* (16 November 1991): 41.

Delaney, Shelagh. *A Taste of Honey.* New York: Grove Weidenfeld, 1959.

Desey, Frank. "Obsession." *Sight and Sound* (May 1995): 33.

Doty, Gresdna A., and Hilly J. Harbin. *Inside the Royal Court Theatre, 1956–1981: Artists Talk.* Baton Rouge: Louisiana State University Press, 1990.

Felperin, Leslie. "*Blue Sky.*" *Sight and Sound* 5.6[n.s.] (June 1995): 56.

Fielding, Henry. *The History of Tom Jones.* 2 vols. Ed. A. R. Humphries. London: J. M. Dent Everyman's Library, 1962.

———. *Joseph Andrews and Shamela.* Ed. Martin C. Battestin. Boston: Houghton Mifflin Co., 1961.

Findlater, Richard. *At the Royal Court.* Derbyshire: Amber Lane Press, 1981.

Gaston, Georg. *Karel Reisz.* Boston: Twayne Publishers, 1980.

Geduld, Harry M. *Film Makers on Film Making.* Bloomington: Indiana University Press, 1967.

Gielgud, John. "Tony Richardson." *The* [London] *Times* (22 November 1991): 20.

Gleiberman, Owen. "Atom's Family." *Entertainment Weekly* 242 (30 September 1994): 38

Gomez, Joseph A. "*The Entertainer.* From Play to Film." *Film Heritage* 8 (1973): 19–26.

Graham, Allison. *Lindsay Anderson.* Boston: Twayne Publishers, 1981.

Halliwell, Leslie. *Halliwell's Film Guide.* New York: Scribner's, 1985.

Harcourt, Peter. "'I'd Rather Be Like I Am': Some Comments on *The Loneliness of the Long Distance Runner*." *Sight and Sound* 32.1 (Winter 1962–1963): 16–19.

Haskell, Molly. "The Long Night of the Suburban Soul." *Village Voice* (13 December 1973): 93.

———. "MOMO Meets Momus." *New York* (24 April 1978): 71.

Haspel, Jane Seay. "Sex and Moral Purpose in *Joseph Andrews*." *Literature/Film Quarterly* 19.2 (1991): 122–26.

Higson, Andrew, ed. *Dissolving Views: Key Writings on British Cinema*. London: Cassell, 1996.

Hill, John. *Sex, Class and Realism: British Cinema, 1956–1963*. London: BFI Publishing, 1986.

Holden, Stephen. "An Angry Man Found Himself in 'Tom Jones.'" *New York Times* (21 August 1994): II.9.

Houston, Penelope. "*Look Back in Anger*." *Sight and Sound* 28.1 (Winter 1958–59): 31-32.

Irving, John. *The Hotel New Hampshire*. New York: Dutton, 1981.

James, Caryn. "An Army Family as Strong as Its Weakest Link." *New York Times* (16 September 1994): C8.

Jones, Edward T. "Checking into While Others Run to Check Out of Tony Richardson's *Hotel New Hampshire*." *Literature/Film Quarterly* 13.1 (1985): 66–69.

Kauffmann, Stanley. "British Tailorings." *The New Republic* (13 May 1978): 27.

———. " England Expects." *The New Republic* (22 October 1968): 32, 47.

Klein, Michael, and Gillian Parker, eds. *The English Novel and the Movies*. New York: Frederick Ungar, 1981.

Lambert, Gavin. "Free Cinema." *Sight and Sound* 25 (Spring 1956): 173–77.

———. "Tony Richardson: An Adventurer." *Sight and Sound* (November 1993): 30–33.

Lassally, Walter. *Itinerant Cameraman*. London: John Murray, 1987.

Lewenstein, Oscar. *Kicking Against the Pricks: A Theatre Producer Looks Back*. London: Nick Hern Books, 1994.

Littlewood, Joan. *Joan's Book: Joan Littlewood's Peculiar History As She Tells It*. London: Minerva, 1995.

Litton, Glenn. "Diseased Beauty in Tony Richardson's *Hamlet*." *Literature/Film Quarterly* IV:2 (Spring 1976): 108–22.

Macdonald, Dwight. *On Movies*. New York: Berkley Medallion Books, 1969.

Manvell, Roger. *New Cinema in Britain*. London: Studio Vista, 1969.

McCaffrey, Donald W. "*The Loved One*: An Irreverent, Invective, Dark Film Comedy." *Literature/Film Quarterly* 11.2 (1983): 83–87.

McCarthy, Todd. "*Blue Sky*." *Variety* (12–18 September 1994): 41.

McVay, Douglas. "Hamlet to Clown." *Films and Filming* 8.12 (1962): 16–19.

Maugham, W. Somerset. *The World's Greatest Novels: Great Novelists and Their Novels*. Greenwich, CT: Fawcett Publications/ Premiere Books, 1962.

Millar, Sylvia. "*A Delicate Balance*." *Monthly Film Bulletin* 43.506 (1976): 50–51.

Milne, Tom, ed. *The Time Out Film Guide*. London: Longman, 1989.

Monaco, James. *The Movie Guide*. New York: Putnam, 1992.

Morley, Sheridan. "Tragedy of the Genius with a Talent for Self-destruction." *Daily Mail* (16 November 1991): 51.

Mullin, Michael. "Tony Richardson's *Hamlet*: Script to Screen." *Literature/Film Quarterly* IV.2 (Spring 1976): 123–33.

Munn, Michael. *Trevor Howard: The Man and His Films*. Chelsea, MI: Scarborough House, 1990.

Osborne, John. *Almost a Gentleman: An Autobiography, 1955–1966*. Vol. II. London: Faber and Faber, 1991.

———. *The Entertainer*. London: Faber and Faber, 1957.

———. "Jimmy Porter, 35 Years On." *The* [London] *Observer* (26 January 1992): 45–46.

———. *Look Back in Anger*. New York: Penguin Books, 1957.

Petrie, Duncan J. *Creativity and Constraint in the British Film Industry*. New York: St. Martin's Press, 1991.

Phillips, Gene D. "Faulkner and the Film: The Two Versions of *Sanctuary*." *Literature/Film Quarterly* 1.3 (1973): 262–73.

Pickering, David. *Dictionary of the Theatre*. London: Penguin/Sphere Books, Ltd., 1988.

Powell, Dilys. "Rebel in Our Midst." [London] *Sunday Times* (30 September 1962).

Quirk, Eugene F. "Social Class as Audience: Sillitoe's Story and Screenplay 'The Loneliness of the Long Distance Runner.'" *Literature/Film Quarterly* 9.3 (1981): 161–71.

Radovich, Don. *Tony Richardson: A Bio-Bibliography.* Westport, CT: Greenwood Press, 1995.

Redgrave, Vanessa. "AIDS Victim Who Inspired Generations of Talent." *Evening Standard* (27 November 1991): 53.

———. "Demeaning a Fine Man." *Daily Mail* (26 November 1991): 26.

———. *Vanessa Redgrave: An Autobiography.* New York: Random House, 1994.

Richardson, Tony. "Directions." *Granta* 122 (10 November 1962).

———. "A Free Hand." *Sight and Sound* 28.2 (Spring 1959): 64.

———. "London Letter." *Film Culture* 2.2 (1956): 16–17.

———. *The Long Distance Runner: A Memoir.* London: Faber and Faber, 1993.

———. *The Long-Distance Runner: An Autobiography.* New York: Morrow, 1993.

———. "The Man Behind an Angry-Young Man." *Films and Filming* 5 (February 1959): 9, 32.

———. "The Two Worlds of the Cinema." *Films and Filming* 7 (June, 1961): 7, 41.

Robinson, David. *The History of World Cinema.* New York: Stein and Day, 1973.

Rollins, Janet Buck. "Novel into Film: *The Loneliness of the Long Distance Runner.*" *Literature/Film Quarterly* 9.3 (1981): 172–88.

Rubens, Robert. "Conversations at the Royal Court Theatre." *Transatlantic Review* 9 (Spring 1962): 5–10.

Russell, Ken. *Fires over England.* London: Hutchinson, 1993.

Sarris, Andrew. *Confessions of a Cultist.* New York: Simon and Schuster, 1970.

Seldes, Gilbert. "The Vandals of Hollywood: Why a Good Movie Cannot Be Faithful to the Original Book or Play." *The Saturday Review of Literature* (17 October 1936): 3–14.

Shakespeare, William. *The Tragedy of Hamlet, Prince of Denmark.* Ed. Willard Farnham. Baltimore, MD: Penguin Books, 1957.

Sillitoe, Alan. *Life without Armour*. London: Flamingo, 1995.

———. *The Loneliness of the Long Distance Runner*. New York: Knopf, 1965.

Sragow, Michael. "Jack Nicholson Catches Fire in 'The Border.'" *Rolling Stone* (18 March 1982): 45.

Taylor, John Russell. *Anger and After*. Harmondsworth, UK: Penguin Books, 1966.

———. *Cinema Eye, Cinema Ear*. New York: Hill and Wang, 1964.

Tookey, Christopher. *The Critics' Film Guide*. London: Boxtree, 1994.

Tynan, Kathleen. "Exit Prospero." *Vanity Fair* 55.2 (February, 1992): 82–85, 116–19.

Wakeman, John, ed. *World Film Directors, 1945–1985*. Vol. II. New York: H. W. Wilson, 1988.

Walker, Alexander. *Hollywood, U.K.* New York: Stein and Day, 1974.

Wardle, Irving, and Allen Eyles. "Tony Richardson." *Independent* (16 November 1991): 49.

Welsh, James M. "Tony Richardson." *International Dictionary of Films and Filmmakers—2: Directors*. 2nd ed. Ed. Nicholas Thomas. Chicago: St. James Press, 1991.

Wollen, Peter. "The Last Wave: Modernism in the British Films of the Thatcher Era," in Lester Friedman, ed. *British Cinema and Thatcherism*. Minneapolis: University of Minnesota Press, 1993.

Woodham-Smith, Cecil. *The Reason Why*. New York: McGraw Hill, 1953.

Young, Colin. "Tony Richardson: An Interview in Los Angeles." *Film Quarterly* 13.4 (Summer 1960): 10–15.

Zimmerman, Paul. "Theatre in the Camera." *Newsweek* (3 December 1973): 113.

CONTRIBUTORS

Linda Costanzo Cahir and Stephen Cahir. Linda holds graduate degrees in English (Ph.D.) and cinema studies (M.A.) from New York University and currently teaches at Centenary College in New Jersey. Fortunately, her husband, Stephen Cahir, a practicing trial attorney, shares her passionate interest in film. She serves as contributing editor of *Literature/Film Quarterly*. She and her husband both wrote multiple entries for *The Encyclopedia of Novels into Film*, edited by John Tibbetts and Jim Welsh (Facts on File, 1998). She is now completing *Solitude and Society in the Works of Herman Melville and Edith Wharton*, forthcoming from Greenwood Press.

Robert Holtzclaw is an associate professor and director of the Film Studies Program at Middle Tennessee State University. He has published on individual film personalities (screenwriter Charles Brackett, actor Edward G. Robinson, and others) and on film genre. He is currently at work on a study of biographical and autobiographical films (as co-author), as well as on a biography of the actor Mark Frechette.

William L. Horne was born in Britain and educated at the University of Wisconsin. He is now an associate professor of mass communications at Towson University in Maryland and has helped to organize several Literature/Film Association conferences at Towson. He has also served as contributing editor of *Literature/Film Quarterly* and is currently working on a book entitled *"See Shooting Script": The Role of the Screenplay in Film Theory and Criticism*.

Bruce Hutchinson is currently pursuing graduate study in film studies at the University of Kansas. He also contributed to *The Encyclopedia of Novels into Film* (Facts on File, 1998).

Edward T. Jones is professor and Chair of English and Humanities at York University of Pennsylvania. He has written books on L. P. Hartley and Peter Brook. A frequent contributor to *Literature/Film Quarterly*, he teaches courses on Shakespeare, theatre, and film.

Paul Meier is an associate professor in the Department of Theatre and Film at the University of Kansas in Lawrence. He has acted in Shakespearean roles and was director for the BBC Drama Repertory Company radio series "*Vivat Regina.*" He taught at the Royal Academy of Dramatic Arts and at the London Academy of Music and Dramatic Arts. He also taught at the North Carolina School of the Arts before moving to Kansas. He recently published an interview with Kenneth Branagh concerning the four-hour *Hamlet* in *The Drama Review*.

Kenneth S. Nolley is a professor of English at Willamette University in Salem, Oregon. Has written especially well on Peter Watkins's *The Journey: A Film in the Global Interest*, in a monograph he edited in 1991 concerning the fifteen-hour Watkins film. Besides serving as dean at Willamette, he has published in *Literature/Film Quarterly*, *CineAction!* and other specialized journals, and he reviews regularly for *Choice*.

Rebecca M. Pauly is a professor of French and Italian at West Chester University in Pennsylvania, contributing editor of *Literature/Film Quarterly*, and past president of the Literature/Film Association. Her publications include *Le Berceau et la bibliothèque*, a study of the autobiographic voice (Stanford French and Italian Studies 62, Anma Libri, 1989) and *The Transparent Illusion: Image and Ideology in French Text and Film* (Peter Lang, 1993).

Gene D. Phillips, S.J., has taught for years at Loyola University of Chicago, where he is a member of the Jesuit Community and has served as contributing editor of *Literature/Film Quarterly* for twenty-five years, since its inception. He is the author of several books on cinema-related topics, such as *The Movie Makers: Artists in an Industry* (Nelson-Hall, 1973), *Ken Russell* (1979), *George Cukor* (1982, both for the Twayne Series), and *Graham Greene: The Films of His Fiction* (Teachers College Press, 1974), followed by *Hemingway and Film* (Ungar, 1980), *Fiction, Film, and F. Scott Fitzgerald* (Loyola University Press, 1986), *Fiction, Film, and Faulkner* (University of Tennessee, 1988), and *Conrad and Cinema: The Art of Adaptation* (Peter Lang, 1995).

Judith Bailey Slagle is an associate professor and chair of humanities at Roane State Community College. She has published several works on the Restoration playwright Thomas Shadwell and recently edited a special collection entitled *Thomas Shadwell Reconsider'd: Essays in Criticism* for *Restoration: Studies in English Literary Culture, 1660–1700* (Fall 1996). She is presently editing a two-volume collection of the letters of Scottish playwright Joanna Baillie.

John C. Tibbetts teaches cinema studies at the University of Kansas in Lawrence and is contributing editor of *Literature/Film Quarterly*. From 1976 to 1985 he edited the magazine *American Classic Screen* for the National Film Society. He has worked for several radio and television stations in the Kansas City area and with Monitor Radio, as well as writing for *The Christian Science Monitor*. Publications include *His Majesty the American: The Cinema of Douglas Fairbanks, Sr.* (co-authored with J. M. Welsh, A. S. Barnes, 1977), *The American Theatrical Film* (Bowling Green University Popular Press, 1985), and *Dvořák in America* (Amadeus Press, 1993). He is co-editor with Jim Welsh of *The Encyclopedia of Novels into Film* (Facts on File, 1998).

James M. Welsh is a professor of English, Salisbury State University, Salisbury, Maryland, founding past-president of the Literature/Film Association, and editor-in-chief of *Literature/Film Quarterly*. In 1973 he hosted, moderated, and co-scripted *The Films of the Gatsby Era*, a thirteen-part series of MGM silent classics produced by the Maryland Center for Public Broadcasting and telecast nationally. He is co-author with John C. Tibbetts of *His Majesty the American: The Cinema of Douglas Fairbanks, Sr.* (A. S. Barnes, 1977) and (with Steven Philip Kramer) *Abel Gance* (Twayne, 1978), and is author of *Peter Watkins: A Guide to References and Resources* (G. K. Hall, 1986). He is co-editor with John Tibbetts of *The Encyclopedia of Novels into Film* (Facts on File, 1998).

INDEX